The Absence of Grand Strategy

The Absence of Grand Strategy

The United States in the Persian Gulf, 1972–2005

Steve A. Yetiv

The Johns Hopkins University Press
Baltimore

The Johns Hopkins University Press
2715 North Charles Street
Baltimore, Maryland 21218-4363
www.press.jhu.edu

Library of Congress Cataloging-in-Publication Data

Yetiv, Steven A.
   The absence of grand strategy : the United States in the Persian
Gulf, 1972–2005 / Steve A. Yetiv.
      p.   cm.
Includes bibliographical references and index.
   ISBN-13: 978-0-8018-8781-9 (hardcover : alk. paper)
   ISBN-13: 978-0-8018-8782-6 (pbk. : alk. paper)
   ISBN-10: 0-8018-8781-X (hardcover : alk. paper)
   ISBN-10: 0-8018-8782-8 (pbk. : alk. paper)
   1. Middle East — Foreign relations — United States. 2. United
States — Foreign relations — Middle East. 3. United States — Foreign
relations — 1981–1989. 4. United States — Foreign relations — 1989–
5. Iran-Iraq War, 1980–1988. 6. Persian Gulf War, 1991. 7. Iraq War,
2003–   I. Title. II. Title: United States in the Persian Gulf, 1972–
2005.
DS63.2.U5Y48 2008
327.73053609'045 — dc22

                                                      2007031771

A catalog record for this book is available from the British Library.

*Special discounts are available for bulk purchases of this book. For more
information, please contact Special Sales at 410-516-6936 or
specialsales@press.jhu.edu.*

Contents

Tables

Preface

All great powers, from the Romans to the Mongols, from the Spaniards to modern-day Americans, have ventured afar, sometimes to plunder and pillage and at other times to defend their security against real and imagined threats. In pursuing their varied goals, they have resorted to multiple approaches, some effective and others calamitous, ranging from the high stakes of unbridled force and hegemony seeking to the low jinks of internal sabotage. And in the process they have shaped and been shaped by their foreign adventures and misadventures. Their tales form the very stuff of history, painted on a broad canvas, one littered with the political carcasses of their enemies — and sometimes their own.

The overarching goal of this book is to paint a portrait of how a great power behaved in a distant land, a great power that is no less important in history than many of the defining powers of eras long gone. The study of great powers in various regions of the world is an ancient practice, but it is also salient in modern world politics. Great powers cannot avoid involvement in regions for a plethora of reasons, including globalization, economic development, civil wars, ethnic conflicts, energy security, proliferation of weapons of mass destruction, and terrorism.

Within this book's thematic context of great-power behavior, it has two general goals. The first is to offer an uncommon exploration of one of the most central concepts in the field of international relations — balance of power — a concept that lies at the core of realist theory and its many offshoots.

The second general goal is to sketch the evolution of U.S. foreign policy toward the Persian Gulf from 1972 through 2005. The Persian Gulf rose like a meteor in the late twentieth and early twenty-first centuries, even though it has always held a special place in the annals of history. It is a region in which the Iran-Iraq War caused more than a million casualties; in which the United States and its allies fought two large wars in a dozen years; and from which significant oil flows to the overly dependent global economy. It is a region in which powerful and corrupt monarchs and dictators fell; in which terrorists were incubated and hatched; and in which the United States, like a political chameleon, attempted to use many approaches for protecting and promoting its interests.

The two goals of this book are intimately related. I begin by examining a key question: To what extent did balance-of-power policy animate the thinking behind, and practice of, American foreign policy in the Persian Gulf region, as compared with other approaches? Through this question, we can explore larger questions about foreign policy, balancing theory, and the U.S. role in the Middle East, and especially the enduring question of the extent to which great powers actually pursue grand strategies.

Ultimately, this book finds, in sharp contrast to many views on the subject, that the United States pursued neither balance-of-power nor hegemonic strategies — indeed, that the United States did not pursue a grand strategy at all from 1972 through 2005. Rather, its behavior could best be captured by a concept that I refer to as reactive engagement. The United States reacted to events that it often did not expect and which caused it to alter its policies, sometimes fundamentally, sometimes clumsily. There was no grand design here, no grand strategies, no consistent set of principles at play. The real story of U.S. foreign policy is about how the United States was slowly dragged into the region by a farrago of events at the domestic, regional, and global level, culminating in the attacks of September 11, all of which set up the invasion of Iraq in 2003.

All this is not to say that the study of grand strategy is not useful. It is critical for a variety of reasons that I discuss later in the book. But single grand strategies certainly do not appear to offer good stand-alone guides to understanding the United States in the Persian Gulf over time.

With respect to the study of balance of power, most research examines whether states balance against other states in their regions or whether great powers balance against one another at the global level. This book does something different. It looks at U.S. foreign policy in a region of the world — and at the United States as a potential balancer from outside that region — and it does so within the context of exploring the grand strategies of great powers.

In pursuing this goal, the book also offers a panoramic view of U.S. foreign policy. The American experience in the Gulf did not begin with the controversial invasion of Iraq in 2003 or even with the eviction of Iraq's forces from Kuwait in 1991. We need to understand the evolution of U.S. foreign policy in order to comprehend why the United States became so involved in this region and why, ultimately, it decided to invade and re-create Iraq.

The Absence of Grand Strategy

Although it is my hope that this book will be of interest to students and scholars of foreign policy, international relations, and the Middle East, it is not a detailed history of American foreign policy in the region. Nor is it a book only about grand strategy and theory. Rather, it uses history to study and illuminate strategy and theory, and vice versa, in the ten episodes it examines. These episodes cover the major policies of the United States from the Nixon administration to that of President George W. Bush in the Iraq war of 2003. In toto, these episodes constitute one longer case study of the foreign policy of a great power.

I worked on this book for more than a decade, and it sure felt like it. In that time I received critical input from many colleagues and friends. I would like to thank the following people for reading parts of the manuscript and giving me those painful but much needed reality checks: Anouar Boukhars, Tom Christensen, Steven David, David Earnest, Betty Rose Facer, Kurt Taylor Gaubatz, David Lake, Peter Liberman, Lenore Martin, Eric Miller, Paul Papayaonou, Anna Rulska, Randall Schweller, and Gary Sick. I extend a special thanks to John Duffield for his detailed comments on an earlier version of the work and to Henry Tom at the Johns Hopkins University Press for his very able guidance. For their research support, I would like to thank Joyce Battle at the National Security Archive and my able research assistants, Tim Breslin, Anna Rulska, and John Torcivia.

No Grand Strategy

Realists of various stripes assume that in a world of anarchy — one with no highly developed and effective government, police, laws, and community above the state level — states must help themselves. Anarchy breeds insecurity among states which pushes them to hedge their bets by balancing against the strongest state rather than bandwagoning (aligning) with it.[1] Balancing is the safer strategy because states fear that a strong state or potential hegemon could eventually threaten them, even if they initially align with it, and that no one can protect them in this scenario.[2] There are many variants of realism, but as one scholar aptly describes it, they may all be seen as ultimately focusing on the balance of power to explain foreign policy, war, and other phenomena.[3]

Various forms of realism are often used to explain international outcomes that result from the interaction of many states. But inferences also can be, and are commonly, made from realism about how great powers or specific states should act, such as with regard to balance-of-power behavior.[4] Thus realism is transformed from a theory of international relations into one of foreign policy, and even of grand strategy, which Colin Dueck rightly describes as a "branch of foreign policy," one that deals chiefly with the underpinnings and architecture

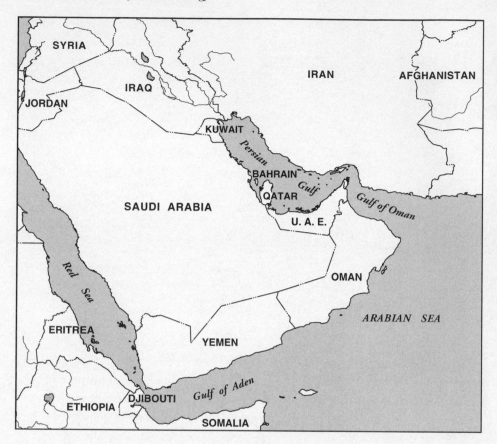

of foreign policy, primarily in areas related to military-security affairs.[5] Grand strategy, in this sense, may be defined as involving a set of core approaches used by major states to protect and advance their interests against a range of challenges,[6] or, in broader terms, as a "conceptual road map, describing how to match identified resources to the promotion of identified interests, and a set of policy prescriptions" to achieve national goals.[7]

Perhaps no region appears to be better captured by realist theory than the Persian Gulf. It is widely seen by scholars and nonscholars as a cauldron of insecurity, as a place of unending conflicts where Iran and Iraq have sought hegemony over the weaker Arab states of Kuwait, Saudi Arabia, Oman, Qatar, the United Arab Emirates and Bahrain, in a bid for dominance in the broader

Middle East and global influence. The region is commonly referred to as unstable, mercurial, and even irretrievably Hobbesian and as the ultimate locale of global realpolitik where security concerns and mistrust dominate. Despite the status of the United States as an external power, its basic security interests increasingly came under threat from actors and events in the region since the late 1970s. Indeed, if there is any region in which we would expect the precepts of realpolitik to dominate and realist theory to guide us well in understanding American foreign policy, it might well be the Persian Gulf.

If balance-of-power realism is adjusted to explain the role of outside powers in regions, we could infer from it that the United States would behave either as an active balancer (a concept that I develop in this book) or as an offshore balancer (which I discuss later in the Introduction).

Students of international relations commonly describe and assess the behavior of great powers in terms of whether they behave as active balancers. Active balancers are concerned about, and seek to maintain, the balance of power in regions as a general and ongoing task, and they aim to balance, using a variety of means, against the strongest actor to keep it in check. Students of international relations have invoked balance of power to refer to great-power behavior in various regions, including Russia's role in Central Asia and the Persian Gulf and U.S. intervention and potential balancing in Central America, in Europe, and in relations with Asia broadly.[8] Thus one scholar asserted that, by "balance of power criteria, the United States should have repaired relations with Vietnam long ago," in the effort to balance against China.[9] Regarding South Asia, another thinker asserted that during the Cold War "the military balance between India and Pakistan — two states unequal in size, population, and resources — was sustained by the two superpowers through both hard and soft balancing."[10]

With respect to the Persian Gulf, scholars and policymakers not infrequently describe U.S. behavior as if it were an active balancer.[11] For instance, one political scientist asserted that U.S. policy for decades was aimed at achieving a "degree of balance between the region's two strongest states, Iran and Iraq."[12] Other thinkers were so convinced that the United States practiced balance-of-power policy in the past that they called on Washington to renew this approach in the future, after its military withdrawal from Iraq. They saw it as preferable to fighting a losing war against Iraqi insurgents and attempting to democratize the Middle East in line with President George W. Bush's doctrine of democratization as an antidote to terrorism and instability.[13] As one analyst put it, "the harsh reality of Gulf security — past, present, and future — remains balance of power politics."[14]

The United States, in his view, would have to act as the balancing power to maintain some loose form of stability well into the twenty-first century.[15]

Core Arguments of the Book

This book makes three key arguments about American behavior in the Persian Gulf which serve as the basis for addressing broader questions. They are supported by the findings of the book, which are laid out in table 5 (in Chapter 10) and discussed in detail throughout the book, especially in Chapter 10.

First, contrary to realist expectations and to the view of some students of international relations, balance-of-power policy was not prominent in American foreign policy toward the Persian Gulf from 1972 through 2005. It was not prominent in its actions in the region or in its motivations as reflected in various primary and secondary sources. In fact, the United States did not often try to maintain the balance of power as a general and ongoing task by playing Iran and Iraq off each other, by balancing against the strongest actor to keep it in check, or by eschewing actions that could engender or worsen an imbalance of power.[16] Rather, it sometimes placated or bolstered the strongest actor in the region in lieu of balancing against it; it took actions that it knew could create or worsen an imbalance of power in the region; or it pursued approaches other than balance-of-power policy. Moreover, in assessments of its approaches, motivations other than those consonant with balance-of-power policy often proved important. In this sense, balance-of-power policy was not prominent in the way officials approached, and thought about, America's role in this critical region.

Second, in line with some realist expectations, the United States was much more inclined to practice balance-of-threat policy or to balance against the most threatening state in the region rather than the most powerful one. However, the record suggests that it sometimes balanced against prevailing threat and sometimes did not.

Third, although the United States was much more likely to balance against prevailing threat than against prevailing power, we can add a temporal dimension to this analysis. Over time, it became much less likely to be animated by balance-of-power policy and to practice it. This is also true of balance-of-threat policy, although to a lesser extent.

These three arguments are about empirical evidence, but they generate a number of questions that I will answer in brief in the remainder of this introductory chapter and then in more detail later in the book: Why was balance-of-power policy not prominent? Why did the United States balance less over time?

If the United States sometimes balanced against threat and sometimes did not, why so? How is it that the United States did not pursue the two most central grand strategies, balance of power and hegemony? What is reactive engagement as a concept?

Why Was Balance-of-Power Policy Not Prominent?

Some thinkers might guess that the United States did not practice balance-of-power policy much in the region because it clashed with balancing against Moscow at the global level. But they would be only half right at best. Sometimes this was true and sometimes it was not. For instance, the U.S.-led invasion of Iraq in 2003 was not consonant with balancing behavior, yet we cannot explain that by virtue of global concerns because the Cold War was long over.

Global-level concerns were sometimes salient, but balance-of-power policy ranked low in America's foreign policy for many reasons. The United States had multiple goals, some at the domestic or even personal level, which often impeded, superseded, or preempted its use and led to policies that ran contrary to exercising balance-of-power policy. They included releasing American hostages held in Lebanon by the Shiite group Hizballah; securing Iraqi business for American farmers and the economy; democratizing the Middle East; and dealing politically and strategically with transnational terrorism.

Balance-of-power policy also ranked low in American foreign policy because policymakers did not appear to privilege it in their priorities, even when imbalances in capability between Iran and Iraq suggested that they should have done so. At times, they were not open to it as an approach and appear not to have even considered it much compared with other motivations. This may have been because it was difficult to tilt toward either Iran or Iraq, even when balancing would have required it, because of poor relations with both states. Yet at other times, Washington engaged or even appeased the regional state that it knew full well was the strongest and most threatening. On that score, the case in point is U.S. policy toward Iraq in the years prior to its invasion of Kuwait in August 1990. The United States pursued a policy of "constructive engagement" with the strongest and most threatening state, Iraq.

Why Did Balancing Decline over Time?

Balance-of-power policy became even less prominent over time, as did balance-of-threat policy, although less so. Indeed, in the 1970s, balancing was much more prominent in U.S. foreign policy, both in practice and as an idea of real-politik under the administration of Richard Nixon, than it would be in subsequent decades. Why? A number of explanations are salient, but four developments contributed significantly to the decline in American balancing over time.

The end of the Cold War made it easier and safer for the United States to adopt nonbalancing strategies that would have threatened Moscow during the Cold War, such as invading its ally, Iraq. The rise of American global power, which was partly tied to the end of the Cold War but also had its own important trajectory, yielded Washington the capability to pursue more aggressive foreign policy approaches in lieu of less provocative balancing approaches. The rise of transnational terrorism generated security challenges at the domestic and transnational level against which balance-of-power policy was not effective or salient. Meanwhile, neoconservatives rose in influence in the United States. Especially during the administration of George W. Bush, balance-of-power policy was eclipsed by notions that were largely foreign to the realist school of thought, such as moral preaching, democratization, and a healthy appreciation for using U.S. military prowess to re-create states in the American image.[17] That became quite manifest with the Iraq war of 2003, which was driven by motivations and approaches that ran largely counter to balance-of-power policy.

Interestingly, although many reasons have commonly been bandied about to explain the invasion of Iraq, there are notions that have received little attention as partial explanations: the United States went to war partly as a result of the same developments that made balance-of-power policy less important over time. The end of the Cold War left the United States largely unchecked in world politics and with greater room to maneuver; the rise of American capability yielded it the potential to make war; the drama of the terrorist attacks of September 11, 2001, provided the impetus as well as increased domestic political support; and the rise of neoconservatism contributed the ideological bedrock and elite political support that helped motivate and facilitate the effort.

When Did America Balance against Prevailing Threat?

If the United States sometimes balanced against prevailing threat and sometimes did not, when did it do one or the other? I offer a brief preview here of three conditions that were important, which I state in general terms.

First, active balancing against threat is more likely when the external actor is unlikely to co-opt the most threatening actor, through a variety of positive incentives. That is, the external actor will tend to try out "nicer" approaches first before moving to balancing.

Second, balancing against threat is more likely when the outside state faces a regional military threat rather than a political or ideological threat. Military threats are more easily recognized and reflect more serious problems for the outside state's interests than do political or ideological threats.

Third, the external actor will be more likely to balance against threat at the regional level if that does not contradict balancing against threat (not power) at the global level. Indeed, as I lay out in Chapter 1, it is important to consider pressures at both the regional and global levels in trying to assess how external actors behave in regions.

Why Did America Not Pursue Grand Strategies?

The foregoing analysis allows a foray into the larger subject of great powers and grand strategies. Scholars differ on the number of grand strategies that states can pursue, but for purposes of an extensive empirical study, it is useful to narrow them down.[18] Christopher Layne sensibly suggests that great powers ultimately "have two grand strategic options," which, in effect, are to pursue extraregional hegemony or to pursue balance of power.[19] It is important to stress that advocates of both offshore balancing and hegemonic strategies agree that the United States has vital interests in the Persian Gulf which must be protected by military power and that these interests include preventing the rise of a single state in the region which can control the world's oil reserves.[20] Thus, both balance-of-power and hegemonic strategies are concerned not only with other global great powers but also with potential regional great powers.[21] To what extent did the United States act as an offshore balancer or a hegemony seeker in the Persian Gulf?

An Offshore Balancer?

Balance of power as a grand strategy can assume different forms. In this book, I explore two of them. Earlier in the Introduction, I argued that the United States did not behave much like an "active balancer." That is one form. However, it is also important to assess in what measure it acted as an offshore balancer — the other form. Both offensive realism and defensive realism, which are two key variants of the core school of realism, would predict that the United States would be an offshore balancer in various regions of the world.[22]

For present purposes, and perhaps more generally, it is important to distinguish between active and offshore balancing. This is because a state may well be an active balancer but not an offshore balancer or vice versa. The offshore balancer is also a rarer form of balancing, especially in modern world politics, in which great powers are more engaged in regions. Thus, we may not observe offshore balancing in practice, but that does not mean the actor was not an active balancer that pursued balance-of-power policy. Most important, both types of balancing assume that a great power will be a balancer in a region, and privilege balancing strategies over hegemonic ones, but they differ in basic ways.

Indeed, the offshore balancer balances chiefly against prevailing power but also sometimes against prevailing threat, and, in the main, it uses military capability for this goal. It acts to deal with a potential hegemon, to "contain it or cut it down to size."[23]

Moreover, rather than being involved in the region all along, it engages from afar in extreme cases to prevent imminent hegemony when local actors are unable to do so; otherwise it would prefer to get other powers to check the aggressor and to remain at a distance.[24] Thus, Britain was chiefly an offshore balancer both in mainland Europe and in the European imperial system in Asia by pursuing a grand strategy referred to by Josef Joffe as "watchful aloofness."[25] Other states qualify as offshore balancers, such as Sweden in the Baltic region during the reign of Charles XI between 1660 and 1672.[26] For its part, the United States acted as an offshore balancer in World War II, proving very reluctant to engage in hostilities until it was literally forced into doing so.[27]

In contrast to the active balancer, the offshore balancer takes a higher risk of allowing hegemony. Robert Art, for instance, argues in his illuminating book *A Grand Strategy for America* that an offshore balancer strategy in the twenty-first century would risk "redoing World War I and World War II."[28] This is chiefly because the offshore balancer does not develop a forward military presence in regions of the world. Nor does it actively manage regional affairs for balancing reasons but rather pursues a last-resort strategy. In fact, it withdraws its forward presence from regions after dealing with a potential hegemon.

As I elaborate in Chapter 1, the active balancer balances in particular ways. It balances against prevailing power, rather than against both power and threat. Moreover, whereas the offshore balancer is concerned only with one key strategic interest, preventing hegemony in a region, the active balancer is concerned with the balance of power, even short of imminent hegemony.[29] Thus, unlike the offshore balancer, it seeks to maintain cooperative relations and arrangements with various states in the region, so as to be able to balance even before a bid for hegemony appears at hand. It works the balance of power with vigor as an ongoing challenge, while the offshore balancer waits patiently and acts only when severe problems arise. Furthermore, the active balancer may develop a forward presence, so as to facilitate efforts to balance, but that is certainly not the case with the offshore balancer.

Of course, states can pursue elements of offshore and active balancing, as even Britain did in its heyday. Thus, as Henry Kissinger described it, "England's policy was based on throwing its weight as the occasion required to the weaker or more threatened side to redress the equilibrium."[30] President Theodore Roosevelt accepted this notion as well. He believed that the United States needed to play a conscious role in Europe's balance of power as a balancer, and he put limited faith in international laws and norms around which collective security efforts could form, in sharp contrast to the position of President Woodrow Wilson.[31]

This book finds that America rarely acted as an offshore balancer in the Persian Gulf. Indeed, in contrast to what we would expect of an offshore balancer, this book clearly shows that the United States increasingly became involved in the region; it used multiple approaches to achieve its ends, including appeasing the strongest or most threatening actors in the region; it developed a forward military presence in the region; and, when it did balance, it did so in a manner often not consonant with offshore balancing.

One partial exception is the 1990–91 Persian Gulf crisis. The United States ultimately did resort to massive force to achieve its ends to check Iraq, which likely had some hegemonic ambitions in the region. In this sense, it acted as an offshore balancer. However, Washington drew on a major political and military infrastructure that it had built over a long period of time and enjoyed a clear forward military presence. The United States was already heavily involved in the region. It was not a last-resort player as it had been in Europe in World War II. Moreover, the 1990–91 crisis had the trappings of a collective security operation, albeit an imperfect and American-dominated one. These points raise questions about the extent to which balancing was predominant in the overall mix of American approaches.

The argument that the United States did not often balance against power in the region, and balanced less over time against either power or threat, raises another question. If America did not act as an active or offshore balancer in the Persian Gulf, does this underscore a problem with balance-of-power theory writ large?[32] To what extent is a test of balance-of-power grand strategies also a test of balance-of-power theory? That is a very delicate question that I pursue in Chapter 11.

An Extraregional Hegemon?

If the United States did not pursue the realist grand strategy of balance of power most of the time, the good news for realist theory is that the United States did not pursue hegemony much, either. Hegemonic strategy differs starkly from active and especially offshore balancing and is the antithesis of what we would expect a realist grand strategy to look like.[33] In his important book *The Peace of Illusions*, Layne argues that since the 1940s the United States has "sought — and to a great extent attained — extraregional hegemony" and that "the story of American grand strategy over the past six decades is one of expansion, and that strategy's logic inexorably has driven the United States to attempt to establish its hegemony in the world's three most important regions outside North America itself: Western Europe, East Asia, and the Persian Gulf."[34] Layne focuses on American strategy in Europe from the early 1940s to the early twenty-first century, leaving a detailed analysis of East Asia and the Persian Gulf to others.[35]

It is very important to stress that Layne does not simply argue that America became a hegemon, which is largely an argument about relative capability in the world.[36] Nor does he argue that it became a hegemon by accident; rather, he maintains that it deliberately pursued a grand strategy of hegemony. That is fundamentally an argument about American intent, the intent to be a hegemon and to pursue hegemony zealously. Layne is certainly not alone in making this judgment about American hegemony seeking, although he develops a new theory called extraregional hegemonic theory to explain America's behavior since the early 1940s.[37] Indeed, inasmuch as thinkers view great powers as pursuing grand strategies of hegemony or at least well-crafted designs, this may be because of how we view history. As Ranke portrayed it, European history since the sixteenth century was a succession of bids for hegemony by one empire or another, and such descriptions are not uncommon in the twenty-first century, with regard to whether American domination will be challenged, for instance, by China or the European Union.[38]

This book fundamentally challenges the thrust of Layne's argument in the case of U.S. foreign policy in the Persian Gulf, as well as that of other thinkers who subscribe to the notion that the United States pursued and sought hegemony in the region. In the process, it also may indirectly challenge broader arguments that refer to American behavior as seeking dominion or primacy or as imperial, which is an even more aggressive and intrusive foreign policy approach than hegemony seeking.[39]

Little evidence suggests that Washington sought hegemony in the Persian Gulf from 1972 through 2005, with the partial exception of the U.S.-led invasion of Iraq in 2003. Quite the contrary, rather than seeking hegemony, it often tried to achieve its goals without involving itself seriously in the region. If anything, it got dragged into the region slowly and largely with little enthusiasm. This scenario contrasts sharply with the way many students of international relations have interpreted U.S. action in the period covered in this book.[40]

To be sure, the Iraq war of 2003 smacked of some elements of hegemony seeking and was a choice that America certainly did not have to make. Nor did the muscular policy that the United States displayed in Iraq emerge overnight. The same factors that led to a decline in balancing in the region created the possibility for the United States to exhibit some aspects of a hegemonic strategy: the rise of American capability, the end of the Cold War, transnational terrorism, and neoconservatism. But I argue in this book that at least three rather critical ingredients were missing from what could be called a hegemonic strategy.

First, the United States did not have a strong intention to be a hegemon. In invading Iraq, it appeared to be motivated less by the trappings of hegemony than by other factors related to the September 11 attacks, to Iraq's record of defiance, and to faulty and selective intelligence.

Second, although Washington's foreign policy may have involved elements of a hegemonic strategy in 2003, it certainly lacked a grand strategy over the broader period of time covered in this book. The notion of grand strategy ascribes to Washington a strategic rationale and outcome that belie how it really approached the region. In fact, its policies and approaches shifted and certainly did not exhibit anything approaching an inexorable or unalterable underlying logic and rationale to which Layne refers or the type of "consistent" effort to expand its power and hegemony which is suggested by a hegemonic strategy.[41]

Third, American foreign policy, if anything, was reactive to events in the region. Indeed, Washington was far more likely to respond to crises and threats that arose than to fashion an organized, forward-looking approach to the region. As a basic guide, table 1 captures the key differences between balance-of-power and hegemonic grand strategies, as well as between active and offshore balancing.

"Reactive Engagement" as the Absence of Grand Strategy

If the United States did not pursue the grand strategies of balance of power or hegemony, what did characterize its behavior toward the region? This is an interesting question. Indeed, what is intriguing is how a country that did not

Table 1. Basic Grand Strategies

	Balance of Power		
	Active Balancing	Offshore Balancing	Hegemony
1. Forward presence	Possibly but not primarily	No	Yes
2. Peacetime role	Yes	No	Yes
3. Forces retracted after balance restored	Largely	Definitely	No
4. Balance against power	Yes	Yes	Not primarily; not unless it serves hegemony
5. Balance against threat	No	Yes, but secondary to balance against power	Not primarily; not unless it serves hegemony
6. Gets other powers to check the aggressor	Possibly	Whenever possible	No
7. Use of force	Sometimes to maintain balance	To prevent imminent hegemony	To assert dominance
8. Intent to dominate	No	No	Definitely and consistently

relish involvement in the Persian Gulf, much less heavy involvement in the post-Vietnam period, increasingly got stuck in the tortuous politics of the region. This is not the story of a grand power pursuing grand visions of hegemony or any grand strategy for that matter. If anything, the vagaries of world politics were more like the tail wagging the superpower dog.

If we needed to describe American behavior, I would coin a new term for this purpose: "reactive engagement."[42] This is neither a new model nor a grand strategy. It is merely a set of concepts. At its core, reactive engagement posits that the United States did not pursue grand strategies of a realist or hegemonic variety. If it pursued any strategy, it was to balance against the most threatening actor, to react against prevailing threat in the region. However, I should stress that balance-of-threat policy was sometimes not pursued, even egregiously breached, and in any case, does not constitute a grand strategy in the literature.[43]

Rather than acting in line with any grand strategy, America most often responded to unexpected, unwanted, and complicated challenges. It engaged most often in reaction. The notion of reactive engagement is intended to conceptualize U.S. foreign policy in the Persian Gulf. However, it may strike a larger note. It may capture the notion that many of the actions of great powers may appear to be part of a larger strategy, or may be conceptualized by thinkers in that way, but are a function largely of events, some random and many unpredictable, to which they must react in a manner that, over time, belies grand strategy. I will develop the concept of reactive engagement in the conclusion of the book, but its trace elements should be evident throughout this work.[44]

Informing Policy Making for the Twenty-first Century

Since the British withdrew their forces from the Persian Gulf in 1971, American behavior has increasingly defined important contours of this region, a region that will become more important in world politics given current projections of rising global oil dependence on the region through at least 2025.[45] U.S. foreign policy in the region directly affects the economic fortunes of all countries, linked by global interdependence, largely because it is an oil-rich region. It is no surprise that major global recessions have coincided with high oil prices caused in part by events in or near the Persian Gulf. The 1973 Arab oil embargo was the first shock; then came the 1979 Iranian revolution, followed by the 1991 Persian Gulf War.

This book informs policy making by exploring the variety of policies that the United States used in the Persian Gulf. And although it does not consciously aim to do so, it also provides some sense of the successes and failures of these policies. It is impossible to determine how the United States should approach regions of the world without a sound understanding of how it has done so in the past.

In particular, virtually under any set of conditions, the United States will have to fashion a foreign policy toward the region. But which policy or combination of policies will it choose? This book does not answer but does inform questions of the following kind, which will remain salient for many years to come: Should the United States become an active balancer, even if that means redoubling its support for unsavory regimes?[46] Should it, as the Cato Institute has argued, "end its policy of trying to manage Persian Gulf security and instead act only as a balancer of last resort if developments in the region pose a serious threat to vital U.S. national security interests"?[47] Can it become an offshore balancer, as many realists and observers would counsel, despite global interdependence and its track record of involvement in the region?[48] Should it try to husband its resources and revert to a policy that relies on regional proxies, as it had done in the 1970s? Might it benefit from pursuing a strategy of hegemony? Can collective security be a sensible alternative? Or might containment work best?[49] Or some combination of the many different approaches the United States has tried?

All these approaches, and others it might pursue, are different and need to be informed by grand theorizing as well as by in-depth analyses of U.S. foreign policy. Washington will not be able to escape the question of how to approach not only the Middle East but also key regions of the world. It is at once inextricably linked to them and yet unable to dominate them. It is linked partly because of global interdependence, which contributes to its far-flung interests, and partly because no other states or set of states can or want to assume its security role. Indeed, European states invented the concept of balance of power in the interstate system, but they are too weak or uninterested to assume the role of balancer in world affairs.[50] Thus, for the foreseeable future at least, Washington must consider playing this role or seeking other strategies by which to meets its goals.

How This Book Contributes

This book seeks to contribute to the literatures on American foreign policy in the Persian Gulf and on grand strategy, but it would be useful to sketch briefly how it fits into the balance-of-power literature. Although balance of power has been influential, it has faced theoretical as well as empirical challenges.[51] Like many other scholars, Stephen Walt believes that states often balance.[52] But, based on a sweeping study of the causes of alliances in the Middle East from 1955 to 1979, he found that states emphasize perceptions of threat more than real capabilities, that "states ally to balance against threats rather than against power alone."[53] This book supports Walt's findings in a rough sense: it finds that the United States was much more likely to balance against threat than against power in the region. But this book differs starkly from Walt in its enterprise.

The overwhelming focus in both theory and practice is on balance of power at the global level. A few scholars have explored balancing at the regional level, but they have not been concerned with the role of great powers outside the region.[54] Walt's balance-of-threat theory offers an effort to explore balancing in a regional

context, but he seeks to examine balancing among global powers or among regional powers, rather than between the regional and global powers, in terms of an
external actor.[55] An exploration of balancing between the two levels is a central
goal of this book.

Moreover, this book considers the extent to which global balancing imperatives might impede regional balancing and vice versa. This is important because
great powers outside regions might not balance in regions because they are
seeking to balance against power or threat at the global level or vice versa.
Neither Walt nor other balancing theorists consider this two-level interaction.

Furthermore, much valuable theoretical work exists on various versions of
balancing, but they are not often tested in real cases.[56] For that matter, although
the literature on grand strategy is burgeoning, it does not include much work that
actually explores the behavior of great powers in detail. For his part, Layne
interestingly tests grand strategy in the case of Europe, but he makes minor
claims on East Asia and the Persian Gulf.[57] This book explores a region and a
time period that have not been examined much in the study of either balancing or
grand strategies.

Beyond Walt, there is also a need for work on the external actor in regions.
Steven David, for his part, significantly enhances our understanding of balancing
behavior in the third world. He shows how domestic-level variables such as the
overriding imperative of autocrats to stay in power affect their external balancing
choices.[58] But his novel work is focused largely on the domestic level within the
context of the third world, not on the role of outside powers in various regions.

Regarding the Gulf in particular, little in-depth analysis exists on even the
distribution of power, much less balancing or active balancing, despite common
references to it and despite its vital role in affecting regional and global security.[59]
The most involved and innovative treatment of balance of power in the post–
Cold War era barely covers the role of outside powers in regions, and it does not
aim to examine the Persian Gulf.[60]

The Scope and Organization of the Book

This book examines key U.S. policies undertaken from 1972 through 2005
toward Iran and Iraq within the larger context of Middle Eastern and global
politics. Chapter 1 explains how the notion of balancer is tested in this book or, in
other words, how we would know if the United States did balance against power
or threat. It also presents a conceptualization that makes it easier to understand

and consider the fact that great powers in regions must consider global and regional pressures when deciding to what extent to balance in lieu of pursuing other strategies at the regional level.

Chapters 2–5 examine the central policies of administrations from Richard Nixon's administration to that of George H. W. Bush. Chapter 2 analyzes the Nixon administration's twin pillar policy (1972–79), which constituted American foreign policy toward the Gulf in the post-Vietnam era.

Chapter 3 turns to the Reagan administration's record. It focuses on three episodes during the Iran-Iraq War: the U.S. tilt toward Iraq (1980–85), the controversial Iran-Contra affair (1985–86), and the U.S. reflagging of Kuwaiti tankers (1986–87).

Chapter 4 explores the controversial policy of constructive engagement toward Iraq carried out by the administration of George H. W. Bush prior to Iraq's invasion of Kuwait in 1990 (1988–90). Chapter 5 looks at the U.S.-led war against Iraq, including Operations Desert Shield and Desert Storm (1990–91), as well as Washington's war-termination strategy at the end of that war (1991).

Chapter 6 analyzes the Clinton administration's policy of dual containment (1992–98), which aimed to contain both Iran and Iraq simultaneously. Chapter 7 discusses Clinton's move toward an approach to Iraq referred to as "containment-plus," which added an official commitment to regime change in Iraq. The Iraq war of 2003, which carried out this commitment in earnest, is addressed in Chapter 8.

Chapter 9 shows that the United States became less likely to practice balance-of-power policies over time. This chapter provides explanations for why this occurred. Chapter 10 cycles back on the book and elaborates its findings, especially the extent to which the United States acted in line with balance-of-power and balance-of-threat policy and the extent to which it pursued the grand strategies of offshore balancing and hegemony seeking. In so doing, this chapter ties the book more firmly into the relevant literature on grand strategy.

Chapter 11 explores some broader theoretical questions. It discusses what this book means for balance-of-power theory more generally and identifies conditions under which the United States did act as an external balancer against prevailing threat.

The concluding chapter addresses a central question generated implicitly by the previous chapters: How can we characterize American behavior in the region? I develop the concept of reactive engagement, which I believe explains U.S.

behavior in the Gulf better than other concepts do and may help explain the behavior of great powers beyond the case of the United States.

The episodes examined in the book are:

1. The Nixon administration's twin pillar policy (1972–79)
2. The Reagan administration's tilt toward Iraq during the Iran-Iraq War (1982–85)
3. The Iran-Contra affair (1985–86)
4. The U.S. reflagging of Kuwaiti oil tankers (1986–87)
5. The Bush administration's constructive engagement toward Iraq (1988–90)
6. Iraq's invasion of Kuwait (1990–91)
7. Washington's war-termination strategy (1991)
8. The Clinton administration's policy of dual containment of Iran and Iraq (1992–98)
9. The Clinton administration's policy of containment-plus (1998–2001)
10. The Iraq war of 2003 (2003–5)

CHAPTER ONE

Exploring Great Powers in Regions

The United States has faced profound threats and attempts at outright hege-mony not only at the regional level from Iran and Iraq but also from outside states at the global level, which has complicated efforts to develop foreign policy toward the region. The Soviet Union played a key role in the international relations of the region in part of the period covered in this book. Hence, we need to consider U.S.-Soviet competition in order to understand American behavior in the Persian Gulf. It may be that the United States did not balance in the Gulf because of pressures at the global level or vice versa.

Moreover, the Cold War is over, but great powers still have vital interests in regions of the world. Indeed, China and Russia have repeatedly asserted the importance of balancing the United States globally, though it is unclear to what extent they do so in reality.[1] Considering both the regional and global levels, therefore, remains important.

Furthermore, the United States must consider how its interests at the global level will be affected by the actions it takes at the regional level and vice versa. This may have always been the case, but it is probably even more so in a world of global interdependence, in which a situation and its ramifications are often not confined to only one state or region. In such a world, the consideration of global-regional linkages becomes even more pressing.

Conceptualizing the Global-Regional Dimension

To understand the role of external actors in regions, it is necessary to explore what is meant by "regional" and "global." Naturally, experts disagree on the meaning of these two concepts. My goal here is simply to identify basic elements that can reasonably be viewed as constituting the regional level of analysis to help us distinguish it from the global level. Such distinctions do not exhaust the different points made in the literature in the past several decades; nor do they settle the many interesting debates on the subject.[2] But they do offer some basis for further analysis in this book at least. In this discussion, I draw heavily on the work of William R. Thompson.[3]

First, we can distinguish the global and regional levels of analysis by the actors that constitute them. The global level consists of the major international powers —for the purposes of this book, the permanent members of the UN Security Council: Russia, the United States, China, France, and Britain. Other states could certainly be included as major or middle-range international powers, but these five states have played an important role in the Gulf and are key actors at the global level, as well. The regional level or subsystem consists of at least two and probably more than two actors. In this book, the Persian Gulf states consist of Iraq and Iran, the two historically most powerful actors in the region, as well as the six members of the Gulf Cooperation Council: Saudi Arabia, Kuwait, Oman, Qatar, the United Arab Emirates, and Bahrain.

Second, as Thompson points out, the pattern of relations or interactions in a subsystem exhibits a degree of regularity and intensity such that a change at one point in the subsystem affects other points.[4] Barry Buzan suggests something along the same lines in asserting that each region consists of states whose major security concerns and perceptions are linked in such a way that those of each state cannot realistically be considered separately.[5] David Lake approaches this issue from another angle. He defines a regional system as a set of states affected by at least one transborder but local externality that emanates from a particular geographical area. Under this definition, although geography is important in defining a region, it may not be sufficient. That is because externalities that pose a perceived or actual threat to states, such as pollution or arms proliferation, may extend beyond a geographical area. Lake prefers to define a region in terms of externalities, asserting that it is the "limited scope of such externalities that differentiates regional subsystems from the global system."[6] Whether one prefers Thompson's approach or Lake's, the intensity and impact of relations at the regional level differ from those at the global level.

Third, the actors in a regional subsystem are generally proximate. This is not a profound point, but it does allow us to delimit the geographical confines of a region. Others believe that regions can be delimited by ideology, religion, ethnicity, or common economic considerations.[7] Obviously, actors at the global level need not be proximate; they occupy a much broader space of interaction and lie at the vortex of myriad religious, ethnic, economic, and other factors. We thus need to rely more on the actors themselves as signposts of the global level of analysis than on the amorphous geographical confines in which they operate.

A fourth characteristic of regions that Thompson and others emphasize is that internal and external observers recognize the region as a distinctive area of operations. This is a subjective element and an interesting bridge to the constructivist literature. Social constructivists, in fact, would argue that irrespective of geography, countries sharing a communal identity constitute a region, regardless of their location.[8] A region, in this sense, becomes what actors see it to be.[9]

Following the work of David Lake and Patrick Morgan, this book aspires to do more than treat regions as sui generis, although it does not go as far as they do in assuming the ability to generalize across regions. The primary focus remains at the international level where outside states play an important role.[10]

Exploring Balancing in a Global-Regional Context

This book examines the role of an external actor in a region and accounts for potentially competing pressures to balance at the global and regional levels against power and threat. This conceptualization is based on four key assumptions.

First, regions are in ways separate from the international system and express their own dynamics. Global space and regional space remain distinct enough to offer sensible levels of analysis. As Barry Buzan put it, regions are different from the "seamless web of relationships that connects all of the states in the international system."[11] In earlier eras, most regions appeared to be less distinct; to display their own dynamics independent of imperial global powers; and to be subordinate to the practices of colonial administration and spheres of influence. This reality changed through a combination of events, including decolonization, the rise of states as sovereign entities in the lesser-developed world, the nation-building process, and international norms that conferred legitimacy on newly developing states.[12]

Second, to say that regions are distinct in some ways does not mean that they cannot be treated as part of a broader global environment. In this book, regions are treated as open systems in world affairs, as areas that can be deeply penetrated economically, politically, and sometimes strategically by outside states. For present purposes, great powers lie outside regions but intervene in them for their own aims, which are sometimes critical. This intervention has an impact on regional dynamics.

Third, external actors, be they Britain, the United States, or modern China, may face pressures to balance against or check other great powers. These pressures can affect their behavior in regions.

Fourth, because they are involved at both the global and regional level, external actors may face potentially competing pressures to balance at both levels. Thus, exploring balancing in a region requires an understanding of both levels and their interactions.[13] It requires that we treat outside states (in this case the United States) as trying to pursue sovereign goals at both the regional and global level, sometimes simultaneously.[14]

A key point follows from these assumptions: if an outside actor such as the United States was not balancing at the regional level, the reason could be that it aimed to balance at the global level and the two efforts conflicted. In that case, the notion of balance of power as grand strategy could be salvaged because balancing was at play, albeit not at the regional level.

Table 2 yields three basic propositions. We can infer from balancing theory that, in its approach toward Iran and Iraq, the United States will independently or with other states

> P1: balance against the strongest state in the region and
>
> P2: balance against the most threatening state in the region.[15]

We can also add the consideration of global pressures to the analysis to see whether it affects the results. On that score, Walt and others have argued that the superpowers will ally with regional powers primarily to balance each other because they are each other's greatest potential threat.[16] Iraq and Moscow were roughly aligned for most of the period covered in this study, although their relations were sometimes strained. That alignment was driven partly by the

Table 2. Predicted U.S. Behavior at the Regional and Global Level

	Global Level	Regional Level
Balance of power	Balance against Iraq's power	Balance against strongest regional state
Balance of threat	Balance against Iraq's threat	Balance against most threatening state

1972 Soviet-Iraqi Treaty of Friendship and Cooperation, which strengthened relations between the two states to some extent until Iraq's invasion of Kuwait on August 2, 1990. The Soviet Union did begin to moderate its foreign policy in the Middle East before its dissolution, but Iraq continued to enjoy strong support among critical elements in Moscow, even well after the end of the Cold War.[17]

Given these realities, the key test here is that if the United States aimed to balance against Moscow at the global level, it would balance against Iraq. To make the test even harder, we could posit that the United States would

> P3: balance against the power or threat (or both) of Iraq (Moscow's client state), even if Iran was more powerful or threatening at the regional level.

Although it is valuable to explore basic propositions about balancing, it is also useful to lay out some propositions that can illuminate the conditions under which an external actor will balance against threat. Stephen Walt discusses conditions under which states balance instead of bandwagon, and other scholars have introduced useful domestic variables to refine the theory.[18] The question remains, however, of when an external actor will balance against prevailing threat in a region rather than pursue a nonbalancing approach other than bandwagoning. I propose that balancing against threat is more likely when

> P1: the external actor believes that it is unlikely to persuade the most threatening actor, through a variety of incentives, in lieu of tougher approaches such as balancing;
>
> P2: the outside state faces a regional military threat rather than a political or ideological threat; and
>
> P3: balancing against threat at the regional level does not contradict balancing against threat (not power) at the global level.

Operationalizing Balancing, Threat, and Power

There are no easy ways to operationalize balancing, threat, and power. Inasmuch as scholars have tested balancing, they have relied primarily on case studies.[19]

Active Balancing

Although it is one thing to posit a few basic propositions, it is another to identify what active balancing behavior would look like if we saw it. In the present work, balancing is reflected chiefly but not solely in an external actor's use of military instruments and statecraft independently or with allies against prevailing power or threat.[20]

In evaluating the episodes in this book, I use the following benchmarks as a guide. These cannot ensure a definitive outcome, but they will offer a better basis for making judgments than would exist without them.

First, the chief objective of the active balancer has been to play local powers off each other in order to ensure a balance of power.[21] In this type of action, and as is roughly consonant with the vast historical record, balancing requires "diplomatic flexibility" and shifts in behavior as power and threat change.[22]

Second, balancing also eschews actions to appease prevailing power or threat. Indeed, doing so would represent one of the most serious indications of non-balancing behavior.

Third, as a conscious balancer, the active balancer will not take or be inclined to take actions that leave one state predominant in the distribution of power; at a minimum, it must be seriously concerned with and consider the possibility that its actions could leave one state predominant in the region.[23] In most situations, failure to exhibit such concern would suggest that balance-of-power considerations are not especially important or outright unimportant.

Fourth, the active balancer most often will take action to redress a problem in the balance of power before a serious threat arises. Indeed, this is exactly how Britain acted in mainland Europe in certain periods of previous centuries, even though its public initially preferred not "to fight conjectural dangers based on what some country might do later on."[24] This is in sharp contrast to collective security action, which requires that a threat become manifest before efforts are made to address it through collective action.

Fifth, most balancing theories, including active balancing and offshore balancing, are state-centric. They assume that states are unconcerned with the ideology of other states. Realpolitik-based grand strategy is nonideological and allows for the potential to reconcile competing differences diplomatically.[25] Moreover, balancing theory does not assume that individuals will play a major role in shaping strategic outcomes across an array of cases. It does not consider the subnational level. Even if a state balances at the international level, balancing theory would expect that it would do so not for individual-level reasons but rather in response to the strategic context.

Sixth, following from this point, balancing will not involve efforts to alter or eliminate the regimes of other states. Insofar as states do engage in balancing action, this action cannot be explained with respect to internal politics and realities. Nor would we expect domestic politics to be a primary reason for their foreign policy behavior in any case if balancing is to be considered a good reason for state action.[26]

Threat

For Walt, threat can be inferred from aggregate power, geographical proximity, offensive capability, and the perceived aggressiveness of intentions.[27] That is quite sensible, but Walt does not seek to measure these variables. Though the approach I offer is not better, it is different in that I directly explore threat perception rather than infer it. I do this by examining the historical record, declassified memos and other primary sources, and the positions of decision makers in order to assess whether the United States regarded Iran or Iraq as more threatening in each case. These combined sources offer a fair portrait of threat. Of course, interviews of decision makers need to be assessed for potential bias or forgetfulness, but they can offer insights into how leaders perceive threats which cannot be obtained from other sources or which may augment existing sources.[28]

Power

For Walt, power is an aggregate concept that encompasses a state's total resources (e.g., population, industrial and military capability, and technological prowess).[29] However, there is no ideal way to measure power.

Randall Schweller effectively uses the Correlates of War (COW) database for examining the balance of power at the global level during World War II, but that database does not include measures for Iran and Iraq for the time period covered in this study.[30] Nor are all its measures sensible for the Persian Gulf context. The best measure for this study is military capability because it captures relative fighting capability.[31] In the war-prone Persian Gulf during the period discussed in this book, military capability fundamentally affected outcomes. With greater military capability, Iran or Iraq might have dominated the region, even though their economies were devastated by war. In Iraq's case, it received more than $30 billion in financial support from Saudi Arabia and Kuwait, which allowed it to fight on despite its economic straits.

Some scholars do measure power, partly by using an indicator for population size, but such a measure would cloud more than illuminate the present analysis. Indeed, by 1990, Iraq fielded a military twice that of Iran, even though it had a far smaller population. Moreover, relative military capability, unlike population, changed significantly in the region over time. Thus, indicators of relative military capability can highlight shifts in the balance of power, which are important to understand in trying to assess whether the United States responded to shifts in power and in threat. Changes in military capability also were more obvious and noticeable to Washington than shifts in population or economic strength, thus allowing a better test of changing American threat perceptions.

One approach to assessing the balance of power is to generate an overall figure of power for all relevant states and then assess each state's percentage of that overall power figure. That is useful if many states are involved, but in the Gulf, Iran and Iraq were the only two powerful states in the period 1972–2005.[32]

Finally, the data on military capability are far more reliable than the data on economic measures or even those on military expenditures. The available information, in any case, shows little relative difference in military expenditures between Iran and Iraq from 1985 to 1991.[33]

Whatever measures of power we do use, they cannot replace case study analysis. Power is hard to understand independent of the context in which it is used. Moreover, some elements of power were critical but not quantifiable in the Gulf. For instance, territorial acquisition by Iraq and Iraq during regional wars was an important source of power.

Although the measurement of power is imprecise, it is quite clear, as this book will show, that Iraq became much stronger than Iran over time. This is strongly confirmed by more sophisticated measures of power created by the U.S. Air Force which account for the quality of combat capability. Indeed, even though Iran had four years to rebuild its military after the 1988 cease-fire in the Iran-Iraq War, and even though Iraq's military was devastated by the 1991 Persian Gulf War, Iraq still had nearly three times the combat capability of Iran in 1992.[34]

On the whole, the present method is far from ironclad, but it combines systematic and case study analysis and offers several broader advantages. It disaggregates one historical period into numerous episodes. By testing both balance-of-threat and balance-of-power policy against ten episodes, we generate many tests within one larger case. The greater the number of episodes or observations, the more credible the findings, ceteris paribus.[35] In addition, by exploring the same region over time, we can control for variables better than cross-national studies can, since a diachronic approach involves more constants and fewer variables.[36] That is, fewer variables change over time than over both time and area. These two advantages also make it easier to determine whether variables existed when balancing was or was not at play.

Testing for Balancing Behavior

A special issue needs to be discussed and clarified up front. First, critics might assert that external actors cannot be sensitive to short-term shifts in the balance of power or that power did not shift in the short term in the Persian Gulf. Yet because of conditions of war in the region, American sanctions against Iran, and international support for Iraq against Iran, the balance of power did often change over short periods of time. Iraq gained significantly over Iran in military capability as the Iran-Iraq War progressed. By 1988, Iraq emerged from the war a military powerhouse, whereas Iran was militarily supine. As the episodes will show, the United States was aware not only of regional shifts in power but also of shifts in threat that were often quite clear.

Even in cases in which the balance of power did not change much, we can still test for balancing behavior. This is because U.S. policies did change toward a nonbalancing approach. Thus, as we shall see, Washington shifted from balancing against Iran in 1982–85 to engaging and even strengthening Iran in the Iran-Contra affair, even though the balance of power in the region did not change much.

Second, as suggested above, some critics might assert that balance-of-power realism would not predict short-term responses to changes in the balance of power or threat but rather an eventual response to them. The episodes of the book are chosen, in part, to address this issue. They are lengthy affairs rather than short-term events. For instance, I did not choose Operation Desert Fox in December 1998, in which the United States bombarded Iraq with cruise missiles to punish its noncooperation with UN inspectors, because the operation lasted only four days. Although I discuss it as part of American policy in the region, it was too brief an event to qualify as an episode. In addition, these episodes include events that had the potential to or actually did change the balance of power or threat, partly because they were not short term but also because they were major events. Even the Iran-Contra affair, for instance, had the potential to shift the balance of power by providing Iran with intelligence and arms to prosecute its assault on the Fao Peninsula in February 1986. In most instances, the episodes involve clear-cut changes in power. By 1988, Iraq was clearly far stronger than Iran. Thus, it is less ambiguous how the United States should have responded if it were balancing at the regional level.

Third, some scholars might argue that regions are not marked by anarchical features, chiefly the absence of higher authority above the state level.[37] That, however, is certainly not true of the Persian Gulf. It is as anarchical as regions come, with no higher authority or set of institutions for redress in interstate conflicts, in contrast to the European Union, which represents the other end of the spectrum and most approximates the hierarchy of domestic politics of any region in the world. Nevertheless, American interests are fundamentally at stake in the region.

Fourth, the episodes are chosen because they had global dimensions, thus making for a more interesting examination of the region as part of an open global system. In part, that made it possible to explore the relation between global and regional balancing pressures, as well as how the United States pursued its various interests in the region without a global context.

Conclusion

Using the approach laid out in this chapter, the book first explores balancing in the pertinent episodes of American foreign policy in the Persian Gulf. Later chapters discuss in greater detail the extent to which the United States pursued extraregional hegemony or offshore balancing. That is not something that can be assessed on a case-by-case basis because these strategies can be discerned only across a longer time period. Thus, we should not expect the United States to be an offshore balancer in each case but rather only in the extreme cases in which a hegemonic threat was imminent. However, although it is not sensible to test for these grand strategies in each case, examining many episodes over time makes it possible to test for grand strategies during the period covered in this book. That said, much of this book focuses on examining the active balancer and balance-of-threat approaches in each case. I then draw on these analyses to make judgments about offshore balancing and the pursuit of extraregional hegemony.

The Nixon Administration's Twin Pillars

The Persian Gulf rose in importance in great-power jockeying during the two world wars of the twentieth century. But it was really after the discovery and large-scale development of oil, chiefly after World War II, that it gained larger global economic prominence. Indeed, the United States started to take stock of Saudi oil not only as an economic resource but also because it could serve as a potential weapon of power by Moscow, whose troops had not yet withdrawn from Iranian Azerbaijan, despite the war's end and Moscow's promises to do so. With this concern in mind, President Harry S Truman approved the completion of the air base at Dhahran, Saudi Arabia, on September 28, 1945, thus launching the U.S.-Saudi strategic relationship in earnest.

The United States was formally committed to Saudi security at least as early as 1947 when Truman and King Ibn Saud made a pact, described in a State Department cable, which pledged that if Saudi Arabia was attacked by another power or under threat of attack, Washington would take "energetic measures under the auspices of the United Nations to confront such aggression."[1] Yet even after World War II, the region remained on the sidelines of global politics, submerged under the more pressing realities of the Cold War. It would take revolution, wars, and terrorism over the next three decades to bring it front and center.

This chapter begins by sketching Moscow's rising profile in the region in the 1970s and analyzing the region's balance of power. It then discusses the Nixon administration's twin pillar policy and explains its importance in U.S. strategy in the region. In doing so, this chapter also provides some background that will help in understanding subsequent American behavior in the region.

In brief, the United States clearly balanced against power at the global level in the 1970s. It was fundamentally focused on balancing against the Soviet Union during the Cold War, and thus it balanced against Iraq. Washington also balanced against threat in the region because it saw Iraq as far more threatening than any other state in the Persian Gulf, largely because it was aligned, even if uneasily, with Moscow. It is less clear, however, that the United States balanced against power in the region. This is because Iran was stronger than Iraq during this time. Global imperatives to balance against power took precedence over balancing against power at the regional level.

The British Withdrawal from East of Suez

Serious American involvement in the Persian Gulf is relatively recent. Britain, not the United States, had military predominance in the Persian Gulf in the post–World War II period. This changed in 1968 when, to America's chagrin, Britain announced that it would withdraw from the area east of Suez, a withdrawal it completed by 1971. The withdrawal was motivated by a number of possible factors, including Arab nationalist challenges, rising American strength, and flagging British strategic and economic capabilities.[2] By 1971, Washington had assumed the responsibility for the defense of Western strategic interests in the Persian Gulf, with Britain playing only a minor role.

British withdrawal left a temporary power vacuum in the region which had to be filled. For decades Britain's hegemony over the Gulf decreased adventurism by regional and global powers. Britain enjoyed military predominance at sea and a monopoly of political control in the region. Others could not sensibly challenge the British position.

After Britain withdrew, smaller Gulf states became more vulnerable to the larger ones. Indeed, as a harbinger of ensuing events, Iraq threatened to occupy parts of Kuwait one week after Britain withdrew its forces. At the global level, the

British departure presaged increased global rivalry, which would fluctuate in intensity, alter the nature of regional interaction, and further complicate the international politics of the Gulf until the Soviet Union's demise. Britain's departure strengthened America's influence in the Gulf and heightened the Soviet Union's fears that Washington would either seize control of Gulf oil or use the region to undermine Soviet security.

In particular, on April 9, 1972, the Soviet Union and Iraq signed the Treaty of Friendship and Cooperation, which provided for the qualified Soviet use of the Iraqi base at Umm Qasr and increased Soviet-Iraqi economic and especially military cooperation. Moscow became Iraq's top arms supplier and helped create the Iraqi army that invaded Iran in 1980 and Kuwait in 1990. Article 9 of the treaty stipulated that the parties would continue to "develop cooperation in the strengthening of their defense capabilities," an agreement so unique that it was not even in Soviet treaties with critical countries such as Egypt and India.[3]

The Soviet-Iraqi treaty greatly concerned Washington because it appeared to challenge all its interests in the region and to alter the balance of power at a time when the United States was trying to determine how to replace Britain as the enforcer of regional security. Indeed, the United States' primary aims in the region were to achieve stability, limit Soviet influence while avoiding confrontation with Moscow, and assure access to Persian Gulf energy.[4]

Episode 1: America's Twin Pillar Policy, 1972–1979

It is not accidental that one month after the Soviets and Iraq signed this treaty, President Nixon and national security adviser Henry Kissinger visited Iran and made a fateful agreement in which Washington promised to provide the shah of Iran, Muhammad Reza Pahlevi, with unrivaled access to U.S. weapons in exchange for his role in protecting U.S. regional security.[5] At the end of the meeting, the president stated that the United States would continue to cooperate with Iran in strengthening its defenses as the best hope for regional stability and security, given that Iran could, among other things, put pressure on Iraq.[6] Whether Moscow's connection to Baghdad or Washington's connection to Iran was more responsible for triggering a regional arms race in the 1970s, that outcome did occur.[7]

The famous Nixon Doctrine, which was enunciated at Guam in 1969, called on states in Asia to assume greater responsibility for their own security, thus relieving the United States of direct involvement in the region.[8] In line with that doctrine,

Washington preferred to delegate responsibility for Persian Gulf security to regional states. In this way, Washington would not need to intervene directly in the region in the post–Vietnam War era, avoiding the potential for costly and unpopular foreign wars. That war had left an indelible mark on the American people and on U.S. decision makers. It hurt the economy, divided the public, damaged American credibility, and most important, cost more than fifty-seven thousand lives. Nixon won the presidency partly on the promise that he would end the war in Vietnam without sacrificing American honor and credibility.

In the Gulf, unlike in Vietnam, the United States could rely primarily on Iran and, to a lesser extent, Saudi Arabia to safeguard regional security and to protect the status quo, which favored American interests.[9] Few Americans understood at the time (or since) that one by-product of the Vietnam experience was that Washington would shy away from more serious and involved efforts in the Middle East.[10] That trend would be radically reversed over the next three decades. As Vietnam faded in memory, as American power grew, and as revolutions and wars erupted in the region, the United States would find itself reacting to events — many of them unpredictable — that drew it into the politics of the region.

In exchange for Iran's stabilizing role, Washington sold the shah copious amounts of conventional weapons, following Nixon's promise to do just that when he visited Iran in May 1972.[11]

The United States adopted a policy that provided, in effect, that it would accede to any of the shah's requests for arms purchases from the United States "other than some sophisticated advanced technology armaments, and with the very important exception, of course, of any nuclear weapons capability."[12]

The shah was entirely right to note, without a hint of understanding that his connection to America would prove controversial with his people, that these arms sales, "whose vastness may prove astonishing," served partly as an indicator from Tehran of strong U.S.-Iranian relations.[13] However, these arms sales also underscored just how critical Washington considered its relations with Iran. Arms sales to Iran accounted for one-third of U.S. sales to the world between 1973 and 1978.[14] Indeed, arms transfers rose from $750 million in 1969–71 to an annual average of more than $2 billion in the 1970s.[15] Not only did the quantity of arms sales increase massively, but so did the quality of weapons sold. The shah was sold F-15 and F-16 fighters, which represented cutting-edge technology in global weaponry. The vast arms sales to Iran that followed from the thrust of the Nixon Doctrine reversed a twenty-five-year approach in U.S. foreign policy which rejected Iran's previous efforts to benefit from massive American arms sales.[16]

The arms sales underscored a key element in the twin pillar policy: a motivation to balance Iraq at the regional level and Moscow at the global level. Balance of power as a motivating notion was stronger under the Nixon administration than it would be for the next three decades, at least in American foreign policy in the Gulf.

Kissinger, the chief architect of the twin pillar policy, described it as motivated largely by balance-of-power concerns, although Iran was important to the related goal of protecting the free flow of oil through the Strait of Hormuz.[17] By 1972, not only had the British withdrawn from the region, but the Soviets were strengthening their position in the Middle East by securing treaties with Egypt and, more important, Iraq. Moreover, states friendly to the United States, such as Saudi Arabia and Jordan, appeared encircled by hostile forces. In order to balance against this array of forces, the United States chose to support the shah of Iran.[18] As Kissinger put it, the "real issue in 1972 was that the required balance within an area essential for the security, and even more the prosperity, of all industrial democracies appeared in grave danger."[19]

Kissinger and Nixon deemphasized the ideological fight against communism that had been prevalent in American politics for more than two decades and instead opted for a realist approach to world politics.[20] Détente (a relaxation of tensions) with the Soviets marked their approach at the global level. It was a different form of containing (checking) the threat from Moscow.[21]

Indeed, not only did Moscow appear to be gaining ground at the global level, but the threat from Iraq was also a concern for Washington at the regional level. For Kissinger, "radical Iraq was being put into a position by Soviet arms to assert traditional hegemonic aims, at just the time that Britain had completed its historic withdrawal of its forces from the Persian Gulf. . . . It was imperative for our interests and those of the Western world that the regional balance of power be maintained so that moderate forces would not be engulfed nor Europe's and Japan's (and as it later turned out, our) economic lifeline fall into hostile hands. We could either provide the balancing force ourselves or enable a regional power to do so. . . . Fortunately, Iran was willing to play this role. The vacuum left by British withdrawal, now menaced by Soviet intrusion and radical momentum, would be filled by a local power friendly to us. Iraq would be discouraged from adventures against Emirates in the lower Gulf, and against Jordan and Saudi Arabia."[22]

Bolstering Iran to check Iraq underscored that the administration thought in terms of balance-of-power realism. However, in actual behavior — and this is

Table 3. The Military Balance, 1972–1980

Total	Men[a]	Army[b]	Tanks	Combat Aircraft
1972 (At the initiation of the twin pillar policy)				
Iran	191,000	160,000	860	160
Iraq	102,000	90,000	860	189
1977				
Iran	342,000	222,000	1,560	341
Iraq	188,000	160,000	1,400	369
1980 (At the outset of the Iran-Iraq War)				
Iran	240,000	150,000	1,735	447
Iraq	243,000	200,000	2,750	339

Source: International Institute for Strategic Studies, *The Military Balance* (London: International Institute for Strategic Studies, various editions).

[a]The active total for "Men" comprises all personnel on full-time duty, including conscripts, long-term assignments from the Reserves, and paramilitary elements when so required by the national authority.

[b]Personnel in the army, not including paramilitary elements.

important to stress—it did not reflect balancing against the strongest actor in the region. Indeed, in overall military capability, Iran was roughly stronger than Iraq in 1972 and at least maintained that position throughout the rest of the 1970s, owing to massive American arms sales, as shown in table 3.

Rather, the American arms sales and strong connection to Iran reflected primarily an effort to balance against Moscow at the global level by checking Iraq at the regional level. Moreover, it represented an effort to balance against Iraq's threat at the regional level, if not Iraq's prevailing power. Iraq was obviously viewed as the much more threatening actor in the region in the 1970s, until Iran's theocratic revolution.

For its part, Moscow eagerly sought to strengthen its position in the Persian Gulf in the 1970s in rivalry with the United States.[23] Its efforts met with mixed success, but it did establish a political and military foothold in the Horn of Africa and in South Yemen from which it could more effectively project military power into the Gulf region.[24] Moscow's gains were militarily insignificant considering that it probably never had the propensity to invade the Gulf region. However, they created the impression that the Soviet Union, rather than the United States, had predominance in global and regional rivalry. The Saudis and Omanis even feared military action by the Cubans and Ethiopians, directed by the Soviets, against the strategically vital Strait of Bab el-Mandeb, which lies at the mouth of the Red Sea.[25]

In a region where perceptions of power and strength are highly significant, Moscow's gains did not go unnoticed, and Iran did help in addressing Washington's concerns about the Soviet Union. Indeed, although America's support of the shah was problematic, it offered the United States some strategic benefits, which Washington recognized and appreciated.[26] As one official pointed out, "It is hard to identify another country in which our interests are better served. We derive numerous benefits from this relationship that contribute to our vital strategic needs . . . in this strategically vital area."[27]

The shah established correct relations with all Gulf states, except Iraq, between 1972 and 1979 and was, by and large, a mediating influence — a development that Iran liked to advertise.[28] These states were made uneasy by the shah's imperialist designs, found his arrogance annoying, and even feared that he might one day turn Iranian power on them. However, they also saw Iran as a stabilizing force in the region, insofar as it helped check real and perceived threats from Iraq and Moscow. On the Gulf's periphery, Iran served as a conduit for improved U.S.-Egyptian relations throughout the 1970s. Between 1972 and 1979, it helped lure North Yemen and Somalia away from the Soviet Union, and Iran's troops also played a role in defeating a communist-backed tribal revolt in Pakistan's Baluchistan Province. In the Gulf, the shah's troops were useful in helping Oman suppress the Dhofar rebellion against Sultan Qabus in 1975 and maintain order thereafter. To some extent, the rebellion had been supported by the Soviets and Soviet client states as a means of undermining Oman's pro-American monarchy. The insurrection, however, was controlled with help from Iran, Britain, the United States, and Jordan. The suppression of the rebellion was viewed by other Gulf states as important to their strategic interests, since Oman's stability was connected to that of the Gulf as a whole. Iran also served as a check on Iraq and South Yemen, which, because of their links to Moscow and their own regional ambitions, were viewed as serious threats to regional security.

With regard to the oil issue, relations between the United States and Iran were tempestuous, but on the positive side, Iran, which was one of the founding members of the Organization of Petroleum Exporting Countries (OPEC) in 1960, refused to join the 1973 Arab oil embargo, though Tehran exploited it to push oil prices higher. Iran's refusal to join the embargo gained it stature in Washington and in oil-consuming nations, as did the shah's open call for an end to the embargo and for earnest efforts to pursue Middle East peace prospects; this position contrasted sharply with that taken by the Arab rejectionist front, which Moscow supported and which was composed of states that were especially hostile to the United States and to Israel.[29] That effort served U.S. interests on the oil front and in challenging radical regional politics from which Moscow and Iraq benefited. Enhancing relations with Iran had the added benefit of decreasing the chances that Moscow could make inroads in Tehran. Moscow had aligned with Baghdad, but it also sought to gain influence with Iran, chiefly by the use of economic instruments, in the hope that Iran's policies would be more favorable toward the Soviet Union. These efforts were noted in Washington.[30]

Yet although the shah had established extensive economic ties with the Soviet Union and was not reluctant to point to positive relations with Moscow at times, he remained, in Kissinger's view, "highly suspicious of long-term Soviet objectives. His nightmare [was] Soviet envelopment of Iran, through client forces in Iraq and Afghanistan."[31] In a meeting with the Soviet ambassador in July 1973, the shah, according to an Iranian official present at the meeting, told the ambassador, who had chided him about major arms purchases from Washington, that a "strong Iran, along with Turkey and Pakistan, could serve as a bulwark to the south of Russia; the Shah made this out to be directed at China, but it is clear that it was about the USSR."[32] Relations with Moscow, which had been at a ten-year low, took a turn for the better in the summer of 1974, but the shah, according to one key cable from Tehran, remained "wary of Soviets' long-term intentions."[33]

To be sure, Carter pursued what some might call a more moralist foreign policy, one that viewed as possible not only coexistence with the Soviets but also the development of a sense of global community.[34] At the global level, Carter moved away from the non-normative, balance-of-power realpolitik that Nixon practiced.[35] However, balancing against Iraq and Moscow still remained important elements in U.S. foreign policy. For instance, although President Carter was more likely to call into question the policy of selling Iraq unlimited conventional weaponry, he did push through the sale of Airborne Warning and Control System (AWACS) aircraft to Iran, against strong opposition in Congress and various branches of government.[36] Moreover, the Carter administration initiated the development of the U.S. Rapid Deployment Force to deal with contingencies, chiefly in the Middle East, although its efforts to protect the region would be increased rather significantly after the Soviets invaded Afghanistan in 1979.

The Crash of the Twin Pillar Policy

The twin pillar policy established the basis for positive relations between Iran and the United States, but the policy proved problematic over time. The problems that arose underscored the difficulty of pursuing balancing politics from afar and relying on proxies to protect American interests, and they presaged an inevitable shift in U.S. foreign policy. America's designs for the region clashed with reality.

The Carter administration, which continued the Nixon administration's twin pillar policy, had challenging relations with Iran from the start. Tehran did serve as a reliable supplier of a high volume of oil, but it proved much more hawkish on oil pricing than Washington found acceptable. In fact, Iran exploited the 1973 Arab oil embargo to drive oil prices higher before calling for it to be ended and continued to push oil prices higher.[37]

Except for a short period in late 1977, Iran continued to be hawkish on oil prices within OPEC.[38] The State Department was even concerned at times that the Soviets might try to capitalize on what they saw as the "coming crunch between US and Iran over oil prices." In August 1974, for example, the American Embassy in Tehran informed the U.S. secretary of state that the shah had emerged as the "most quoted defender of current oil prices" and Americans as the "most vocal objectors."[39] Yet Washington was also concerned that pressing Iran strongly to lower oil prices might damage relations with Iran, which was important to American security in the Gulf.[40] The United States preferred instead to use diplomacy and positive incentives. Indeed, it is reasonable to believe that arms sales to Iran helped coax the shah to agree to the request from Washington that Iran stop pushing for higher oil prices at OPEC meetings.[41]

U.S.-Iranian tensions started to become more serious in the period from 1975 to 1979, as did domestic-level opposition against the shah. The shah's grandiose plans for regional power proved challenging to the United States, as well as to other actors that resented Iran's rising military strength, such as Saudi Arabia.[42] Riyadh did not trust the shah and, according to State Department reports, doubted the stability of his regime.[43] It also sought to send Iran a strong signal that Riyadh, although interested in cooperating with Iran, was ready to react to any Iranian efforts at regional hegemony or intrusion.[44]

At times, the shah appeared more willing to take American arms than advice. He based his security approach less on joint U.S.-Iranian goals than on Iran's goals alone, which may well have included an effort to dominate the region, even at America's expense. Indeed, in line with long-standing Iranian preferences, the shah would sometimes assert that he preferred no foreign power or influence in the Persian Gulf, and Washington understood that point as a clear reference to the American role in the region, as well.[45]

Nor was Washington discriminating in its arms transfers. Concern mounted in the U.S. Congress regarding the pace, scope, and implications of Iran's massive, American-supported military buildup. The shah's dismal human rights record also raised questions about the morality of supporting his regime. His disregard for basic American values as reflected in the repressive, far-reaching, and shady nature of his secret police, SAVAK, was viewed as troublesome in some American quarters.

However, given American fears of Soviet power and of the ambitions of regional actors such as Iraq, morality took a back seat to American strategic interests in the Persian Gulf, as it did in most other regions around the globe. In retrospect, it does appear that U.S. support of the repressive shah contributed to his downfall. The close American connection helped paint him as a puppet of America and therefore as a leader less likely to preserve the interests and integrity of Iran.

The twin pillar policy was dealt a lethal blow by the events of 1979, which are important for understanding not only the precipitous demise of this strategy but also subsequent U.S. foreign policy in the Persian Gulf. The Iranian revolution swept away the Pahlevi monarchy and replaced it with Ayatollah Khomeini and the Islamic Republic of Iran. The Persians, who were once ruled by the greatest of kings and oversaw one of the largest empires in history more than 2,500 years ago, would now be ruled by a cleric who had great visions for an Islamic republic.[46] In many quarters in the Middle East, it was believed that the United States would take the necessary steps to save the shah.[47] The prime minister of Bahrain, reflecting the general sentiment in the Gulf, was baffled that America could be "brought down to its knees" by a religious fanatic, and he questioned American reliability.[48] The shah's imperialist stand in the Gulf was not appreciated by the Gulf states, but he at least was a devil they knew. Khomeini, who was affected by an almost Marxian belief that the masses would prevail over their oppressors and that governments per se would diminish in importance, actively encouraged the overthrow of the Gulf monarchies, whose secular, Westernized rule he viewed as shameful.[49] He promised to vouchsafe Islam not only to the Middle East but also to the world.[50] Iran was predominantly Shiite, but the more secular Arab Gulf states in the region were under Sunni leadership. In the case of Iraq until Saddam's regime was eliminated in 2003, and Bahrain as well, Sunni leaders ruled over a predominantly Shiite population. This situation presented Khomeini with the opportunity to subvert Sunni leaders by appealing directly to their people.

In the period following the revolution, Iran appeared bent on dominating the region, overthrowing Arab Gulf monarchies, and eliminating U.S. regional influence.[51] Not only did it reject any American overtures, but it wanted to be rid of American interference, which was prominent in its history from the time that the popular prime minister Mohammad Mossadegh was removed by a CIA-assisted coup assisted by the CIA and replaced by the shah of Iran in 1953. The Saudis in particular also feared that the Iranian revolution would create a "military vacuum" that Moscow could exploit.[52]

Initially, however, the Iranian revolution did not generate serious tensions between Iran and Arab Gulf states. Although radicals in Iran's government entertained a more ambitious foreign policy vis-à-vis the Arab Gulf states, Iran's overall threat was confined as long as the Gulf states appeared not to challenge the fundamental bases of the revolution. Iran even sought to maintain relations with Arab states.[53] However, the underlying incompatibility of Iran's foreign policy with the policies of the more moderate Arab Gulf states eventually became manifest and would be widened by the Iran-Iraq War. As with the Chinese, French, and even Russian revolutions, Iran's revolution transformed a moderate, monarchical, and basically agrarian state into one mobilized for conflict and ultimately war.[54]

The revolution eventually disrupted security interactions that for a decade had served as the foundation for relative stability. It also made the Gulf the focus of larger trends in the Middle East, such that Soviet influence on the Gulf's periphery gained a new meaning for the security of the Gulf. Prior to the revolution Saudi Arabia had been concerned about the shah's increasing military strength and regional ambition, but it shared with Iran an interest in checking Soviet influence and in ensuring regional stability. Consequently, the two countries often tacitly cooperated with each other.[55] The revolution, however, put Saudi-Iranian relations on a path toward increased tensions and, in the 1980s, open conflict.

Saudi legitimacy rested on Riyadh's role as the guardian of the two most holy sites of Islam, namely, Mecca, the birthplace of Islam, and Medina, where the prophet Muhammad launched his mission in God's service.[56] Unlike Pahlevi Iran, revolutionary Iran challenged Riyadh's claim as the champion of Islam by offering an alternative Islamic model that rejected the monarchical Islamic state and offered a theocratic one in its place. The clash between these two approaches to Islamic governance created serious frictions, as would Al Qaeda's even more radical vision of Islamic rule with Riyadh's monarchical rule.

In the postrevolutionary period Iran's relations with Oman, Bahrain, and Iraq also deteriorated. Iran withdrew its forces from Oman, where they had played an important security role, and threatened to revive its historical claims to Bahrain, which the shah had renounced. More important, the revolution eventually produced effects that undermined Iran's relations with Iraq, relations that had been relatively stable. The weakening of relations between Iran and other regional actors assumed greater importance because it coincided with the perception that Moscow was on the move and that America was weak. The Iranian revolution considerably heightened fears of Soviet intentions. Leaders in the Gulf and observers outside the region felt that Soviet moves in the Horn, southern Arabia, and Afghanistan were part of a long-term effort to encircle and subvert the Gulf.[57] For their part, the Saudis publicly expressed their hope for regional stability, but privately they were concerned that the chaos in Iran would create greater leftist influence and lead over time to Soviet domination.[58]

The fall of the shah forced a reluctant and unprepared Washington to seek alternate means for protecting its interests in the Gulf. The collapse of Iranian oil production in the postrevolutionary period led to a tripling of oil prices, which damaged American interests and accelerated the need for increased U.S. involvement in the region.

As the remaining pillar, Saudi Arabia became more important in this strategy. Although Riyadh lacked Iran's military capability and considerable troops, it did have anticommunist credentials, a strategic location, and relative clout in the Arab world. These factors made it an attractive replacement for the fallen Iran within a makeshift approach to protect American interests in the region, but even that approach was bedeviled largely by the political headwinds blowing through the broader Middle East to which American mini-designs would be vulnerable. The Saudis had always been wary of a close association with Washington, and political developments in 1978 and 1979 made Riyadh even less willing and able to align itself with the United States.[59]

First, the disruption caused by the revolution was exacerbated by the residual effects of the Camp David peace process. The Camp David Accords isolated Egypt, the only Arab state willing to make peace with Israel, from the Arab world and from Persian Gulf actors in particular. Perceptions on the treaty differed in the Arab world, but many saw President Anwar Sadat's peace with Israel as selling out the Arab cause, breaking with Arab multilateral pressure on Israel, and appeasing the Americans and Zionists.

On April 7, 1979, Egypt announced the recall of its ambassadors to Bahrain,

Kuwait, Qatar, Saudi Arabia, and the United Arab Emirates.[60] Later in the month Saudi Arabia and Kuwait broke diplomatic relations with Egypt, an action that Egypt reciprocated. Political and security relations between Egypt and Arab Gulf states would be restored in the late 1980s in response to the imperatives of the Iran-Iraq War. However, for almost a decade, Egypt, which had become more important to Washington as a result of its peace with Israel, would remain isolated from most of the Arab world and unable to play an effective moderating role. To make matters worse, Iraq grew in power as Egypt was ostracized. As a sign of this, the two emergency Arab summits aimed at dealing with Egypt's break with the Arab world were held in Baghdad.[61]

Second, internally, the Saudis were faced with two attempts to undermine the royal family's authority. The first attempt was the November 20, 1979, seizure of the Grand Mosque of Mecca, Islam's holiest shrine, by several hundred armed Muslim zealots. Eight days after this event, while the Saudi National Guard was still battling the zealots at Mecca, disturbances erupted in Saudi Arabia's oil-rich eastern province in a second attempt to undermine the country internally. These disturbances constituted the first political challenge posed by the Shiites to the Saudi regime and were viewed as serious enough by the royal family to prompt the dispatch of twenty-thousand troops to the area.[62] The Mecca incident further called Saudi stability into question and raised some doubts as to whether the Saudi government would last even a few months.[63]

The armed men who seized the Grand Mosque in Mecca criticized the Saudi royal family for being corrupt and for not adhering to the tenets of Islam.[64] It was not coincidental that similar criticisms emanated from Iran. In addition, in the period after the Shiite uprising in the eastern Saudi oil province, Radio Tehran attempted to foment discontent among Saudi oil workers, even calling for the overthrow of the monarchy on December 11, 1979. In a demonstration on February 1, 1980, in Saudi Arabia, Saudi Shiites carried pictures of Khomeini, a scene that was repeated in Bahrain.[65] Although, in retrospect, it appears that the threat to Saudi stability had been much exaggerated, Saudi self-confidence and its reputation as a regional security asset came under question.

Third, the rise of the Arab rejectionist front further reduced Saudi influence. This front, composed of hard-line Arab states such as Syria and Libya, had pressured the more moderate Saudis to distance themselves from the United States. Given the perception of Soviet momentum in global rivalry, the precarious situation in Iran, anti-American sentiment generated by the Camp David peace process, and the fear of the entrenchment of Soviet influence on their southern borders, the Saudis were inclined to appease hard-line Arab states rather than to tilt toward the United States. This propensity was reinforced by Saudi questions about U.S. credibility and by American doubts about Saudi stability.[66]

Fourth, Saudi influence also decreased because the shah's fall created an opportunity for Saddam Hussein to assume the mantle of Gulf leadership. Iraq's influence on Saudi Arabia increased substantially from 1978 to mid- to late 1979, which further limited Saudi action. Although the Saudis feared Iraq less than they did Iran under its supreme leader Ayatollah Khomeini, Iraq was still viewed by them as a military and political threat, and they saw themselves as subject to the balance of forces between Iran and Iraq.[67] Along with Kuwait and Oman, they even felt it necessary to mollify Iraq after allowing the U.S. access rights.[68]

The Iranian revolution threatened Saudi Arabia and attenuated its leverage by making it more dependent on Iraq for security purposes. Despite fears of Iraq, the Saudis needed Iraq against Iran, and despite fears of Iran, they needed Iran against Iraq. In this sense, Saudi Arabia lacked a reliable security policy because it could not trust its would-be protectors and constantly had to adjust its balancing act. Given the prevailing political and security climate, the Saudis even had serious doubts about whether the United States, on which they had relied for outside support, could come to their aid in a serious crisis.

The combination of these factors placed Riyadh in a position of weakness domestically and regionally. This weakness hurt U.S. interests because the Saudis were more likely than other Gulf states to support them and Riyadh assumed a much more important role in twin pillar policy after the shah fell. The balance sheet looked bad: the primary pillar, Iran, had fallen; the secondary pillar, Saudi Arabia, could not act effectively as a second pillar and was, in fact, less stable than it had been in the past.

Conclusion

The twin pillar policy was initiated shortly after the 1972 Soviet-Iraqi treaty was signed. That treaty helped solidify the alignment between Moscow and Iraq. Clearly, Washington sought to balance against Moscow by balancing against Iraq. Moreover, it was much more concerned with Iraq's threat than its power at the regional level. Although the twin pillar policy did not balance against power at the regional level, it did balance against power at the global level. It served to balance Moscow's power and Iraq's threat while also serving other American objectives.

Overall, balance-of-power policy was important as a general thrust of the Nixon administration's foreign policy, although détente also infused a healthy respect for the potential of interdependence and linkage to give Moscow a vested interest in the status quo, thus containing it. Nixon's foreign policy, unlike Eisenhower's, did not seek to transform Soviet society.[69] In that sense it reflected one element of balance-of-power policy—that the internal politics of states were not of great concern but their external power was. Many decades later, President George H. W. Bush would view Iraq in a similar way at the end of the 1991 Gulf war, quite unlike his son in the 2003 invasion of Iraq.

The twin pillar case offers an interesting baseline from which to compare subsequent episodes. Indeed, as we shall see in the next chapter, the regional and global environment in which the United States had to fashion its policy in the Persian Gulf changed radically in 1979 and in the 1980s. Not surprisingly, its strategies toward the goal of protecting its interests in the Persian Gulf also changed.

CHAPTER THREE

The Reagan Administration and the Iran-Iraq War

History is sometimes shaped by the sheer, grinding flow of minor events and processes and at other times forged by grand events, shocks to the system, sometimes in the same time period. In the Middle East, the events of 1979 were shocks and need to be understood if we are to make sense of the subsequent history in the region, the rise of the American regional profile, and the strategies that Washington chose to deal with complex threats to its security. Indeed, historian David Lesch has gone so far as to describe 1979 as the year that shaped the modern Middle East.[1] This chapter sketches these critical events and then turns to an analysis of American behavior during the Iran-Iraq War.

America Alters Course

In retrospect, it perhaps seems odd that, even after the shah departed Iran on January 16, 1979, President Carter initially believed that Iran could still be a factor for stability and asserted that the Soviet Union shared the American desire for a stable Iran.[2] The view of high-level officials was that the United States and Iran shared a strong interest in a noncommunist Iran, which could serve as a basis for wary cooperation.[3] Washington also continued to believe that the Iranian military would support pro-American forces in Iran. From February to November 1979 Washington tolerated Iran's massive human rights violations, pursued a military-training relationship, and cultivated the Iranian "moderates" whom it expected would gain power.

Throughout 1979, U.S. policymakers tried to rebuild relations with Iran, hoping that conciliation would elicit Iranian cooperation on a variety of issues.[4] This notion would later motivate the Iran-Contra scandal, in which the United States sought to exchange arms to Iran for American hostages in Lebanon, over which Iran had influence. As late as October 1979, the Defense Department announced that it had resumed the delivery of spare parts to Iran for American-built military aircraft.[5] Furthermore, Washington believed that it might secure the offices of another pillar, be it Saudi Arabia, Iraq, Pakistan, or even Israel.

The seizure of the American Embassy in Tehran on November 4, 1979, altered Washington's approach to the revolutionary regime.[6] In the throes of revolutionary fervor, and angered by America's acceptance of the shah into the United States for medical treatment, Iranian militants stormed the embassy, captured fifty-two American citizens, and held them for 444 days in what would become a national and international drama.

The Iranian revolution and hostage crisis renewed American interest in formulating a new approach for Gulf security and seriously altered the climate of U.S.-Iranian relations. In October 1979, President Carter saw no prospects for U.S. military intervention anywhere in the world, but the hostage crisis helped change his views.[7] It became clear that American interests abroad could be threatened enough to warrant military intervention.

In an attempt to bolster diplomatic efforts to free the hostages, the United States built a twenty-one-ship naval force around the Gulf. Carter also asked the Joint Chiefs of Staff for a list of military force options against Iran. The president recognized the inadequate state of American military capability when, on November 24, 1979, the Joint Chiefs of Staff informed him that the United States was unable to release the hostages.[8] This state of affairs was perhaps best highlighted by the abortive attempt to rescue the hostages in June 1980.[9] The failed mission underscored perceptions of America as inept, as incapable of protecting its own citizens and security.

It is not clear whether the United States could have freed the hostages even with a more developed military capability, but these foregoing events made it evident that when the shah of Iran fell, the United States lacked its own military capability for Gulf contingencies because it had counted on proxies to defend its goals.

The hostage crisis, the Iranian revolution, and the broader Soviet threat motivated serious U.S. efforts to gain access to forward-basing facilities in Southwest Asia.[10] At the time, America's military presence consisted of only a noncombatant flagship and three destroyers. These events also helped convince Pentagon analysts to hasten development of the Rapid Deployment Force (RDF). The National Security Council (NSC) met on February 28, 1979, in part to propose the RDF's formation, and by April the Department of Defense was preparing plans.[11] By November 1979, Carter's fiscal year 1981 defense request would push legislators to decide about funding a rapid deployment force for the first time.[12]

Yet, for all these efforts, no consensus developed on a long-term policy to enhance the U.S. military presence, and no specific programs for expanding it were approved. Deep disagreement existed over how to proceed, which continued until the Soviet invasion of Afghanistan.[13] As one official noted, the United States was still "starting from scratch in building Carter's security framework."[14]

At the global level, Moscow was busy, as well. After determining the anti-American nature of the Islamic revolution, it began to court Iran, assuming that if Iran was anti-American, it might be pro-Soviet.[15] Emboldened by previous political and strategic gains and by American failures, Moscow invoked the 1921 Soviet-Iranian treaty that allowed it to intervene in Iran if Soviet security was threatened, and in November 1978 it warned the United States against intervening in Iran.[16] Some U.S. officials saw this bold action as presaging a more active Soviet effort to influence Iran's revolutionary forces.[17] The United States responded by declaring that it had neither the desire nor the ability to intervene in Iran, which was viewed as weak by many regional and some American officials.[18] The Saudis were especially disappointed and reportedly considered reestablishing diplomatic relations with the Soviet Union.[19] This must have been partly a political ploy, but it did reflect Riyadh's serious annoyance with the United States.

Moscow's efforts, which would have played havoc with the regional balance of power and threat if they succeeded, failed until the November 1979 Iranian hostage crisis. That event temporarily changed Iran's view. In the month after the seizure of the American Embassy in Tehran, M. Mokri, Iran's ambassador to the Soviet Union, initiated a visit to Moscow, during which he described prospects for Soviet-Iranian relations as "the very best."[20] For his part, Soviet foreign minister Andrei Gromyko assured the Iranian ambassador that Moscow "would not remain neutral" if the United States attempted "armed aggression" against Iran.[21]

The Soviet Union did not succeed in making serious inroads with Iran, partly because of revolutionary Iran's preference to tilt "neither East nor West."[22] However, while the enigmatic ayatollah was trying to secure Iran's revolution against domestic opponents, the Soviets invaded Afghanistan, further undermining U.S. security in the Gulf. Moscow might well have invaded and occupied Afghanistan only to ensure the stability and pro-Soviet orientation of the Marxist Afghan government that it had propped up by coup in 1978. However, its troops did come about 320 miles closer to the Gulf, which placed them on Pakistan's doorstep. This move generated fears that Moscow's ambitions stretched beyond Afghanistan. The Russians had always wanted a warm-water port as well as influence in the Persian Gulf, as exemplified in their rivalry with Britain in Asia, which Rudyard Kipling dubbed the "Great Game."[23]

The perception of Soviet political and military gains in Angola, Ethiopia, South Yemen, and now Afghanistan, coupled with Washington's loss of Iran as an ally and the unending hostage crisis, further damaged U.S. credibility.[24] Analysts feared an increase in Soviet influence or an outright military invasion of the region; the spread of Islamic fundamentalism; the ascendance of Iran or Iraq to regional hegemony; an alignment of anti-American radical forces around Syria, Libya, and Iraq; and the weakening or collapse of the generally pro-American Saudi regime.[25] Fears that dominoes would fall to Moscow — fears that had been muted by the rise of détente — resurfaced, and the Truman Doctrine was back in vogue after appearing to have been rendered historically obsolete by President Carter's notions of coexistence with the Soviets.

Not long after the invasion, on January 23, 1980, President Carter issued the Carter Doctrine, one of the most forceful statements of his presidency, which indicated a major change from the noninterventionist U.S. role of previous decades. It committed the United States to deter or respond to "outside" threats to Gulf security.[26] That commitment would soon be expanded under President Reagan. Concerned with global and regional threats to Gulf security, Washington was determined not only to improve its capability to deter "outside" pressure on the Gulf but also to deal with pressures arising within the Gulf.[27] In that spirit, President Reagan stated in October 1981 that there was "no way" the United States could "stand by" and see Saudi Arabia threatened to the point that the flow of oil could be shut down.[28]

These commitments were impressive in terms of rhetoric, but this was not the

United States that would reverse Iraq's invasion of Kuwait in 1990 or overthrow Saddam's dictatorship in 2003. It was a much weaker power, something that we tend to forget given the major rise of the United States in the post–Cold War world. The RDF had not been developed in full; regional actors were incapable of providing much logistical support for U.S. military efforts; and the edifice of American security was shaky.[29]

The United States had begun formally developing some capability in the region after 1945 when President Roosevelt met King Abdul Aziz al-Saud, and certainly by the 1970s, but these efforts were accelerated primarily in the 1980s. From 1979 to 1990, Washington was forced to develop major capability and regional support to protect its interests.[30] In essence, it reacted to events in the region by creating the potential for a forward military presence. In addition to the RDF, the U.S.-operated naval and air base at Diego Garcia in the Indian Ocean was upgraded, the "scale and pace" of U.S. periodic naval force deployments increased, and America gained access to key regional military facilities.[31] Washington's ability to project force improved considerably between 1980 and 1991, aided by the development in Saudi Arabia of a $200 billion military infrastructure.[32]

In 1979, however, all these developments were barely a mirage in the minds of American strategists, and U.S. interests were subject to the vagaries of regional politics. It is in this context that the United States had to react to Iran's revolution and Iraq's invasion of Iran in September 1980. The invasion touched off a ferocious war with an estimated one million casualties which ended in a cease-fire in 1988. During the war, the United States tried a variety of different strategies for protecting its interests and ensuring regional stability. The Iran-Iraq War further drew the reluctant United States into the region and accelerated American defense efforts for Gulf contingencies.[33]

The Iran-Iraq War

Iraq's invasion had the trappings of both a defensive and an offensive act, although it was probably more the latter than the former, despite the failure of the UN Security Council to identify Iraq as the aggressor.[34] Although the reasons for Iraq's decision to invade were multifaceted, it can be viewed as a function of three factors: Iraqi fear, opportunism, and miscalculation.[35]

In contrast to popular perception, and to his determined stance in the Iran-Iraq War, Khomeini was not militarily oriented. In contrast to the shah, whose military expenditures were extraordinary, Khomeini severed the extensive arms relationship with Washington, shut down U.S. military facilities on Iranian soil, and even spurned Soviet arms offers. In addition, he executed or imprisoned many of his top officers and placed much less trust in Iran's regular, better trained military than in the ideologically motivated Revolutionary Guard. Unlike the ancient Persians, who defeated the Greeks militarily in order to protect and expand their vast empire, Khomeini sought to spread the ideas of the Iranian revolution politically before his hand was forced in war by Saddam Hussein. Although Khomeini used force internally, he asserted that even the export of Islam was to be conducted nonmilitarily.[36] From Iraq's perspective, however, Iran was profoundly threatening.

Iran and Iraq were different in many ways that contributed to conflict. For instance, Iraq's Sunni tradition clashed with Iran's Shiite legacy (Islam had split into these two main branches in the seventh and eighth centuries AD), and Iraq's Arab heritage differed significantly from Iran's Persian background. In addition, Iran and Iraq had long-standing territorial disagreements over control of the Shatt al-Arab waterway (the confluence of the Tigris and Euphrates rivers, where the first civilization of humankind was believed to have been developed). Finally, Saddam and Khomeini hated each other for a variety of reasons, one of which was that Iran's theocratic rule was opposed to Iraq's more secular regime, which Khomeini saw as illegitimate. Iraq feared Iran because, unlike the shah, Khomeini's revolutionary theocracy sought to subvert Iraq's predominantly Shiite population and to spread Islamic fundamentalism throughout the Arab Gulf, thereby undermining Iraq's influence. In fact, Saddam had been battling Shiite elements supported by Iran which sought the overthrow of his regime. Although it may well be that Iraq's Shiites were more loyal to Iraq than to transnational Islam, Saddam could not have known how Iran's meddling might have affected his predominantly Shiite population, just as the United States, oddly enough, would not know this answer until after it eliminated Saddam from power in 2003 and faced Iran's efforts to subvert Iraq's Shiite groups.[37]

In addition, as the other major power in the Persian Gulf, Iran posed a moderate short-term military threat to Iraq and possibly a more significant longer-term threat in the event that Iran emerged intact from its revolutionary chaos. Since the future was unknowable, Saddam probably preferred to hedge his bet by dealing with Iran sooner rather than later.

These situational factors may have led Iraq to believe that war would come sooner or later, a belief that greatly enhanced its interest in attacking Iran. As history suggests, states are more inclined to attack others if they feel that war is inevitable and that the balance of power is shifting against them.[38] Indeed, Saudi Arabia's King Fahd asserted that, prior to Iraq's attack on Iran in 1980, Saddam told him, "It is more useful to hit them [the Iranians] now because they are weak. If we leave them until they become strong, they will overrun us."[39] Iran's military forces had been weakened significantly by the revolution, by arrests of leaders believed to be too close to the shah, and by subsequent U.S. sanctions and the cutoff of the strategic relationship that sustained Iran's American-built air force.

Although Iraq viewed the revolutionary chaos in Iran as an opportunity to reduce the long-term Iranian threat, it probably also aimed to advance its own inflated foreign policy agenda — but not for economic reasons, as would be the case when Iraq invaded Kuwait in 1990. Iraq's economy was booming, flush with oil revenues that allowed Saddam to build the military. Rather, Saddam's attack was intended to deal Iran a blow so that Iraq could make territorial gains around the Shatt al-Arab and possibly beyond. Saddam may have also believed that such gains could hurt the credibility of Iran's revolutionary regime, while burnishing his own image among his people, in the Persian Gulf and throughout the Middle East. Indeed, Saddam sought to consolidate his rising position in the Arab world. The Baghdad summit in November 1978, which showcased Saddam's leadership and power to Arab leaders, helped establish Iraq in that regard.[40] Its influence over Saudi Arabia increased from 1978 to mid- to late 1979, partly because of Iraq's growing influence in the Arab world but also because Iran's threat to Saudi Arabia made Iraq more vital to Riyadh.[41] Iraq's growing status in the Arab world was enhanced by its success in tapping Arab-world disaffection with the 1979 Egyptian-Israeli peace treaty. In March 1979, Saddam hosted another all-Arab conference, which, in part, evicted Egypt from the Arab League for its treaty with Israel.

Iraq became the beating heart of the Arab world, with Saddam at its helm. And it may, therefore, have been natural in Saddam's view for it to confront the Persian enemy that historically had been at odds with great Arab powers. Most Gulf states quickly accepted Iraq's February 1980 pan-Arab charter, which, among other things, embodied Saddam's regional ambitions and called for a "new Arab order," as Iraq's foreign minister Tariq Aziz would describe it in September 1990 during the Gulf crisis.[42] In part, this charter called for the rejection of any foreign military presence in the Gulf and represented an effort to decrease and even eject U.S. regional influence. Saddam's ambitions, however, came to no good end.

Like so many dictators in history, he grossly miscalculated in deciding to invade Iran, perhaps because he was overtaken partly by hubris. It appeared that Iran, caught in the throes of revolution, would swiftly or eventually capitulate. Saddam believed that the war would be over in weeks, thus leaving Iraq dominant over Iran, or at least with substantially increased influence.[43] But Iran saw Iraq's attack as a vicious attempt to seize territory and possibly to neutralize the glorious Iranian revolution, and it could not go unpunished. Iran mustered soul and limb to fight off the Iraqi attack.

On September 28, a mere five days after the invasion, Saddam, sensing Iranian counterpressure and strength, halted his forces and announced his willingness to engage in peace negotiations.[44] The implacable dictator became much more flexible after running into a wall. By November 1980, Iraq's war effort was altogether stymied, and Iran turned the conflict into roughly a stalemate. Thereafter, Iran sporadically threatened the Arab Gulf states not only because they aided Iraq in the war but also because Khomeini's worldview predisposed Iran to undermine them.

Episode 2: America's Tilt toward Iraq, 1982–1985

Until late 1981, the United States remained neutral on the Iran-Iraq War, perhaps privately hoping that both states would lose the war. The vague notion at play, sometimes referred to as benign neglect, was that the war, though generating some instability, could weaken both states. Since both states were anti-American in general, weakening them could serve American realpolitik, especially since it seemed hard to imagine that the United States could develop good relations with them.

For his part, the ayatollah would not openly cooperate with the United States; nor would Washington dare seek to approach Iran in any public and formal manner. Such efforts held little chance for success while running the risk of becoming liabilities at the domestic level in both states. After the hostage crisis, relations between the two states were entirely dysfunctional, partly because of the psychological shrapnel of the hostage crisis, the retaliatory measures taken by Washington against Tehran, and the negative perception of Iran among the American people and of Americans by the Iranian people.[45] In fact, Khomeini claimed that the hostage crisis helped the United States and its regional agents undermine the

Iranian revolution in its infancy, suggesting that the United States was behind the Iraqi invasion of Iran.[46]

For its part, Iraq had been part of the communist bloc and an ally of the Soviet Union. It made little sense for Washington to try to enhance relations with Baghdad at the time. Doing so might have provoked Moscow at the global level, even though Soviet-Iraqi relations had begun to weaken in the late 1970s, and simply angered Iran even more, a state that the United States mistrusted but did not want to antagonize unnecessarily. Meanwhile, Saddam did not want to risk his rising profile in the Arab world, especially among its hard-core states, by being seen as anything but tough on the United States.

Washington's tacit approach of benign neglect in the war did not last too long. By late 1981, Iran was increasingly viewed as a significant regional threat. In 1982, it recaptured its own territory that Iraq had seized earlier in the war, sparking warnings from U.S. intelligence agencies of Iraqi defeat.

In 1982, Washington began to tilt slowly toward Iraq in order to balance against Iran.[47] In February 1982, the Reagan administration took steps to increase its support of Iraq by removing it from its list of state sponsors of terrorism. In addition, in response to the Iranian threat, it passed along to Iraq satellite imagery and communications intercepts on Iran's positions and allowed American arms to be sent to Iraq from Jordan and Kuwait.[48] The intelligence provided by the United States allowed Iraq to fortify defenses that protected the critical area of Basra and proved critical to Iraq's ability to fight the war, but Iraq remained in trouble on the battlefield.[49] Indeed, by mid-1982, Iran's military had sported a series of victories that raised the prospect that it might actually win the war and free itself to turn its revolution on the Gulf monarchies.[50]

For its part, the United States had added reason to tilt toward Iraq. American perceptions of the threat from Iran were shaped by the Iranian revolution and the hostage crisis. For many policymakers and citizens, these events cast Iran as a zealous, irrational, and hateful regime. Seen through the prism of these events, an Iranian victory in the Persian Gulf seemed all the more ominous.

By the spring of 1983, the tide of war had clearly turned in Iran's favor. Iran expelled Iraqi forces, seized small parts of Iraqi territory, and shelled Iraq's key cities of Basra and Baghdad.

Aside from providing Iraq with arms sales, the United States had already modified its neutral stance in the war. However, the tilt in Iraq's direction intensified in 1983, as reflected in various memoranda. They underscored how important it was to favor Iraq in order to prevent Iran from winning the war, an issue that became vital because, as one high-level memo put it, the "Iranian strategy of bringing about the Iraqi regime's political collapse through military attrition coupled with financial strangulation seems to be slowly having an effect."[51]

In that context, the United States initiated Operation Staunch on December 14, 1983, to stop arms transfers to Iran and check the growing threat posed by that state.[52] It also enhanced sanctions against Iran when, on March 30, 1984, the Department of Commerce imposed antiterrorism controls on Iran. They prevented the sale of any dual-use items or technical data to Iran, items that were intended for civilian use but did have potential military uses.

Washington also considered various options for tilting toward Iraq and began to pursue some of them.[53] They included providing Iraq with intelligence information and selling it dual-use items. Although U.S. policy forbade the sale of defense items to Iraq, the administration did sell it more than a hundred helicopters, asserting that they were for civilian use, and also reportedly transferred to Iraq military supplies stored in Europe, particularly spare parts and various specialty items.[54] Washington also allowed Iraq to purchase U.S. agriculture products, valued in the hundreds of millions, in the form of Commodities Credit Corporation guarantees. These guarantees would become controversial after the Iran-Iraq War when Baghdad started to flex its muscles in the Middle East and Washington was accused of having tried to ingratiate itself with the aggressive Iraqi dictator.

The United States also increased high-level contacts with Baghdad. In a ninety-minute meeting with Saddam Hussein on December 20, 1983, Donald Rumsfeld, who as secretary of defense under George W. Bush would become one of the strongest proponents for overthrowing Saddam after the September 11 attacks, told Saddam that the United States and Iraq shared interests in preventing Iranian and Syrian expansion. The CEO of the multinational firm G. D. Searle & Company at the time, Rumsfeld was acting as a presidential emissary. He delivered the thrust of a memorandum from President Reagan which urged a change in U.S. policy toward greater cooperation with Iraq. The meeting was described in a then secret memo as representing a "positive milestone in development of U.S.-Iraqi relations."[55] Rumsfeld asserted that the United States did not want a war outcome that weakened Iraq's role or enhanced the interests and ambitions of Iran.[56] Soon after, covert shipments of military and dual-use items were sent to Iraq through Jordan, Egypt, and Kuwait.[57]

The United States also reestablished diplomatic relations with Iraq in November 1984. In a meeting between Secretary of State George Shultz and Iraq's deputy prime minister, Tariq Aziz, both gentlemen agreed that the threat from Iran was serious and needed to be checked, and Shultz assured Aziz that the United States would work with its allies on dealing with Iran and in particular on curbing the flow of Eastern arms to Iran.[58]

Although Iran posed a military threat, it also presented an ongoing political threat. Iraq wanted to end the war in the weeks after it initiated it, but Khomeini, who wanted Saddam out of power, adamantly refused until July 1988. Thus, even though Iraq was the initial aggressor, Iran appeared more threatening over time for its uncompromising stand. More important, Iran sought to overthrow the monarchies of the Persian Gulf. Since they were important to global oil stability, this represented a threat to the United States. Indeed, if Kuwait or Saudi Arabia fell under Iran's influence, Iran could gain enough control over oil prices to use them as a political weapon against the West. It could literally drive prices to a point of causing a global recession. States that control oil don't usually want to use it for political purposes because this can hurt them as well, but Iran's revolutionary regime might well have been tempted to use any newly gained influence over oil for political means. As a price hawk, Iran preferred higher oil prices than did the price doves such as Saudi Arabia, and it could have translated its regional power into influence in global oil markets.[59]

Moreover, Iran supported Hizballah in Lebanon, which bordered on a terrorist group that aimed to undermine Arab-Israeli peace. Although Iran began to moderate its foreign policy to some extent in 1984, it was still fundamentally anti-American and antimonarchical, and the administration clearly saw it as the major threat, as did the Gulf Cooperation Council (GCC) states, which also balanced with the United States against Iran.[60] They never really trusted Saddam and even feared his intentions, but revolutionary Iran made Saddam look good in their eyes. He could serve as a bulwark between them and Iran, which wanted to eliminate their regimes. Caught between Iraq and Iran, they clearly preferred Iraq — a reality that would change 180 degrees just a few years later when Saddam's forces invaded Kuwait.

Furthermore, the war served to moderate Iraq. If Saddam saw himself as the powerful leader of the Arab world in 1979, his travails in the war humbled him inasmuch as he could not survive the war without the help of others. He even strove to bring Egypt, which he had tried hard to isolate in 1979, back into the Arab fold; he participated in the Arab summit in Fez, Morocco, in 1982, which took a more conciliatory tone toward Israel than previous Arab summits; and he embraced relations with the United States, against which he railed in 1979. Of course, he would resume his effort to dominate the region when Iraq invaded Kuwait in 1990, but so long as the Iran-Iraq War raged, he moderated his foreign policy position and tolerated a number of strange bedfellows.

Balance-of-power policy does not explain the U.S.-led balancing against Iran in 1982–83, reflected in Operation Staunch in 1983 and its tilt toward Iraq. Iraq was far stronger than Iran in military capability. However, balance-of-threat policy does explain American action. As Iran's threat increased and Iraq moderated its position, the United States responded with actions to balance against Iran.

The United States began to change its approach toward Iran in 1984 and 1985. Although it did attempt, intermittently and quietly, to contact and cultivate moderates in Iran from 1979 through the 1980s, this effort was most pronounced in the Iran-Contra case.[61]

Episode 3: The Iran-Contra Affair, 1985–1986

The Iranian revolution and the related hostage crisis seriously damaged U.S.-Iranian relations, but the United States essayed to repair them at various times. It still held the position, albeit reluctantly, that it would meet with any authorized representative of Iran to explore the issues that divided the two states. The Iran-Contra affair represented this approach at a supercharged level.

The affair damaged the presidency of Ronald Reagan, which in other ways was viewed as successful on the foreign policy front. The scandal broke when it was disclosed that the United States, in August 1985 and thereafter, had participated in secret dealings with Iran with the support and encouragement of Israeli officials and intermediaries. The United States, through various American officials and foreign actors, had agreed to sell Iran arms in exchange chiefly for Iran's promise to effect the release of seven American hostages held in Lebanon, who were abducted in seven separate incidents between March 1984 and June 1985.[62] They were being held by Hizballah terrorists over whom Iran was believed to have influence.[63] To add to the problem, the arms exchange became linked to another of the Reagan administration's foreign policies: the proceeds from these sales were to be diverted to the U.S.-backed Contra rebels, who were seeking to overthrow the communist-leaning government in Nicaragua.

The affair assumed scandalous proportions for four key reasons.[64] In some measure, U.S. actions ran counter to declared U.S. policies and laws. The United States had declared an embargo on arms sales to Iran and sought to isolate it because of the hostage crisis. Although some restrictions on Iran were lifted on January 19, 1981, the United States maintained the embargo on arms transfers.

Selling arms to Iran not only broke the U.S. arms embargo but also derailed U.S. relations with Arab states, which saw Washington's actions as hypocritical and nonsensical. Arab states had strongly believed that the United States was balancing against Iran and supporting Iraq in order to keep Iran in check because U.S. officials had stressed this point in high-level meetings with Arab officials in the early 1980s. For instance, during his visit to Baghdad in 1983, referred to earlier, Rumsfeld told Saddam that the United States was encouraging others not to sell weapons to Iran and would continue to do so.[65]

Beyond the problem with breaking its own arms embargo, the government also had taken a strong stand against negotiating with terrorists directly or indirectly. On January 20, 1984, the secretary of state designated Iran a sponsor of international terrorism, accusing it of involvement in the October 1983 bombing of the U.S. Marine barracks in Lebanon which killed 243 marines. Subsequently, the United States pushed other states even harder to stop arms sales to Iran. Thus, trying to sell Iran arms in order to gain its support in releasing the U.S. hostages was doubly problematic: it involved dealing with a terrorist state and appeasing, rather than opposing, terrorists in Lebanon.

For its part, Congress passed the first Boland Amendment on December 21, 1982. It prohibited the Department of Defense and the Central Intelligence Agency from using funds to overthrow the Nicaraguan government. Later, in October 1984, Congress cut off all funding for the Contras and prohibited any American agency from supporting their efforts. The Iran-Contra affair violated the Boland Amendment and offended some members of Congress who had supported the amendment.

The affair, though conducted with the knowledge of higher-ranking officials, was executed in secrecy by what appeared to be lower-ranking NSC officials. They were depicted by the Tower Commission Report, the official investigative report on the affair, as reckless cowboys, "taking control of matters that are the customary province of more sober agencies such as the C.I.A., the State Department and the Defense Department."[66] Their actions were not the ideal reflection of a well-honed policy process; nor were they prudent because they precluded important policy inputs that might have prevented the scandal in the first place.

Nonbalancing and the Iran-Contra Affair

The behavior of the United States toward Iran in this period runs contrary to patterns of behavior inferred from balancing theory if we focus only at the regional level. At that level, balance-of-threat policy would involve the United States balancing against Iran rather accommodating it (because Iran was the more threatening actor), and balance-of-power policy would involve supporting Iran (because Iraq was the stronger actor), but not by cultivating moderates. Indeed, over the years, Iraq's military, especially its air force, had become superior to Iran's. Years of inadequate maintenance, problems in obtaining spare parts for its American-built aircraft, and attrition in the war had combined to make Iran the weaker state militarily. This imbalance was clear from the numbers of military personnel and arms (see table 3) and was widely recognized among military analysts.

Iran was more threatening than Iraq because its interests conflicted with those of the United States, whereas Iraq and the United States were on better footing. Iran was the more threatening actor even though it was not performing well on the battlefield at the time and, from the American viewpoint, faced a possible struggle for succession at home. As one high-level memo titled "US Policy toward Iran" asserted: "[A] dynamic political evolution is taking place inside Iran. Instability caused by the pressures of the Iran-Iraq war, economic deterioration and regime infighting create the potential for major changes in Iran."[67] That instability was a cause for concern in Washington: high-level officials, including national security adviser Robert McFarlane, had feared that, if Khomeini should die, a struggle for succession would follow and that the United States would have no policy or leverage to affect post-Khomeini events in Iran, especially if the Soviets had gained influence.[68] The "US Policy toward Iran" memo indicated that they had: "The Soviet Union is better positioned than the U.S. to exploit and benefit from any power struggle that results in changes in the Iranian regime."

The United States aimed to create a strategy that would promote cooperation with Iran, an approach that Colin Powell, then assistant to Secretary of Defense Caspar Weinberger, described as Kissingerian in its proportions.[69] His description underscored just how difficult it would be to carry out this strategy. Indeed, Powell was proud of Weinberger's response to the Iran-Contra strategy, which Weinberger had written across the top of the cover letter of the memo containing the first sketch of the strategy: "This is almost too absurd to comment on. . . . It's

like asking Qaddafi to Washington for a cozy chat," referring to the implacable —
and strongly anti-American — Libyan dictator.[70]

For his part, Weinberger praised the policy objective of blocking Moscow's
efforts to increase its influence with Iran, but he asserted that under "no circumstances" should the United States ease its restriction on arms sales to Iran.[71] In
his view, a policy reversal "would be seen as inexplicably inconsistent" by those
nations that the United States had urged to refrain from such sales and "would
likely lead to increased arms sales by them and a possible alteration of the strategic balance in favor of Iran" while Khomeini was still the "controlling influence."[72] Secretary Shultz agreed, asserting on June 29, 1985, that the "U.S.
Policy toward Iran" memo had exaggerated Soviet advantages over the United
States in gaining influence and that arms supplies from the West were "not likely
to retard Iranian overtures to the Soviets but could ironically prolong the Iran-
Iraq war." He concluded, "Given the disparity in size between Iran and Iraq, this
could ultimately mean an Iranian victory, and a fresh burst of energy for anti-
Americanism throughout the region."[73]

Despite these concerns, the arms-for-hostages approach was accelerated from
March to May 1985. In fact, on January 17, 1986, President Reagan signed a top-
secret "Finding of Necessity," declaring that the covert sale of arms to Iran was in
the country's interest.[74] These sales continued even after Iran's major victory at
the strategic Fao Peninsula in February 1986. In the United States and the
Persian Gulf, that victory clearly created the appearance of Iranian regional
domination and threat.

Oddly, on February 27, 1986, the State Department circulated a briefing
memo that asserted: "[After] almost six years, it is clear that the only way to bring
Iran to its senses and to the negotiating table is to cut off its munitions."[75] It is
not clear from the memo whether State Department officials were fully aware of
the broader range of the Iran-Contra affair, although a prior State Department
memo in May 1986 suggests concern that the arms sales may have been used to
fund activities that were prohibited by legislation.[76]

Iraq eventually repulsed the Iranians, but the outcome might have been different if Iran had been able to translate its initial victories into more sustained
ones. The Fao victory was important on the ground and also at sea because it
completely cut off Iraq's access to Gulf waters. It also put Iran in a position to
attack one of the three key centers in Iraq — Basra, which is about fifty miles from
Fao — and threatened to cut off some of Iraq's supply and communication routes.
Iraq was thus at a major strategic disadvantage at this point in the war.[77]

However, Iran was unable to hold the Fao Peninsula and to take Basra. If it had been successful in moving into these areas, Iran would have threatened the vital oil fields of the Persian Gulf. Even if it did not actually proceed into these oil fields, its military position would have given it increased influence over the Arab Gulf states and made it an effective hegemon in the region. An ayatollah in Iran was one thing, but an ayatollah influencing the oil pipeline of billions of people whom he considered infidels was quite another. Even the shah of Iran, who was considered an American ally, preferred much higher oil prices than were acceptable to Washington, so the United States had to be even more concerned about Khomeini. As one State Department memo noted, an "Iranian victory would be a severe setback" for the United States and "an extremely important event in the Middle Eastern and Muslim worlds."[78] In particular, officials in the State Department feared that the balance in the Iraq-Iraq War could be shifting toward Iran, a state that had been denounced for terrorism.[79]

While the State Department was expressing its fears about the dangers of Iran's military gains, Iran launched the Al Dawa offensive that took the Fao Peninsula on February 9, 1986. Meanwhile, the first 500 TOW antitank guided missiles were shipped to Iran on February 17–18, 1986; another 500 followed on February 27, while the United States was still considering trading another 4,000 TOW missiles; later in October, even more were delivered.[80] Irrespective of their actual military significance, and there is question as to whether they reached the battlefield in time to influence the Fao attack, these arms deliveries underscored a neglect of balancing considerations in U.S. strategy. And, in fact, there is good reason to believe that the Iran-Contra affair strengthened Iran at a time when it was especially threatening in the region, chiefly by the transfer of intelligence information. As one former NSC official in charge of Iranian affairs put it, the intelligence given to Iran helped the Iranians "gain a more accurate sense of Iraq's defenses," which in turn helped them plan the Fao offensive at the southeastern tip of Iraq, while the TOW and HAWK missiles helped Iran resist the inevitable Iraqi counterattack.[81]

The Iran-Contra affair was entirely contrary to the thrust of balancing and in fact threatened to do the exact opposite of what balance-of-power or balance-of-threat policy would suggest. But one proviso is important here. To some extent, the United States sought to balance against Moscow at the global level. In theory, by co-opting Iran through a more accommodative approach, it could prevent Moscow from penetrating Iran and strengthening its regional position in the global balance of power.[82] As mentioned earlier in the chapter, at the time, the

United States believed that Iran might soon be facing a struggle for succession, and one of its concerns was that Moscow might capitalize on this state of affairs. As one declassified memo stated, "Our primary short-term challenge must be to block Moscow's efforts to increase Soviet influence now and after the death of Khomeini."[83] Or, as one official put it in a memo to the director of the CIA which became a basis for the arms-for-hostages approach: "Iran has, in fact, now begun moving toward some accommodation with the U.S.S.R. Our urgent need is to develop a broad spectrum of policy moves designed to give us some leverage in the race for influence in Tehran."[84] The memo then notes, "The time may now have come to tilt back—at least via our allies—to ensure the Soviets lose . . . potential access to the clergy."[85]

Clearly, the administration was concerned with Soviet gains in the Middle East and what that would mean for the global balance of power. The Middle East was a critical region in global rivalry, and fears had developed in the late 1970s, and continued into the 1980s, that the balance of power—or as the Soviets would refer to it, the correlation of forces—was moving strongly in Moscow's direction. In this sense, the arms-for-hostages approach was one in which U.S. balancing against the Soviet Union at the global level did preempt U.S. balancing against Iran at the regional level, thus partly salvaging this case for balancing behavior.

However, we should also note that U.S. action was driven largely by motivations that had little to do with balancing. Indeed, in addition to the pursuit of better relations with Iran by cultivating Iranian moderates, Reagan identified the Iran-Iraq War as one of the four reasons for the arms-for-hostages approach. Cultivating Iranian moderates was viewed as enhancing U.S. leverage to end the war, even though it undermined U.S. relations with Arab Gulf states that, by and large, supported Iraq against Iran.[86]

The driving motivations behind the Iran-Contra case were to obtain the release of the American hostages in Lebanon and to help the Contras in Nicaragua with funds obtained from the arms sale to Iran.[87] The issue of the hostages was especially important. Multiple sources close to President Reagan noted that he raised it on almost a daily basis as if he were obsessed with it.[88] The congressional report on the Iran-Contra affair concluded that the president was "too influenced by emotional concern for the hostages," which the president himself recognized.[89] For Weinberger, the president's "very human concern for the safety of the hostages led him to agree with the very bad advice he was getting—that there were some moderate factions in Iran that he could work with, which, of course, was totally untrue."[90] Robert Gates, then deputy CIA director, asserted that there appeared to be "little question that, personally, Reagan was motivated to go forward with the Iranian affair almost entirely because of his obsession with getting the American hostages freed."[91]

Not only was Reagan heavily focused on the hostages, but he put significant and daily pressure on his subordinates to do something about them.[92] As his frustration mounted over the failure to save the hostages, he became more likely to support the Iran strategy.[93] As Shultz saw it, Reagan bought into the Iran-Contra scheme because of his determination to free the hostages.[94] Reagan was not absorbed with the international dimensions of U.S.-Iranian relations or of Middle East politics in which balance of power could have been a relevant concern; rather, he was focused at the individual level. Certainly, the powerful role of an emotive president regarding an issue such as hostages does not conform in the least with any notions of state-centric balancing.

Of course, some may question whether the arms-for-hostages approach was official policy. This is not an insignificant point. Balance-of-power policy refers to the behavior of a state, not a subgroup within it. Evidence, however, shows that the arms-for-hostages approach was official enough to make it a legitimate test of balancing behavior. Although Weinberger and Secretary of State George Shultz were out of the loop at junctures, the approach had high-level support.[95] In a series of classified memos, high-level officials considered the arms strategy from 1984, when the NSC started to exert pressure for a new approach, into early 1986.[96] Shultz and Weinberger were alerted to this new, potential initiative, although they disapproved.[97] In fact, according to McFarlane, they met along with the president and vice president four or five times in the family quarters of the White House to discuss the arms sales, even though Bush would later describe himself as out of the loop on this strategy.[98]

Shultz and Weinberger, who often disagreed, argued strongly to the president against trying to trade arms for hostages in December 1985 and January 1986, but the approach continued.[99] In his description of one meeting on the arms initiative, Shultz underscored high-level involvement: "The President, the Vice President, the Director of Central Intelligence, the Attorney General, the Chief of Staff, the National Security Advisor all had one opinion and I had a different one and Cap [Weinberger] shared it."[100] Reagan was not only clearly involved in key aspects of the approach, but he also issued two formal findings authorizing arms shipments to Iran in November 1985 and on January 17, 1986, after having decided as early as August 1985 that the United States would allow such sales.[101]

Reagan may well have been out of the loop on aspects of the approach and on tactics. On that score, Shultz did write during the scandal that Reagan did not grasp the nature of the arms-for-hostages swaps, while national security adviser John Poindexter held to the position that Reagan did not know that the proceeds from the arms sales would go to the Contras.[102] Nonetheless, he appeared quite aware of significant aspects of the strategy.

Episode 4: Reflagging Kuwaiti Tankers, 1986–1987

The United States did not balance after Iran's Fao attack in 1986, but by 1987 it began to do so for several reasons. Although Iran's victory eventually proved less significant, Iran continued to reject a cease-fire in the Iran-Iraq War. In fact, Khomeini swore, even as late as 1987, that he would drink from the poisoned chalice before he would allow the war to end with Saddam Hussein still in power, and he maintained that Iran would fight until victory in a divine cause against the Iraqi aggressors.[103] He stressed his determination to continue the war at a time when Iraq was pressing hard for the superpowers and for Iran to bring an end to it and when Iran was facing substantial international pressure and mounting economic problems at home.[104]

By September 1986, Iran increased attacks on Kuwaiti tankers in retaliation for Kuwait's support of Iraq in the war, pushing Kuwait to ask both Moscow and Washington to reflag its tankers. These actions were perceived in Washington as evidence of Iran's "intent upon becoming the dominant power in the Gulf" and expunging the United States from the region.[105] Even under the shah, Iran aimed in some measure to achieve these goals, but under Khomeini it sought to do so more aggressively and in the absence of any context of cooperation with Washington.

Moreover, Iran laid mines in the Gulf and bought Chinese Silkworm land-to-ship missiles, one of which it tested in February 1987. They gave Iran the ability to sink merchant ships transiting the narrow Strait of Hormuz, through which much of the world's oil flows. Stoppage in tanker traffic, or the mere threat of it, could spike world oil prices in a manner that Washington wanted to avoid.

Whatever Iran intended by these actions — and it may well have seen them as defensive insofar as Washington was tilting in Iraq's favor — the United States viewed them as a clear threat. Its response in late 1986 and 1987 reflected balancing against threat. Washington "reinvigorated" Operation Staunch, and GCC states provided increased political and military assistance for U.S. transit operations and forces.[106] In addition, as Shultz made clear in various memoranda, the

United States provided Iraq with, as he put it, "limited, but useful, amounts of intelligence," a policy that would continue.[107] This policy was motivated partly by Iran's refusal to end the war, despite significant international pressure and its ongoing hostilities. Interestingly, in this memo responding to questions from the State Department, Shultz noted, "Iraq is the only country which can exert direct military pressure on Iran. We decided that the stakes involved in the outcome of the Iran-Iraq war were great enough to justify supplying some intelligence to Iraq."[108]

In early March 1987, the United States officially agreed to reflag Kuwaiti tankers after a U.S. team was sent to the Gulf in February to assess the potential for such an operation.[109] In doing so, the United States wished, in part, to defeat what former assistant secretary of state Richard Murphy asserted was "Iran's hegemonistic plans for the Gulf" and also to reestablish credibility with Arab Gulf states after the Iran-Contra debacle.[110] But at the global level, it also sought to deny the Soviet Union a more extensive protective role.[111]

The reflagging policy helped dispel beliefs that the United States was uninterested in stopping the Gulf war, and it probably created the perception in some quarters that Washington helped constrain Iran. The policy itself was clearly aimed at Iran: it weakened Iran's significant naval advantage over Iraq and undermined its ability to retaliate against Kuwait for its support of Iraq while doing nothing about Iraq's air attacks on Iran's installations and tankers.

Overall, U.S. credibility increased significantly, and its ties to Arab states improved. Only Washington proved capable enough to take action to control Iran. The Europeans, as aptly observed by a senior U.S. diplomat, saw a real risk in "actually having to confront the Iranians."[112] The U.S. commitment expanded in potentially dangerous ways. Initially it was limited to protecting reflagged Kuwaiti tankers, but it expanded to assist NATO warships that came under attack and finally to support all neutral shipping.[113]

The U.S. reflagging policy was militarily risky, as suggested by the Iraqi warplane attack on the frigate *USS Stark* in May 1997 and the U.S. accidental downing of an Iranian civilian airbus, which Khomeini apparently saw as deliberate.[114] Moreover, by benefiting Iraq, the reflagging also compromised U.S. interests with Iran. Indeed, Tehran may well have been confounded by the fact that the United States just one year before could have sought an arms-for-hostages trade and then moved to balance against it strongly. Therefore, it was not surprising that several high-level visits took place between Iran and Moscow in early 1987, following the U.S. decision to reflag Kuwaiti tankers, and that two days after the U.S. naval escort of tankers commenced, Hashemi-Rafsanjani, the Speaker of the Iranian parliament, for the first time played down prospects for "normalization of relations" with the United States.[115]

Although the United States balanced against the threat from Iran by pursuing the reflagging of Kuwaiti tankers, it did so in other ways, also. In March 1987, House Joint Resolution 216 asserted that Iran was gaining the upper hand in the war, and a congressional report later that year suggested that Iran could even win it.[116] Partly as a result of this concern, joint U.S. military maneuvers with GCC states increased in frequency. The United States also enhanced cooperation with Iraq, which included providing it with targeting information, assistance with planning long-range air attacks on Iran, and tactical military advice for battlefield operations.[117]

Heightened tensions in Saudi-Iranian affairs added to American concern about Iran, even though it was America's reflagging effort and Saudi support of Iraq that contributed to Iran's ire. The Iranian revolution put Saudi-Iranian relations on a path toward increased tensions and, in the 1980s, open conflict. Unlike Pahlevi Iran, revolutionary Iran challenged Riyadh's claim as the champion of Islam by offering an alternative Islamic model that rejected the monarchical Islamic state and offered a theocratic one in its place. The clash between these two approaches to Islamic governance, and between Sunni Saudi Arabia and Shia Iran, created frictions in Saudi-Iranian relations which were dramatized by the Iran-Iraq War and erupted in earnest in July 1987 over the annual pilgrimage to Mecca.

Riyadh faced an ongoing potential for Iranian-inspired subversion, but in 1987 that threat became starkly evident. The pilgrimage to Mecca was disrupted by a riot that was touched off when Saudi security units moved in to stop a forbidden political demonstration by Iranian pilgrims in front of the Grand Mosque. Despite considerable evidence to the contrary, Iran's president, Hashemi Rafsanjani, a close friend of Khomeini's from his early days in exile and later a key adviser, denied that Iran instigated the subversion.[118] He asserted that the Saudis were to blame and called on Iranians as "the implementers of divine principles" to overthrow the Saudi royal family in revenge.[119] This appeal to the people of Iran caused alarm across the Gulf and in certain Western quarters. Iran wanted once again to destabilize Saudi Arabia and challenge its rule over Islam's holy places.[120] The Mecca crisis pushed the Saudis to sever relations with Iran and nearly put the two states in military conflict.[121] This imbroglio concerned Washington. Although it did not want Riyadh and Tehran to become too close, it also did not want Tehran to undermine Saudi stability. The latter situation could threaten global oil stability and cause dangerous spikes in oil prices.

The United States continued to balance against the Iranian threat. By September 1987, President Reagan had decided that the ongoing Iran-Iraq War, Iran's rejection of efforts to end it, and its support of terrorism posed a serious threat to American national security interests and that pressure on Iran should be maintained.[122]

Conclusion

The Iran-Iraq War can be broken down into several episodes that offer a mixed bag of America's approaches for protecting and advancing its interests. The United States tended to practice balance-of-power policy at the outset of the war. The Iran-Contra affair, however, tended to be the near opposite of balancing. It aimed to placate, even appease, Iran and in a manner not consistent with balancing behavior. The arms-for-hostages approach failed to achieve its objectives and instead caused a major scandal. Partly in order to salvage itself after this scandal but more so because of Iran's rising threat, the United States tilted against Iran by reflagging Kuwaiti tankers.

To be sure, the Iran-Contra scheme also aimed to preclude Moscow's potential influence in Iran, which may have helped Moscow in the global balance of power. That effort did not conflict with balancing threat at the regional one, but it did conflict with balancing power. The reflagging effort helped Iraq (the stronger but less threatening actor) because it prevented Iran from attacking oil tankers from Iraq and from Kuwait and Saudi Arabia, which supported Iraq. Thus, although the U.S. preempted Moscow's near-term threat, it benefited the far stronger regional state, and one allied with Moscow no less.

Balance-of-power policy was not apparent in this case. Iraq was clearly the stronger power in the region, yet the reflagging policy supported Iraq and even made it stronger against Iran. We would have expected the United States to balance against Iraq, and yet it did something closer to the opposite. The reflagging case ran against the grain of balance-of-power policy, as would the policy of constructive engagement to which we now turn.

CHAPTER FOUR

The Bush Administration and Constructive Engagement

At the extremes, states can placate or confront other states in the effort to get them to do something that they otherwise would not do — the classic definition of a power or influence. Placating others can be a sensible strategy if it achieves this goal, but it can fail and simply strengthen the strongest actor. That is roughly what occurred in American foreign policy toward Iraq from 1988 until Iraq invaded Kuwait in August 1990. After the Iran-Iraq War, the United States tried to alter Iraq's behavior with a strategy that leaned strongly toward placating it in the hope of co-opting it. Iraq's bellicose and threatening behavior after the war was not met by a change in U.S. strategy toward balancing but rather the opposite.

Episode 5: Constructive Engagement, 1988–1990

At the outset of its tenure in 1989, the administration of George H. W. Bush reviewed previous U.S. policies in the Persian Gulf and decided in what was called National Security Review 10 not to shift away from the policy of tilting in Iraq's direction. Rather, it adopted a policy of "constructive engagement." It was motivated by the fact that Iraq, as one official put it, emerged from the war as the "most powerful country in a key part of the world" for the United States, and so the "feeling at the time" was that the United States needed to "develop a workable relationship with Saddam Hussein."[1] Based partly on this logic, National Security Review 10 recommended that the United States use various economic and political inducements to alter Iraq's behavior.[2] These recommendations were formally adopted by President Bush in National Security Directive 26 in October 1989.[3]

The U.S. policy of constructive engagement did not work as anticipated. Not only did the United States fail to achieve a workable relationship with Iraq, but Saddam became increasingly aggressive from 1988 to 1990. It is important to understand that Iraq was far stronger and more threatening than Iran during this time period and that key American officials fully understood this.

Although it may have been hard to balance with Iran against Iraq, given difficult relations with Tehran, it certainly was possible to decrease support for Iraq, to move toward less accommodation and more containment. Thus, the option of engaging in greater balancing behavior was available but not pursued.

Iraq Gains the Upper Hand in the Balance of Power

Iraq had grown immensely in military capability during the Iran-Iraq War, although it did not actually achieve its war objectives. States around the world wanted Iraq to be strong enough to deter Iran, which appeared more threatening than Iraq most of the time. They were concerned that Iran, infused with the outsized revolutionary zeal of Ayatollah Khomeini and his ardent followers, could win the war, so they took some steps to weaken it beyond the U.S. sanctions that were slapped on Iran during the hostage crisis of 1979 and in the 1980s. States were also driven to support Iraq by the profit motive. The Soviet Union and France in particular became Iraq's number 1 and 2 arms suppliers, respectively. Iraq, thus, obtained a variety of arms and other military items during the war.

By the end of the war, the American, Western, and Arab tilt toward Iraq and against Iran, as well as the effects of war, had weakened Iran compared with Iraq (table 4). Kenneth Pollack, who served as a CIA analyst in this period, asserts that he and his colleagues were concerned about this imbalance and about the possibility that "the devastation of Iranian military power meant that, for the first time, Iraq was effectively unrestrained in how it could pursue its regional ambitions."[4]

Table 4. *The Military Balance, 1980–1992*

Total	Men[a]	Army[b]	Tanks	Combat Aircraft
1980 (At the outset of the Iran-Iraq War)				
Iran	240,000	150,000	1,735	447
Iraq	243,000	200,000	2,750	339
1983 (Coincident with Operation Staunch)				
Iran	235,000	150,000	1,210	90
Iraq	342,000	300,000	2,300	330
1985 (Concomitant with the Iran-Contra affair)				
Iran	555,000	250,000	1,000	95
Iraq	642,000	600,000	2,900	580
1987 (During the reflagging mission)				
Iran	645,000	305,000	1,000	60–160
Iraq	1,000,000	955,000	4,500	500–800
1990 (Prior to Iraq's August 2 invasion of Kuwait)				
Iran	504,000	305,000	500	185
Iraq	1,000,000	955,000	5,500	689
1992 (At start of dual containment)				
Iran	600,000–750,000	500,000–530,000	700–800	200–230[c]
Iraq	600,000–800,000	400,000–500,000	2,900–3,100	330–360

Sources: Off-the-record interviews; U.S. Department of Defense, *Conduct of the Persian Gulf War* (Washington, DC: April 1992), 154, 157; International Institute for Strategic Studies, *The Military Balance* (London: International Institute for Strategic Studies, various editions).

[a] The active total for "Men" comprises all personnel on full-time duty, including conscripts, long-term assignments from the Reserves, and paramilitary elements when so required by the national authority.

[b] Personnel in the army, not including paramilitary elements.

[c] Excluding the 112 aircraft flown to Iran in the 1991 war. Probably fewer than 50% of U.S. aircraft were serviceable.

The Shifting Balance of Threat

Iraq had gained the edge in the regional balance of power, but it had also become the more threatening actor in the region.

After the 1988 cease-fire, the balance of threat changed significantly. Iraq emerged as a major and unambiguous threat. The United States clearly understood that Iraq's intentions in the Gulf, in the broader Middle East, and even toward America were dangerous.

In several speeches, beginning with a famous one on February 24, 1990, Saddam spearheaded a new offensive against the United States. He may have considered the fact that most Arab leaders and elites viewed the decline of the Soviet Union as a sign of a new era of American hegemony at the global level, and Israel's hegemony in the region, and that the time was ripe to capitalize on these perceived concerns about American and Israeli power by challenging the United States. Saddam, perhaps intoxicated by his own descriptions of Iraq's great victory against Iran in what was really a fruitless and bloody war, called on Arab states to offset U.S. power and on the United States to withdraw from the region and eschew involvement in Arab affairs.[5] That was quite a demand from an actor that had tilted in his favor during the Iran-Iraq War.

Saddam's February speech smacked of bravado, but Iraq did seem to have something brewing in its basement. In fact, the United States issued its first major warning in February 1989 that Iraq was seeking to develop nuclear weapons, even though the warning did not reflect an administration shift toward a tougher policy on Iraq.[6] Israel's bombing of Iraq's nuclear reactor at Osirak in 1981 had set Saddam back significantly in the quest for nuclear weapons, but he was indefatigable in his pursuit, no matter the cost. What he learned from the Osirak attack was to build the nuclear program underground and in multiple facilities to make it harder to destroy. Had Israel not bombed Iraq's nuclear facilities or had Iraq not invaded Kuwait in 1990, Saddam may well have developed nuclear weapons before he could be stopped. In fact, UN inspectors asserted that Iraq may well have been close to developing a nuclear weapon in 1991 and might have succeeded were it not for the U.S.-led war against Iraq. The United States had earlier believed that it would be many years before Iraq developed weapons of mass destruction, suggesting that it had an uncanny ability to misestimate which suggests that it had a tendency to underestimate Iraq's potential in this area.[7]

In foreign relations, Saddam appeared perfectly willing to provoke Western powers. In March 1990, Iraq hanged an Iranian-born British journalist, Farzad Bazoft, who worked for the London weekly newspaper the *Observer,* for apparent espionage. The act itself was, of course, inhumane, but it also sent a signal to the West that Saddam was calling the shots and that he was bold enough to engage in such effrontery against Britain.

Not much later, American and British officials seized high-tech devices and machinery destined for use in Iraq's multi-billion-dollar effort to develop nuclear weapons and a long-range supergun — the biggest gun of its type ever to be built which could deliver its deadly nonconventional payload thousands of miles, with Iran and Israel as potential targets.

In addition, Iraq did not noticeably demobilize its army after the war and used chemical weapons and torture on its own people in an effort to depopulate Iraqi Kurdistan.[8] The gravity of these acts put Saddam in a new light. Using chemical weapons in the war with Iran might be loosely explained by the brutal nature of war and by the fear of losing the war, but using such weapons on unarmed citizens of Iraq was another matter altogether.

Saddam, however, appeared to want to extend his campaign against his own people, possibly to Israel. On April 2, 1990, he announced that Iraqi scientists had developed advanced chemical weapons that could "eat up half of Israel" if it tried to "do anything against Iraq."[9] The State Department, fairly quiet until now, called the statement "inflammatory, outrageous and irresponsible," although the administration sought to shield Iraq from potential congressional sanctions for using chemical weapons against its Kurds and for its threat against Israel.[10] It may be true that Saddam only intended to deter Israel from launching any attacks against Iraq, but his statement was incendiary, especially given the experience of the Jewish people with extermination partly by chemicals during the Holocaust. Certainly, it reflected a level of bravado and perhaps recklessness which added to the impression that Iraq was a dangerous threat to American interests in the region.

Saddam, however, did not restrict his invective to Israel. In fact, Israel, as usual, was a useful rhetorical target, but Saddam's real attention was focused far closer to home, in his own neighborhood. In May, he criticized the Gulf states, particularly Kuwait, for waging economic war against Iraq, ignoring oil production quotas, keeping oil prices down, refusing to forgive Iraq's war debts from the Iran-Iraq War, and failing to extend postwar reconstruction credits.[11] In the months preceding the 1990–91 war, he issued various threats against Kuwait, backed by military maneuvers. He even asserted, in conjunction with a diatribe against perceived Kuwaiti efforts to "sabotage" Iraq's economic interests, that it is "more painful to have one's head cut off than one's sustenance."[12] In retrospect, it appears that he was suggesting that Kuwait could hurt Iraq economically but Iraq could eliminate Kuwait as a state.

The United States increasingly recognized that Iraq, in addition to being the strongest Gulf state, was now the chief threat in the aftermath of the Iran-Iraq War. As Colin Powell would later recall: "Iran represented less of a problem to our interests than Iraq in 1988."[13] In March 1989, one internal study asserted that, although Saddam was dangerous and difficult, Iraq was the strongest state in a region vital to U.S. interests.[14] In the fall of 1989, the administration conducted a study on Saddam and found that he was a "a very bad man": "This is an aggressor, this is a man who has weapons of mass destruction . . . and the question is whether by offering some inducements . . . we might be able to bring him inside the tent."[15]

Secretary of State James Baker noted that the United States did get somewhat "tougher" with Saddam from February to August 1990.[16] In addition, according to an internal memo, Baker did assert to April Glaspie, the U.S. ambassador to Iraq, in early 1990 that the United States and Iraq would be at odds if Iraq continued to engage in threatening behavior in the region.[17] However, Washington remained in a conciliatory mode. At a September 1989 meeting of the National Security Council (NSC), national security adviser Brent Scowcroft summed up the administration consensus that there would be little lost by building ties to Iraq. This view was reflected in National Security Directive 26.[18] As Scowcroft put it, "We wanted to see if we could transform Iraq into a moderately responsible leader in world politics. We knew Iraq was rich and that it would initiate a massive reconstruction program and we saw no reason why U.S. business shouldn't be there."[19] At the same time, although the United States could benefit from Iraq's economic reconstruction, it saw various inducements as helping to convince Saddam to discontinue his programs aimed at developing weapons of mass destruction.[20]

The thrust of the policy was not illogical, although hindsight has a way of making failure look like stupidity. Appeasement was not rare in world history, or in the modern Middle East.[21] Yet few people at the time could have predicted that Saddam would dismiss the policy and invade Kuwait. Rather, it made at least some sense to believe initially that he could be enticed to join the Western fold so as to gain support for rebuilding his war-ravaged economy. Such expectations reflected the broader tenor of U.S. foreign policy in a changing world. In 1989 and 1990, walls were collapsing in Eastern Europe, as reflected in the fall of the much hated Berlin Wall and of one communist regime after another; East and West were coming closer together, as underscored by the unification of Germany and by the myriad growth of ties between former antagonists; the Soviet Union was in the last phases of its existence; and global cooperation appeared to be on the rise. It is also important to note that the residue of Vietnam remained a factor in American foreign policy and there was much talk in the 1988 election of American decline. The concern was that the United States had overextended itself in world politics and that this was hurting its economy.

It also made some sense to avoid a tough approach toward Iraq because the United States had more important objectives at the time. American attention was not focused on Iraq but rather on the historic events taking place in the Soviet Union and Eastern Europe. The United States, as one official describes it, had its "mind on other things and was not interested in containment."[22]

Little did anyone know that the liberal notion of unification, reflected in an evolving process that led to the historic merger of East and West Germany in October 1990, would take on a new meaning as Iraq annexed Kuwait in August 1990. This is not the type of unification that the United States had in mind.

Not only did the policy of constructive engagement mesh with the thrust of U.S. foreign policy in an evolving post–Cold War world, but it also could have yielded other benefits. Indeed, the United States also accommodated Saddam because Iraq was a significant market for U.S. agricultural products.[23]

Nonetheless, the key point is that the administration did not check Iraq more strongly, despite increasingly recognizing its predominant military strength and even though "no one was under the illusion that Saddam was other than bad news."[24] The view was that pressuring a strong Iraq would be counterproductive; instead, the United States continued to pursue constructive engagement as a means of influencing Saddam's behavior.[25] That effort was coupled by a directive from President Bush in January 1989 authorizing an Export-Import Bank line of credit that totaled nearly $200 million to support Iraqi grain exports to the United States.[26] The United States's incentives for Iraqi moderation had included the continuation of the Commodity Credit Corporation program, which, through the U.S. Department of Agriculture, had assured American exporters of $1 billion in support to facilitate grain shipments to Iraq.

By October 1989, the administration was reconsidering its approach and had become more "pragmatic and cautious."[27] The last approval of commodity credits to Iraq came in November, although more credit extensions were discussed thereafter but not pursued.[28] Yet it is important to note that Secretary Baker set in motion the request for new guarantees in October 1989 even as evidence was arising — which was recognized in memos and minutes of meetings within the departments of State and Agriculture — that Iraq may well have diverted monies for the purchase of agricultural commodities to the purchase of military hardware and even nuclear-related equipment.[29] It is also noteworthy that in February 1990, six months before Iraq invaded Kuwait, John Kelly, assistant secretary of state for Near East and South Asian affairs, was sent to Baghdad to meet with Saddam. He delivered a conciliatory message from Washington encapsulated in President Bush's confirmation on January 17, 1990, of a policy of placating Iraq. Kelly told Saddam that the United States sought to strengthen ties to Baghdad.[30]

Saddam's February 1990 speech in which he laid out his vision of the post–Cold War world for the Middle East cast the United States as a great enemy and should have been the death knell for constructive engagement. The United States may have believed that it had, as one analyst put it, worked with "nasty dictators before and that Saddam was a bastard but he could be its bastard," but that speech should have been a good indication that he "could not be America's bastard." Nevertheless, the policy of constructive engagement continued until Iraq's invasion of Kuwait.[31]

In fact, even as late as May 1990, just two months before the invasion, Kelly argued against taking a tougher stance.[32] Whatever its initial merits, the conciliatory approach was failing to persuade Iraq to become more moderate, but it was unclear what might replace it. Direct balancing against Iraq with Iran was a nonstarter, given U.S.-Iranian tensions. Nor was there much appetite around the world for balancing against the Iraqi threat. The United States, therefore, had the choice of unilaterally taking stronger actions against Iraq and moving away from the conciliatory approach or staying on course. A tougher approach would have conformed with balancing approaches, even if belatedly.

On April 16, 1990, the State Department's deputies committee dealing with Iraq met and produced a memo for wider circulation on May 16, 1990. That memo did list a variety of options for getting tougher on Iraq. They included banning American purchases of Iraqi oil, ending intelligence cooperation with Iraq, aiming to "sponsor or encourage further action on Iraq's human rights policies," isolating Iraq, and even normalizing relations with Iran. One advantage of the last option was that it could send Iraq a "strong signal."[33] In this sense, the administration did consider options for taking a stronger stand against Iraq, although it did not take much action.

Staying the course also had the advantage of not having to alter an entrenched policy and to deal with special interests. In May, the administration's attempt to cut the second half of the $1 billion loan guarantee to Iraq, one of its few actions to cool the relationship with Baghdad, was defeated by the U.S. Senate. Senator Robert Dole from Kansas, a major exporter of grain to Iraq, had led the fight in the Senate. In April, he had also led a trip to Iraq with four other senators who, while giving Saddam a letter denouncing attempts to develop weapons of mass destruction, also told him, in a transcript released by the Iraqis, that President Bush supported their trip and did not support a tougher campaign against Iraq.[34]

In hindsight, Washington's approach of constructive engagement proved to be nonconstructive. The United States seemed to be trying to move away from its Iraq policy while continuing to send Iraq signals that it wanted positive rela-tions and did not object seriously to its dubious behavior.[35] The issue would become moot, in any case. Iraq's invasion of Kuwait on August 2, 1990, changed everything. We can surmise that the invasion, by suggesting the failure of U.S. efforts to appease Iraq in the late 1980s, made the United States more likely to take a strong stand against Iraq not only to compensate for its past mistakes but also because Iraq revealed itself as surprisingly incorrigible in an embarrassing contrast to prior U.S. appraisals.

Iran Weakens and Mellows

While Iraq was flexing its muscles, Iran, which had been so threatening during the war, changed its tune somewhat by the end of the Iran-Iraq War. By mid-1988, Khomeini reconsidered his stubborn approach on the war, with its high human, economic, and strategic costs. He accepted UN Resolution 598, which called for a cease-fire, in July 1988 but described his acceptance of it as having drunk from "the poisonous chalice."[36]

Iran and Iraq suffered inestimable war-related damage to infrastructure and incurred serious debt. This debt was also much harder to service: Iran resched-uled about $9 billion in debt in 1994 but borrowed another $20 billion in 1994–95.[37] The final Iranian government report placed the war's direct economic dam-age as equal to twenty years of the country's oil revenue at the 1983 earning level of $20.5 billion, and 52.85 percent of the economic damage was indirect.[38]

To be sure, the threat from Iran remained after the war. Its nuclear program, support of terrorism, potential threat to Gulf shipping, and clear efforts to under-mine the Middle East peace process remained serious problems. But militarily it was far weaker than Iraq after the cease-fire in the war. In fact, Iran watchers in the CIA viewed Iran as being "flat on its back."[39] Iran appeared to moderate its foreign policy. After Khomeini's death, President Hashemi Rafsanjani, though hardly a dove, repeatedly stressed the importance of economics over ideology. Less moderate elements in Iran argued for a more confrontational foreign policy, but the regime had virtually no support for renewed conflict with its neighbors.[40] Iran's economic problems circumscribed the nature of its foreign policy and put limits on how ambitious it could be in the region.

After the Soviet Union and its socialist allies fell from power, Iran had, as Shireen Hunter puts it, "no alternative to the West as a source of technology and financing for its economic reconstruction."[41] It even expressed interest in joining the World Trade Organization, more than three-quarters of whose members came from developing or least-developed countries.[42] This situation provided some further incentive at the time for Tehran to moderate its foreign policy in the region. As Shaul Bakhash observes, there was "a realization among the president's advisers and certainly in the new Parliament that one of the issues that [had to] be dealt with to attract foreign investment and expand the economy [was] Iran's relations with the U.S."[43]

In addition, Iran remained relatively isolated politically, which exacerbated its economic problems and left it more vulnerable in war. Tehran had attempted several times since the 1979 revolution to break its isolation, without great success. In 1984, for instance, Khomeini appeared to moderate Iran's foreign policy, chiefly because Iran was suffering military setbacks, was unable to obtain spare parts and equipment thanks to American pressures, and was interested in generating international support for its war position.[44]

Conclusion

U.S. behavior toward Iraq from 1988 to 1990 was far from a balancing against power or threat. Instead of balancing against the strongest and most threatening actor in 1988, the United States was motivated in part by Iraq's prevailing strength and threat to try to accommodate it. Had U.S. behavior conformed to balancing, it would have stopped tilting toward Iraq after the Iran-Iraq War or some time thereafter. In fact, one internal document had recommended precisely that. It asserted that rather than building up Iraq in order to counter Iran the United States should try to play Iran and Iraq off each other to generate a form of "balance of power between the two" and in the process Washington should end support for Iraq.[45]

Despite these recommendations, however, American policy toward Iraq continued to be conciliatory up to the invasion of Kuwait. Even after it became clear that Saddam sought to develop nuclear capability, the Bush administration provided Iraq with agricultural products, military intelligence, and financial access. Rather than focusing its efforts solely on much-needed postwar economic reconstruction, Iraq used American economic support for military purposes, a fact known to at least some American officials.

The conciliatory approach toward Iraq after the Iran-Iraq War failed to change Iraq's behavior. In fact, it may have led Saddam to believe that the United States would not react very strongly to his invasion of Kuwait in 1990. After all, if it had been placating him, despite his threatening behavior, would it be alarmed enough about the invasion of Kuwait that it would send a massive force to the region to reverse the invasion? Would it sacrifice blood and treasure to save what many saw as an illegitimate monarchy in control of a big oil well?

It is hard to explain U.S. behavior by arguing that the United States was balancing at the global level. It is true that Soviet-Iraqi relations were not as strong in the 1980s as they had been in the 1970s. It is also true that U.S.-Soviet relations were stronger in the late 1980s than they had been earlier. But, even so, accommodating Iraq would be the opposite of balancing against Moscow at the global level.

All these realities, in any case, would change rapidly when Iraq invaded Kuwait and presented the United States with yet another shocking event to which it would have to react. This was an event that it did not predict and which would radically alter whatever existed of the policy of constructive engagement and, more important, would change the entire trajectory of American foreign policy in the region and of the international relations of the Persian Gulf. Indeed, virtually nothing of any magnitude which followed in the region was unrelated to the 1990–91 Persian Gulf crisis, including the U.S. invasion of Iraq in 2003 and its subsequent occupation of that country.

CHAPTER FIVE

The Iraq War of 1991

In August 1990, Iraq stunned a world still basking in the evanescent glow of the fall of communism and the end of the Cold War. Its brutal and unabashed invasion of Kuwait was a clarion signal that a new world order had certainly not yet dawned, much less shined, and might not be in the offing at all.

Iraq's invasion motivated a massive U.S.-led deployment of forces to Saudi Arabia, called Operation Desert Shield, to protect Saudi Arabia from Iraq, followed in January 1991 by Operation Desert Storm, which evicted Iraqi forces from Kuwait. These operations were consonant with the end goal of balance of power, which is to prevent a regional hegemon from arising. However, the strategy that the United States used to reach this end goal was more consistent with collective security than with balance-of-power politics. In this sense, the 1991 Gulf war case is partly balance-of-power policy at play, although it is much more a reflection of balance-of-threat policy.

The Background of Iraq's Invasion of Kuwait

It is vital to explore in brief the background of the invasion of Kuwait to gain a clearer picture of why Iraq invaded Kuwait and why its invasion created such a threat to American regional and global interests. What follows is a sketch of the underlying, intermediate, and immediate causes of Iraq's invasion.

The underlying or long-standing causes were important. Iraq believed that Kuwait was, in fact, part of Iraq. The merger of Iraq and Kuwait after the 1990 invasion wed the two countries and, in Iraq's mind, fixed history.[1] Under Ottoman rule, Iraq was not a unified or independent state. Rather, it consisted of three disparate provinces — Mosul, Baghdad, and Basra. From Iraq's perspective, Kuwait was always part of Basra under the Ottoman Empire. Kuwait, however, viewed such Iraqi claims as a smokescreen for aggression. After all, the royal family had established an autonomous sheikdom in Kuwait in 1756, and Iraq, for that matter, was artificial as well, having been carved out of the Ottoman Empire after World War I in an ad hoc manner.

Iraq's Baathist Party ideology also may have played a role in its decision to invade Kuwait. This ideology sought to sweep away artificial borders between states, and Saddam wanted to unite the Arab world behind Baghdad. He would even assert that it was during war that the Iraqi army "rose to the level of the [Islamic] mission," trying in a Herculean feat to pass off Baath Party ideology as something holy.[2]

We can surmise that Saddam's personal ambitions, beyond state or institutional interests, further pushed Iraq to invade Kuwait. A few months before the outbreak of the war, he spoke in typical terms of Iraq achieving great "glory," calling on the faithful to play a role in this unfolding history.[3]

These underlying motivations for war may well have been at play, but intermediate causes were also important. Indeed, the Iran-Iraq War devastated Iraq's economy and left it heavily indebted to Kuwait and Saudi Arabia. These countries had loaned Saddam considerable amounts of money for the war against revolutionary Iran. Estimates suggest that Iraq began that war with US$35 billion in reserve and ended the war $80 billion to $100 billion in debt. Interestingly, Iraqi foreign minister Tariq Aziz claimed shortly after the invasion of Kuwait in 1990 that Baghdad had to "resort to this method" of invasion because its economic situation had deteriorated and it had no alternative.[4] Kuwait was quite a tempting economic prize. In Saddam's mind, gaining control of Kuwait could provide the economic impetus to help reconstruct Iraq and placate some of his enemies at home and a restless population that had suffered much during the Iran-Iraq War.

In invading Kuwait, Iraq did not have to worry as much about exposing itself to Iran, its archenemy, because Iran was now weakened. We can surmise that this made the invasion more plausible.[5]

Moreover, Iraq's huge standing army, expanded during the Iran-Iraq War, could not be effectively reintegrated into the shaky Iraqi economy after the war. And like Napoleon, Saddam may have understood that an idle, restless army could pose a much greater threat to his regime than one kept busy in war. Much better for him to keep his outsized army involved in Kuwait than to allow it to conjure up ways to overthrow him after the very costly Iran-Iraq War.

The Iran-Iraq War, especially Iran's victory at Fao in 1986, also taught Iraq that its short coastline was a major vulnerability, compared with Iran's massive coastline and somewhat developed naval capability. That made control of Kuwait more enticing. It would give Iraq much greater access to the Gulf and thus would strengthen it against Iran, which, for all Iraq knew, might harbor great resentments at being attacked by Iraq in 1980 and might once again be at war with Baghdad in the future.

However, although underlying and intermediate causes were important, the more immediate causes were related to Iraq's growing tensions with Kuwait. At the Arab League summit meeting in May 1990, Saddam attacked Gulf states, especially Kuwait, for ignoring oil production quotas, keeping oil prices down, refusing to forgive Iraq's war debts from the Iran-Iraq War, and failing to provide war reconstruction credits.[6]

Despite the fact that Iraq attacked Iran in September 1980, Baghdad repeatedly argued that it sacrificed greatly to check Iran's threat to all Arab states, especially the Gulf monarchies, which Khomeini wanted to overthrow through political means. Tariq Aziz, in fact, repeatedly asserted to the U.S. ambassador to Iraq, Joseph Wilson, that Iraq "defended the Arab nation against the Persian onslaught with the blood of its sons."[7] Thus, from Iraq's perspective at least, Baghdad deserved Arab allegiance and economic support, and Kuwait could not expect to get a free ride on Iraq's military back.[8]

The Kuwaitis and Saudis were not particularly forthcoming with postwar economic support, and Iraq's economy was devastated, so Saddam sought to push oil prices higher by limiting production by members of the Organization of Petroleum Exporting Countries (OPEC). By agreeing to production quotas, the members of OPEC, which included the Gulf states, could affect the price of oil. The lesser the amount of oil they pumped, the more expensive oil would be on the market. States that sought a shorter-term fix were more interested in pumping a large amount of oil, whereas those with a longer-term view were less interested in doing so.

Saddam was unhappy with Kuwait. Kuwait indirectly lowered oil prices by pumping too much oil, some from the Rumaila oil field over which Iraq laid joint claim. Iraq accused Kuwait of slant-drilling into this oil field: by starting oil wells on their side of the Iraqi-Kuwaiti border and angling their oil equipment under the border, the Kuwaitis could draw on oil from Iraqi sources. Interestingly, in January 2001, Aziz would reflect on the past and assert that Kuwait "got what it deserved" in 1990 because it was undermining Iraq's oil prices and slant-drilling.[9] Since Iraq received almost all its revenues from the oil industry, any changes in the price of oil affected its economy. In 1979, prior to its invasion of Iran, Iraq had enormous oil revenues from a booming global oil market, but in the late 1980s, the opposite situation prevailed. The oil market was in the doldrums owing to a glut of oil on the market, resulting in oil prices that by 1986 had dropped below $10 per barrel. Saddam went so far as to describe Kuwait's behavior as a conspiracy against Iraq's economy and that of the Arab world in favor of Israel.[10]

Oddly, Saddam also justified the invasion by citing the Kuwaiti emir's dissolution of the 1986 Kuwaiti National Assembly, as if he were concerned about democratic practices in the Middle East. As reflected in initial communiqués from Baghdad, Iraq asserted that it would support a popular revolution against the illegitimate Kuwaiti monarchy, organize elections, and then withdraw.[11]

Kuwait was reluctant to bend to Saddam's brinkmanship, perhaps not recognizing his seriousness. With 100,000 well-trained troops, and 350 tanks poised on the Kuwaiti border, Iraq appeared ready to launch an invasion. But despite this show of force, neither the CIA nor Arab leaders were predicting an invasion. On July 25, the U.S. ambassador to Iraq, April Glaspie, met Saddam Hussein. In responding to Saddam's queries about U.S. intentions, she made the now infamous statement that the United States had "no opinion on the Arab-Arab conflicts, like [Saddam's] border disagreement with Kuwait."[12] Although Saddam asserted in an interview in 1992 that he saw her statement as providing a green light to invade Kuwait, it is unclear to what extent we should view his statement at face value, given the gravity of his invasion and the fact that conspiracy theory ran strong in Baghdad. Why should we assume that Saddam saw a "green light" when he was just as likely to see a trap at play?[13]

What is clearer is that Glaspie's remarks — and subsequent ones by Margaret Tutwiler, the State Department spokesperson, and John Kelly, assistant secretary of state for Near East and South Asian Affairs, before the House Foreign Affairs Committee two days before the invasion — underscored broader administration policy. That policy of conciliation may very well have contributed to Saddam's belief that even if he was not being given a green light per se, at least his invasion would not lead to a dramatic response by Washington or to war over Kuwait.[14]

On August 2, 1990, 140,000 Iraqi troops and 1,800 tanks invaded Kuwait, spearheaded by two top-notch Republican Guard divisions.

Episode 6: Iraq's Invasion of Kuwait and U.S. Action, 1990–1991

The 1988 cease-fire in the nearly decade-long Iran-Iraq War left a number of issues unsettled in Iran-Iraq relations, which had explosive potential. Iraq sought to settle them after it invaded Kuwait. Whereas prior to the invasion Iraq rejected Iran's conditions for peace, only three weeks after it Saddam accepted them. Evidently, he hoped that Iran would violate the international embargo against Iraq and sought to secure his eastern front so that he could confront the U.S.-led alliance more effectively. Iraq withdrew from 2,200 meters of Iranian-captured territory; engaged in an exchange of prisoners of war; ceded to Iran rights over part of the Shatt al-Arab waterway, over which they had a long-standing rivalry; and agreed to resume diplomatic relations.[15]

Iraq's invasion of Kuwait further altered the regional balance of power in Baghdad's favor. By incorporating Kuwait into Iraq, the latter country enhanced its geography and access to the Persian Gulf. Iraq had always lacked such access, and securing it offered Iraq the ability to project its power more effectively. Moreover, with Kuwait under its belt, Iraq now controlled 19 percent of the world's oil, which could help it deal with significant budget deficits, as would the fact that it no longer had to repay Kuwait for sizable loans incurred during the Iran-Iraq War. Finally, Iraq's military position had improved in the region as a whole as it absorbed Kuwait into Iraq.

Balancing against Threat

The U.S.-led coalition did balance against Iraq's prevailing threat, albeit within the broader and partly defining apparatus of collective security. The invasion had enhanced Iraq's position in the regional balance of power, but Iraq also clearly posed a serious future threat. Indeed, the fear was that Iraq might invade Saudi Arabia as well, which would leave Iraq in control of approximately 44 percent of the world's oil. If left unopposed, Iraq might gain enough capability to further shift the regional balance of power, blackmail other Arab states into supporting its inflated foreign policy agenda, and threaten Israel, to which the United States was committed.

Down the road, Iraq might also take actions to raise global oil prices, which could facilitate efforts to build weapons of mass destruction and which would drive the global economy into recession, a problem that the United States was already facing. Thus, even though the United States received only 8.7 percent of its oil from Iraq and Kuwait combined, Iraq's invasion still posed a serious threat. In a world of global interdependence, oil prices are set in markets, and these prices apply around the world, regardless of how much oil any one state receives from the Middle East or any other region. As General Khaled bin Sultan, the commander of Saudi forces, put it, Saudi Arabia may have been a target, but even if not, Iraq would have been in a position on "all important matters — particularly oil policy and foreign affairs" to "dictate terms."[16]

Riyadh ultimately appreciated the potential Iraqi threat, but allowing Western soldiers onto sacred soil could anger the powerful religious leaders in the kingdom, which saw Saudi Arabia as the protector of the two holy shrines of Islam at Mecca and Medina. This concern in part explains King Fahd's hesitancy in accepting an F-15 squadron that Bush offered him on August 2, 1990, and his repeated assertions that U.S.-led forces would be "temporary in nature" and would leave "Saudi territory immediately at the request of the Kingdom."[17]

However, although Iraq strongly denied any designs on Saudi Arabia, citing its nonaggression pact with the Saudi kingdom of March 1989 and excellent bilateral relations,[18] the United States and Saudi Arabia were doubtful. They even doubted statements made by Iraq to Palestinian Liberation Organization leader Yasser Arafat and King Hussein that Iraq had no designs on Saudi Arabia, a message they relayed to King Fahd.[19]

For its part, the United States was anxious to move to deter a possible invasion of Saudi Arabia and was deciding which forces to send there. But it needed to know that it could rely on the Saudis. Pressure from the United States and the Iraqi threat had already inclined Saudi Arabia to give the go-ahead for U.S. forces.[20] King Fahd did not want to wait for an "unambiguous" threat from Iraq, as some of his advisers had counseled, noting that the Kuwaitis had done just that.[21] CIA photographs revealed to him that Iraq's forces were less than 250 miles from Saudi oil fields and within striking range of Riyadh. Fahd did discuss the crisis in general with members of the royal family, but he made a critical, final decision virtually alone for the first time in his fifty years in public life to allow U.S. forces mass entry into his kingdom.[22] President Bush was convinced that Iraq had Saudi Arabia in his sights, which added energy to his counteroffensive.[23] He would assert on August 8 that he believed that economic sanctions "in this instance, if fully enforced, [could] be very, very effective," but no single thing tipped Washington's hand in sending troops to Saudi Arabia, except perhaps the fact that the Iraqis headed south toward Saudi Arabia when "they said they were withdrawing."[24]

The Saudis did agree to host American forces en masse, thus putting at loggerheads two goals: securing themselves against outside threats and not appearing to be American lackeys domestically. After the Saudis gave the nod, President Bush began to inform the public of the U.S. approach. In an address to the nation on August 8, 1990, he asserted that U.S. goals included the unconditional withdrawal of all Iraqi forces from Kuwait; removal of a puppet regime put in place by Iraq and restoration of Kuwait's legitimate government; continuation of the long-standing and historical role of protecting regional stability; and the protection of the lives of Americans abroad.

In sharp contrast to the 2003 war, which was launched by the administration of George W. Bush in the broader war on terrorism, the dominant U.S. national concern in 1990 was the threat that the Iraqi invasion posed to global, and in turn U.S., economic interests through the "potential domination of the energy resources that are crucial to the entire world."[25] Scowcroft maintained that two fundamental things had motivated U.S. behavior: the United States' "key interests in the Persian Gulf which required that under no circumstances could Saddam get control of oil, and on top of that the horror of what Saddam was doing in Kuwait."[26] For his part, Baker stated that the fundamental reason that the United States fought the war was that secure access to Gulf oil has been a national interest of the United States "all the way back to Roosevelt."[27] Indeed, in an effort to secure UN support for the U.S.-led use of force, Baker had argued at the United Nations on November 29, 1990: "Saddam's actions, the vast arms he possesses, the weapons of mass destruction he seeks, indicate clearly that Kuwait was not only not the first but probably not the last target on his list."[28]

The United States was concerned about what the invasion meant at the global level as well as at the strategic level. Bush and some of his advisers believed that failure to check Iraq's aggression would encourage even more challenges to the status quo, which favored the United States, and to global stability and that the use of force could succeed.[29]

Balancing at the Global Level?

The Bush administration was focused at the global level when Iraq invaded Kuwait, but its response to Iraq's invasion was not aimed in the least at balancing against the Soviet Union. At the time, Washington sought to integrate it globally and facilitate its transition away from communism. If the United States was balancing against Iraq to balance against threat at the global level, we would have expected such action in 1988 or 1989. At that time, the Soviet Union was clearly perceived as more threatening than would be the case in 1990. In fact, the new world order concept promulgated by President Bush featured enhanced relations with other great powers, especially Moscow. The Soviet Union had not yet disintegrated, but the nature of U.S.-Soviet relations had already changed dramatically.[30] That Moscow lent Washington unprecedented support during the Gulf crisis further makes it hard to conclude that U.S. action in the crisis reflected a balance-of-threat approach aimed at the global level. It is this support from Moscow, and many other states around the world, which helped establish the Gulf case as history's best example of collective security.

Collective Security versus Balance of Power in History

The United States did practice elements of balance-of-power policy, but the picture is more complex because its broader effort took place in the context of collective security, which differs from balance-of-power policy in important ways.[31] These differences become apparent when we assess the role of collective security in American history.

The American approach during the 1990–91 Gulf crisis had historical antecedents in President Woodrow Wilson's ardent advocacy of collective security. In January 1918, as part of its rationale for entering World War I, the United States issued a fourteen-point statement explaining how the "Great War" might be transformed into "the war to end all wars." In his fourteenth point, Wilson called for a "general association of nations to be formed under specific covenants for the purpose of affording mutual guarantees of political independence and territorial integrity to great and small states alike."[32] Collective security became a central concept of this soon-to-be League of Nations, a precursor to the United Nations.

Wilson presented collective security as an alternative to old-world balance-of-power politics, asserting in an address to the U.S. Senate in 1917 that "there must be not a balance of power, but a community of power."[33] In various speeches, he asserted that balance-of-power policy was forever discredited as a way of keeping peace, given its connection in his view to the outbreak of World War I.[34] For Wilson, balance-of-power tactics allowed strong states to dominate and exploit weaker ones, creating enduring instability.[35] Under the nineteenth-century balance-of-power system, the five powerful actors of the European system agreed to cooperate in order to balance against the strongest actor among them, but they sanctioned European domination of others.[36] Wilson saw balance-of-power politics as secretive, manipulative, and power-dominated.[37]

Wilson understood well the challenges of creating a new world order. On several occasions, he shared his concern with other leaders about how or even whether the League of Nations could function effectively, given the problems inherent in collective action.[38] But he did not expect the U.S. Senate to reject American participation in the league by a vote of 98 to 2. Wilson's internationalism ran ahead of American public opinion. America remained too isolationist in 1920 to embrace a notion such as a world league or collective security, which violated President George Washington's warning against getting the United States stuck in entangling alliances.[39]

Wilson's view of balance-of-power policy and his promotion of his Fourteen Points did not make him a hero in Europe, much like President George W. Bush's messianic brand of foreign policy did not earn him accolades on the other side of the Atlantic and around the world. French statesman Georges Clemenceau asserted cynically, "God himself was content with ten commandments. Wilson modestly inflicted fourteen points on us . . . the fourteen commandments of the most empty theory!"[40] Collective security had failed under the League of Nations in part because the United States had refused to join the league, but it would be revived in its clearest form in the 1990–91 Gulf crisis.

Collective Security versus Balance of Power in Practice

For Wilson, collective security clearly differed from balance-of-power politics. For modern thinkers, collective security and balance of power have some similarities, but they differ in important ways.[41]

Collective security does not require that alliances be formed in advance to stop potential aggressors (except in the broad sense that collective security arrangements may deter aggressors). They are activated only after aggression has taken place.[42] Balance-of-power politics in pre–World War I Europe allowed the stronger European states — Britain, Austro-Hungary, Russia, France, and Germany (after 1871) — to balance one another even when no clear threat had manifested itself, as they would in subsequent periods in history.

Under collective security, unprovoked aggressive use of force by one state against another is illegal. Articles 39–46 of the UN Charter require all members to make available to the Security Council, "on its call and in accordance with a special agreement or agreements, armed forces, assistance and facilities, including rights of passage, necessary for the purpose of maintaining international peace and security." The UN charter also includes a series of articles that outlaw the threat or use of force, except in cases of self-defense or for purposes of collective security, and which call on states to contribute to collective security. Of course, under balance-of-power approaches, the aggressive use of force is not only legal per se but is sometimes recommended to ensure a balance of power. In this sense, collective security is much more dependent on normative rules than is balance-of-power politics, which is guided by power, force, and the self-help rules of anarchical world politics. It is not grounded in a legal requirement and architecture but rather by a commonly perceived interest.[43]

Under collective security, aggressive actors are to be checked by collective action under the auspices of a world organization — initially the League of Nations and later, beginning in 1945, the United Nations. The UN Charter requires that all states that join the United Nations agree to accept responsibility for punishing egregious violators of international law, even if their own individual interests are not threatened, unlike balance of power, in which states balance when their interests are threatened. Article 10 of the League of Nations charter, which formed the legal heart of collective security, pledged to protect all members against aggression. According to collective security, an attack on one is viewed as an attack on all. States act under a legally binding, codified commitment that applies to all that are party to the charter or institution.[44]

Historically, collective action involving myriad actors also differed from balance-of-power politics, which often involved only a few self-interested actors rather than a community of nations and was guided by power and force rather than by international laws and organizations.

The Gulf Case: Collective Security in Action

Following from the foregoing discussion, it is fair to say that the 1991 Gulf war represented a case of collective security as much as balance-of-power politics. Indeed, collective enforcement has been put in motion three times in the combined history of the League of Nations and the United Nations, and the Persian Gulf case represented the most significant success, even considering a predominant American role.

As mentioned earlier, under collective security, alliances are formed after aggression takes place. This was the case in 1990. In fact, the United States had outright failed to balance against Iraq's capability before the invasion, but it did spearhead the U.S.-led coalition after Iraq became an open aggressor when it invaded Kuwait.

Iraq's invasion and occupation of Kuwait were also labeled as illegal by numerous UN resolutions. Resolution 660 was the first and, with the exception of a Yemeni abstention, it unanimously condemned Iraq's invasion and demanded that Iraq "withdraw immediately and unconditionally all of its forces to the position in which they were located on August 1, 1990."[45] Thereafter, economic sanctions were imposed on Iraq (except for humanitarian or medical purposes) under UN Resolution 661, adopted on August 6. Meanwhile, the United States was busy creating the anti-Iraq coalition and lobbying for additional UN resolutions. The UN authorization to wage war against Iraq, passed on November 29, 1990, was the first such authorization since 1950, when the absence of the Soviet Union at the Security Council allowed for the United Nations to effectuate collective security against North Korea in defense of South Korea.

More than thirty nations joined together under UN auspices and in line with international law against Iraq. The United States leaned more toward collective action rather than unilateralism because it sought to punish aggressors through a community of nations — an effort that bedeviled the League of Nations in the 1930s. Reflective of his view during the crisis, Bush noted in late January 1991 that "what was, and is, at stake is not simply our energy or economic security and the stability of a vital region but the prospects for peace in the post–Cold war era — the promise of a new world order based upon the rule of law."[46] Through a U.S.-led but collective military response to Iraq's violation of international law, the United Nations achieved the purpose originally envisioned by the architects of the post–World War II era. "Now we can see a new world order coming into view," Bush pronounced to Congress in his victory speech on March 6. "A world where the United Nations, freed from the cold war stalemate, is poised to fulfill the historic vision of its founders. . . . The Gulf War put this new world to its first test. And my fellow Americans, we passed that test."[47] Checking the offensive use of force was the overarching principle of Bush's new world order, which rested heavily on the rule of law, although, as Bush recounts, "this objective remained distinctly secondary in our public explications of our purposes in the Gulf crisis."[48]

Although the U.S.-led operation proved to be the best case in history of UN collective security, it was hardly a pure case. The United States sought to promote collective action, but it did not commit to responding to all acts of aggression against sovereign states as collective security requires in theory. Nor did Washington forsake unilateralism or want to surrender aspects of its sovereignty.

It remained ready during and after the crisis to pursue its interests unilaterally if need be, with or without the United Nations or the U.S. Congress for that matter. Collective security ran risks for the United States because it was difficult to exercise and could limit U.S. influence over outcomes. Moreover, it left the coalition vulnerable to defection by any of its members, which might decrease its credibility, whereas unilateral action could avoid such a potential weakness.

For Bush, the United Nations was the appropriate international body for handling the Gulf crisis, provided it did not curtail American power significantly. Bush and Scowcroft noted that building an international response led the United States "immediately to the UN, which could provide a cloak of acceptability" to U.S. efforts and "mobilize world opinion behind the principles" the United States wished to project.[49] In this sense, collective action was in part a public relations strategy. Multilateral action also added credibility to the U.S.-led approach and made it harder for Saddam to paint U.S. efforts as another example of Western imperialism.

Episode 7: The War-Termination Strategy, 1991

At the end of the 1991 Gulf war, Washington was faced with difficult choices regarding the termination of the war. Overall, balance-of-power concerns played a secondary role at best in these war-termination decisions.

Rather than marching on Baghdad or even continuing the campaign long enough to destroy Saddam's Republican Guard divisions, the United States and its allies chose to end the ground war at 100 hours. On March 3, after a blistering campaign in the air and on the ground which sent Iraqi forces haplessly in retreat, General Norman Schwarzkopf, who commanded U.S. forces, met with Lieutenant General Sultan Hashim Ahmad al-Jabburi, Iraq's vice chief of staff. They aimed to arrange a cease-fire in the war. For this meeting at Safwan air base, Schwarzkopf was joined by General Khaled bin Sultan of Saudi Arabia, while the Iraqi general was joined by ten senior officers, with commanders from other Arab states, Britain, and France present as well.

Many observers in the United States and around the world argued in retrospect that the U.S.-led coalition should have marched on Baghdad. And even some generals such as Schwarzkopf himself noted that doing so would have been easy because American forces would have been "unopposed, for all intents and purposes."[50] Subsequent history painfully showed that invading Baghdad was easy, though not rebuilding it.

Marching on Baghdad was never seriously considered in 1991. It was widely believed that Saddam would be hard to find, that such an operation would have entailed unacceptable potential casualties, and that, even if successful, finding an alternative Iraqi regime to lead a post-Saddam Iraq would be hard.

Moreover, the UN mandate that governed Operations Desert Shield and Storm did not allow for such action, and America's Arab allies, some of which would not even fight Iraq during the war, would have opposed it. American decision makers were concerned that Washington would have been acting without international support. And they also wanted to avoid getting bogged down in the Gulf.[51]

The administration was also concerned about dismembering Iraq. Colin Powell received a cable from the U.S. ambassador to Saudi Arabia, Chas Freeman Jr., asserting, "We cannot pursue Iraq's unconditional surrender and occupation by us. It is not in our interest to destroy Iraq or weaken it to the point that Iran and/or Syria are not constraining it."[52] And Powell's views as well as those of Scowcroft mirrored that position. As both Powell and Scowcroft made clear, balance of power was considered insofar as the United States did not want to split Iraq apart so that Iran would emerge too strong.[53]

Yet most of the decision makers who were interviewed on *Frontline* several years after the invasion made clear, as did the record, that balance of power was one of many of the administration's motivations, and it was not very important.[54] As Baker put it, the United States was "interested in having a united Iraq. But balance of power was not a large element in the decision on going to Baghdad."[55]

Balance of power also was not critical in the decision to end the Gulf war at 100 hours. As one official put it, "there was a legitimate debate about going another 24–48 hours against Iraq's Republican Guard divisions. But balance of power was not an issue."[56] Some of America's key generals, including Schwarzkopf himself, wanted more time to finish the job, if not to march on Baghdad altogether.

Yet Powell observes, regarding an Oval Office meeting prior to the end of the war, that "no one in the room disagreed with the tentative decision to stop the war. Jim Baker was concerned about its effect on world opinion of pointless killing. Brent Scowcroft thought that fighting beyond necessity would leave a bad taste over what was so far a brilliant military victory. Cheney said that what mattered was achieving the coalition's aims."[57]

As Robert Gates notes, Powell, and some others, believed that more attacks, after the surrender of thousands of Iraqi soldiers, would look like a massacre and would be "un-American" and "unchivalrous."[58] Indeed, when he met with President Bush to discuss ending the war, he emphasized that the United States did not "want to be seen as killing for the sake of killing," noting, "We're within the window of success."[59] For his part, Bush believed that Iraqi forces were more devastated than they were and was concerned about exceeding the coalition's mandate.

Balancing was also not critical in the decisions about how to terminate the war. Freeman evidently pressed the Bush administration for a war-termination strategy, but no real action was taken because, in Freeman's view, the Bush team was concerned that the coalition would break down if such a strategy were formulated and leaked. For his part, Schwarzkopf, according to Freeman, who interacted with him at the time, was very "agitated" when he received little direction from Washington regarding the cease-fire talks at Safwan; Iraqi generals must have "walked out of Safwan with smiles on their faces, wondering why the U.S. position was so apolitical." Schwarzkopf wanted instructions from Washington on how to negotiate and in the absence of such direction was forced to treat the talks in military rather than political terms.[60]

It is hard not to see the contrast with the U.S. decision to launch war on Iraq in 2003, which I explore later in the book. All the concerns that made a march on Baghdad nonsensible in 1991 seemed to be eclipsed in 2003. The world, of course, had changed profoundly, but it is interesting to contrast the positions of the two Bush administrations in terms of the potential dangers of marching on Baghdad. The administration of the elder Bush was clearly concerned about these dangers, even when it had the ability to march on Baghdad and to eliminate Iraq's regime, whereas the administration of George W. Bush downplayed these dangers, even though it had to launch a war effort from the start and did not have forces ready to invade Iraq, as was the case in 1990. Nor did it have international support to do so, unlike in the 1991 case.

Conclusion

The American-led response to Iraq's invasion of Kuwait clearly involved balance against threat. Iraq posed a far greater threat than Iran as a result of its invasion of Kuwait. The United States also pursued balance-of-power policy insofar as Iraq's invasion further shifted the balance of power in Iraq's favor. However, collective security was a key element of the U.S.-led approach. At a minimum, the United States utilized the collective security mechanism of the United Nations to pressure Iraq and then to evict it from Kuwait. The United

States' action at the United Nations was a significant element of its global strategy. Although Washington may have launched Desert Storm even without UN approval, we cannot ignore that U.S.-led efforts were made under the auspices of the United Nations. Throughout the crisis, they were guided, if not defined, by its charter and by specific resolutions against Iraq.

Collective security and balance of power are not altogether mutually exclusive, but a fairer interpretation is that collective security was enough at play to diminish the extent to which we could say that balance-of-power policy was in practice.

The U.S.-led approach during the 1991 and 2003 wars differed significantly, partly owing to the role of the United Nations. Its role was limited in the 2003 war and even obstructive of U.S.-led efforts to launch war but was important in the 1991 conflict. Interestingly, both Bush presidents saw the Gulf conflicts in which they were involved as test cases for the United Nations. While the United Nations failed the test for George W. Bush, it passed the credibility test for the elder Bush.[61] In his words, Desert Storm was "a victory for the United Nations, for all mankind, for the rule of law, and, for what is right."[62] A new era appeared to be in the offing for George H. W. Bush, but it would not be very long before Saddam's Iraq was once again at war with American forces and yet another Bush was promoting notions of a new world order, although of a vastly different variety that included a grandiose effort to democratize the Middle East. But before that would occur, the United States and the United Nations would be in a dangerous long-run tango with Saddam Hussein, a man who seemed never to go away, even under the most trying of circumstances.

CHAPTER SIX

The Clinton Administration and Saddam Hussein

Despite the disastrous Iraq war and stringent postwar UN sanctions, Saddam Hussein was not overthrown and actually oversaw what appeared to be an ambitious program of postwar economic and military reconstruction. His resilience as a leader complicated U.S. foreign policy, but Iraq was not left to engage in adventurism. Rather, it faced containment first by the administration of the elder Bush and then under the Clinton administration's strategy of dual containment. As its ambitious name suggested, dual containment aimed to contain Iran and Iraq simultaneously, as if containing one at a time were not enough trouble already. Primarily for this reason, the United States departed from a strategy of containment, which, as Robert Art writes, "aims to hold the line against a specific aggressor that either threatens American interests in a given region or that strives for world hegemony."[1] Dual containment also differed from containment and certainly from balance of power in that it may well have involved the first serious thought about regime change in Iran or Iraq or both, although the administration was not explicit about it.[2] Even so, dual containment represented a stronger line than previous policies and did include efforts to overthrow Saddam Hussein, if not change the regime in Iraq altogether.

Iraq and Iran under the Clinton Administration's Watch

The Iranian revolution and the Iran-Iraq War produced military imbalances by strengthening Iraq, while the Persian Gulf War helped restore the military balance by weakening Iraq. As we shall see in the next two sections of this chapter, Iran and Iraq were weakened but were not viewed by Washington as being in a hopelessly defensive position or as sufficiently constrained.

The Case of Iraq

The Clinton administration's position was that Iraq did have the intellectual infrastructure to produce weapons of mass destruction (WMD) and that, although its conventional military capability had been drawn down, it was still strong and dangerous. Iraq's military capability would have been less problematic had its intentions changed after the 1991 war, but this did not appear to be the case.

Clearly, Iraq was greatly weakened. Desert Storm and postwar UN sanctions, as well as subsequent American policy, helped restore the balance of power in the region, which had been thrown out of balance in the 1980s. It is important to understand the several ways in which Iraq was weakened.

First, UN Resolutions 687 and 707 called for critical UN sanctions that impeded Iraq's ability to restore its military capabilities. Referred to as the "mother of all resolutions" for its record length, Resolution 687 mandated full disclosure of all of Iraq's ballistic missile stocks (with a range of more than 150 kilometers) and production facilities, all nuclear materials, and all chemical and biological weapons and facilities as well as cooperation in their destruction. Paragraphs 10 through 12 required Iraq to "unconditionally undertake not to use, develop, construct, or acquire" WMD. Resolution 687 also forced Iraq to accept the UN-demarcated border with Kuwait, the inviolability of Kuwaiti territory, and UN peacekeepers on the Iraq-Kuwait border.[3] Iraq's compliance with Resolution 687 was a prerequisite for lifting or reducing sanctions against it.[4] Resolution 688, also passed in April, condemned ongoing aggression by Saddam's regime against the Iraqi Kurds and Shiites, whom President Bush had urged to rise up against Saddam. Although it did not mandate any actions, Resolution 688 was the basis for another element of Saddam's containment: the establishment of a no-fly zone to protect these oppressed groups. American concern with Iraq's gross human rights violations in this area led the United States, Britain, and France to declare a no-fly zone over southern Iraq in August 1992, which applied to fixed-wing aircraft and helicopters. Operation Northern Watch, meanwhile, was put in motion to protect the northernmost 10 percent of Iraq, where the Kurdish minority lived. All in all, approximately 60 percent of the country was under no-fly zones.

Second, Saddam's problems extended to maintaining sovereignty over Iraqi territory. In northern Iraq, the Kurdish insurrection succeeded for the first time in taking several major urban centers including the oil facilities at Kirkuk and, at the height of the rebellion, a majority of Kurdistan territory. Although Saddam crushed the rebellion in early April 1991, it sapped Iraq's energy and created nearly one million refugees, concentrated primarily on the Iranian and Turkish borders. This human tragedy generated support for an international effort, code-named Operation Provide Comfort, and led the coalition allies to create safe havens against Iraqi attacks. The influx of allied troops further compromised Saddam's freedom of action in his own country.

In the south, Saddam met the postwar Shiite uprising with an unprecedented crackdown. Even during the Iran-Iraq War, the Baath Party and Saddam's state police maintained control of southern Iraq. But Desert Storm changed this by weakening Iraq's military capability and logistics as well as Saddam's credibility, while temporarily raising the spirits of his detractors until he crushed their resistance.

Third, over time, UN sanctions deprived Iraq of oil revenues and a role in affecting decision making in global oil markets. Although Baghdad circumvented this ban to some extent, it successfully deprived Iraq of billions of dollars with which it could rebuild its conventional capabilities and develop nonconventional weapons.[5] UN sanctions prohibiting arms transfers and related materials further hindered Iraq's ability to restore its conventional capability to prewar levels.

Fourth, partly as a result of UN sanctions, Iraq's living standards were cut to half the prewar level. Inflation reached 250 percent over prewar levels, and the Iraqi dinar was devalued more than 900 times its value from 1990 to 1993 and ran virtually unchecked thereafter.[6]

Fifth, economic deprivation, resulting from two regional wars and from postwar UN sanctions, worsened Saddam's internal problems. He not only had to quell the troublesome Kurds and Shiites but also had to keep his own officers content, a task that became increasingly difficult. Iraq's economic plight contributed to dissatisfaction among the people, in the army, and even within Saddam's Tikriti ruling family. Desert Storm and UN sanctions made Iraq more vulnerable to a coup or internal family problems than ever before and reduced the circle of advisers on whom Saddam could count.[7] Saddam's problems accelerated after the war and were made clear by mid-1995 as evidenced by the March 1995 coup attempt against Saddam.[8] The small revolt was crushed repeatedly over three weeks. However, it was the first time since the rise of Saddam's Baath Party in 1968 that a Sunni tribe traditionally loyal to Saddam attempted a coup. Shock waves rippled through Iraq.[9]

The high-level defections to Jordan in August 1995 of Lieutenant General Hussein Kamel Hassan Majeed, the architect of Saddam's war machine and military buildup, and Lieutenant Colonel Saddam Kamel Hassan Majeed, the head of his personal guards, confirmed the weakening of Saddam's traditional Sunni power base.

Sixth, at the strategic level, Desert Storm and postwar UN sanctions weakened Iraq in the conventional arena, undermined its nuclear program, and damaged to some extent its biological and chemical programs. Prior to Desert Storm, Iraq had a formidable conventional force, which enabled it to affect events in the Gulf region and the broader Middle East. By the war's end, the world's sixth largest air force had been decimated, and Iraq's army was halved in size. Iraq lost an estimated 2,633 tanks of 5,800; 2,196 artillery pieces of 3,850; and 324 fixed-wing combat aircraft of an estimated 650–700. Its navy, which was not particularly formidable but dangerous, was destroyed. Furthermore, postwar UN sanctions decreased Iraqi capabilities by reducing the operational readiness of forces that survived Desert Storm. However, Iraq did retain about 50–60 percent of its prewar military capability and reconstituted a total of 28 of its prewar 57 divisions. As a result, it remained the strongest military in the Persian Gulf region.[10]

In the nuclear area, postwar UN inspections, as suggested earlier in this book, revealed that Iraq had been closer to developing nuclear weapons than believed. Inspectors found a multi-billion-dollar nuclear program that could have produced a nuclear weapon not in ten years, as some U.S. intelligence agencies had thought, but in three to four years had Iraq not invaded Kuwait.[11] Iraq initially defied the UN resolution requiring full disclosure of nuclear materials, but over time the UN Special Commission and the International Atomic Energy Agency (IAEA) made substantial progress toward eliminating its programs of mass destruction.[12] Experts believed that all major parts of Iraq's nuclear program were destroyed or seriously damaged either by Desert Storm or by UN inspection teams, including Iraq's nuclear reactor, major nuclear labs, calutron project, and centrifuges. Its uranium mine was also located and its processes for turning uranium ore into oxide controlled.

However, Baghdad retained the human intelligence capability to support a major nuclear program as well as substantial dual-use technology and working designs for a centrifuge system. In the 1980s and before, it had developed experience in how to defy internal inspections and to protect its program from external attack. Some analysts speculated that Iraq retained an underground reactor or centrifuge cascade, despite the failure of UN inspectors to identify such facilities.[13] While highly improbable, Iraq also had the potential to buy nuclear fuel and technology or even a nuclear weapon from former Soviet republics. At a minimum, Saddam's continuing interest in obtaining nuclear weapons necessitated long-term monitoring as described in UN Resolution 715 to prevent Iraq's program from taking off again.

Prior to the Persian Gulf War, Iraq had the most advanced chemical warfare program in the Arab world. After Desert Storm, it retained the ability to produce chemical and biological weapons, despite the severe damage imposed by allied air forces on its principal chemical-agent facility located at Samarra and its main biological warfare research complex at Salman Pak. Were UN sanctions to be lifted, Iraq could restore its former chemical weapons production in less than one year and produce biological weapons within weeks. Indeed, CIA director James Woolsey asserted that neither the war nor postwar inspections were enough to degrade seriously its chemical and biological capability.[14]

Iraq initially pledged to accept UN Resolution 687 and took some actions to meet some of its obligations, but, after doing so, it quickly called for the lifting of the UN embargo.[15] Its temporary and incomplete cooperation was a tactical strategy to rid it of UN sanctions without really complying. According to one official, Iraq displayed "no apparent intention" of relinquishing its WMD programs. Rather, it engaged in sporadic concealment and "pretended cooperation."[16] Saddam also refused to allow the United Nations to control Iraq's overseas oil sales and to use proceeds for humanitarian purposes and for funding UN operations in Iraq.

Saddam appeared to retain his enduring ambitions regarding Kuwait as well. The Iraq-Kuwait border dispute was settled in legal terms in the postwar period, but Iraq was unsatisfied. The postwar UN commission that was designated to redraw the border redrew it in a manner that disadvantaged and angered Iraq. Kuwait was given a larger portion of the Rumaila oil field, over which Kuwait and Iraq lay joint claim. It also retained control over Warba and Bubiyan islands, which are Iraq's only current access point to the Persian Gulf and which Kuwait has considered its rightful possession, one usurped by Iraq in 1932 and 1973.[17]

Iraq continued to assert that it would eventually conquer Kuwait. Despite warnings from the UN Iraq-Kuwait Observer Mission, the Iraqi army repeatedly violated Kuwaiti territory in 1993, and Iraqi forces shot machine guns along the Saudi border, which alarmed the royal family.[18] In October 1994, Saddam sent Republican Guard divisions south to the border with Kuwait, forcing the United States to mount Operation Vigilant Warrior and to quadruple the American presence in the region to deter a possible invasion. Saddam may have been engaging in brinkmanship, but the United States had already been burned once in 1990 and did not want to take any chances.

The Case of Iran

For its part, Iran had mellowed and had become far less orthodox in exporting the revolution to other states in the neighborhood and beyond. Still, it did resurge in other ways, and we need to understand that dimension within the context of a moderating foreign policy.

Tehran embarked on a postwar five-year, $10 billion military rebuilding program, despite severe economic problems, and acquired modern conventional weapons mainly from Russia, China, and North Korea; it continued to develop its biological and nuclear capability and its already effective chemical weapons program. This course of action was not peculiar given major defense expenditures by Iraq and Saudi Arabia but was viewed in Washington as significant, especially given Iran's other foreign policy actions. Indeed, in 1992, Iran annexed the three islands of the Greater and Lesser Tunbs and Abu Musa, to which it held historical claim. Although Khomeini, and even the shah of Iran, had raised the issue of sovereignty over the islands, Iran had heretofore not taken such strong actions.

For their part, the Gulf Cooperation Council (GCC) states, while at the same time trying to continue a rapprochement with Iran, repeatedly asked it to withdraw from the islands or to agree to international arbitration to resolve its territorial dispute with the United Arab Emirates.[19] The row over Abu Musa, though serious in its own right, also reflected the broader rivalry between Iran and Saudi Arabia, each attempting to fill the power vacuum left after the defeat of Iraq.

Iran also began increasing troop strength and deploying antiaircraft missiles on the islands at the entrance to the Gulf in November 1994. From America's perspective, Iran sought to develop the capability to interdict traffic in the 34-

mile-wide Strait of Hormuz, marked by 2-mile-wide channels for inbound and outbound Gulf tanker traffic.[20] Closure of the strait would require the use of alternative routes (if available), such as the Abqaiq-Yanbu pipeline across Saudi Arabia to the Red Sea. But that would impose higher transportation costs and greater lag times for delivery.

Iran suggested that its actions were partly directed against Israeli threats on Iran's nuclear facilities.[21] Irrespective of motive, the action heightened fears in Washington that Iran sought regional dominance.[22] Iran demonstrated the ability to interdict or shut down oil traffic, a capability enhanced by antiship missiles and submarines, its long coastline dominating the strait, and its position on the Greater and Lesser Tunbs and Abu Musa. Of course, Iran understood that the United States would respond strongly if it sought to disrupt Gulf shipping. Yet Iranian deputy foreign minister Abbas Maleki asserted that while Iran supported the stable flow of oil, it reserved the option to shut the strait down if threatened.[23]

Iran's military buildup and actions on the islands at the Strait of Hormuz were only part of the problem. Tehran and Washington remained on opposite wavelengths on various issues. Iran opposed the Middle East peace process and Israel's right to exist, at a time when Washington was keen on jump-starting the peace process. Washington also saw Iran as a serious exporter of international terrorism, especially with respect to the Palestinian-Israeli conflict, in which it helped finance and arm Palestinian rejectionist groups as well as Hizballah in Lebanon, which periodically lobbed Katyusha rockets into northern Israel, claiming that it was responding to Israeli strikes on Lebanese targets.

In addition, Tehran opposed the U.S. military presence in the Persian Gulf region, viewing it as its own backyard in which the imperialistic United States was a trespasser. Khomeini, of course, promoted an Islamic Iran rather than a glorified Persian Iran, but Iran's ancient glory added to its disdain for another great power in its perceived realm of influence.[24] That was a historical impulse. Iran had viewed with disfavor the British empire in India and in the Gulf and the Russian empire on its northern borders and tried to play the two empires off each other, so as to preclude their individual or joint influence arising from the Anglo-Russian Entente of 1907. Having been a playground for global rivalry until 1926 when Reza Shah, founder of the Pahlevi dynasty, restored full sovereignty, Iran remained sensitive to the ambitions of outside powers.

On the Central Asian front, Iran launched a diplomatic and economic offensive aimed at gaining a foothold in the republics. In response, the Saudis, reflecting an increasingly assertive foreign policy, sent Foreign Minister Prince Saud al-

Faisal to tour the region in order to push the Saudi position.[25] This relatively new arena of rivalry for these states added yet another dimension to the complex international politics of the Middle East region.

Considered together, some of these factors alarmed the Bush administration, as they would the Clinton administration throughout the 1990s. In 1992, CIA director Robert Gates claimed that Iran's "behavior in rearming its military and developing a strategic deterrent [was] ominously analogous to Iraq's action in the 1980s — and could pose a grave threat to regional stability."[26] President Clinton described Iran as a "threat not only to its neighbors, but to the entire world," and his views were echoed by other administration officials, including Secretary of State Warren Christopher.[27]

Although the administration viewed Iran in this manner, it is important to understand as well that, in some ways, Iran moderated its foreign policy. After Desert Storm, it again sought to break its global isolation through a rapprochement with GCC states and the development of economic relations with the West. This effort made sense because the Iran-Iraq War had left Iran economically devastated and war-weary.

Unlike Iraq, which dealt with its war-torn economy by seeking a quick fix in Kuwait, Iran recognized that it needed Western support to reconstruct itself after the devastating Iran-Iraq War. Thus, it had to jettison major parts of its policy of "neither East nor West," made famous by the ayatollah. As Lawrence Freedman and Efraim Karsh point out, Iran's "earlier call for the removal of Gulf regimes . . . had been replaced by appeasing statements underlining the peaceful nature of the Iranian revolution and Tehran's good will towards the Gulf monarchies."[28] Indeed, Saudi Arabia and Iran initiated an important rapprochement that accelerated in earnest in the spring of 1997.[29] In early 1992, responding to some moderation on Iran's part, the Bush administration even considered lifting sanctions on Iran selectively in order to trigger improved relations, but the National Security Council, after assessing American options, decided that such efforts would be politically intractable in Washington, given strong anti-Iranian sentiment.[30]

The election of Muhammad Khatami as president of Iran in May 1997 reflected the slow mellowing of Iran's revolution, which had already been demonstrated in elections for Iran's parliament in which reformers won significant victories. The reform movement in Iran came to be defined by Khatami's presidency from 1997 to 2005.[31] Khatami did believe that Gulf security should be the province of regional states and remained predisposed to question the U.S. role in Iran's backyard. But, as an avowed reformer, he was more inclined than his predecessors to seek better relations with the West and even called for the "wall of mistrust" between Iran and the United States to be torn down.[32] In his famous interview with CNN in January 1998, he even drew a parallel between the American and Iranian revolutions, describing them both as struggles against oppressive forces. He also moved that same month to reverse Iran's previous position and to support Palestinian participation in a Middle East peace process, acknowledge Israel's legitimacy, and hold out prospects for a broader regional peace if the Palestinian goal of self-determination was met. As a result of these actions, Secretary of State Madeleine Albright "concluded that Iran no longer belonged in the same category as Iraq. The time was ripe to move beyond dual containment," even though, under Iran's constitution and in reality, Khatami had limited power.[33] He enjoyed popular support, but the key organs of government, including the military, intelligence, police, and judiciary, were under the control of the Supreme Leader Ayatollah Khamenei. He and the archconservatives who supported him remained quite hostile to the United States.

Indeed, as had occurred in the past, hostility in American and Iranian domestic politics made any shade of rapprochement hard to accomplish. The domestic obstacles to, and costs of, such an approach made it hard to exercise, much less exercise with success, particularly given that Khatami might not be able to deliver on well-intentioned promises in Iran's complex domestic context. And the history of such efforts did not yield much hope either, the Iran-Contra affair being the most obvious case in point.

Episode 8: The Nature of Dual Containment, 1992–1998

When President Clinton took office in January 1993, Iraq was already in a political, economic, and military box. It faced American containment and UN sanctions under Resolution 687 in particular, even before the policy of dual containment was enunciated. For its part, Iran was already under numerous military and economic constraints that extended back to the hostage crisis during President Carter's term. All military exchanges and most economic forms were prohibited, although trade between the two states was higher than one might expect. Diplomatic relations were severed in 1980, and Iran was placed on the State Department's list of state sponsors of terrorism in 1984.

In this sense, although the administration described dual containment as a radical departure from previous American policies, it did continue some of the previous policies against Iran and Iraq, and it did not go as far as some hawkish officials would have preferred.[34] These officials believed that the United States should be more active in removing Saddam Hussein through a "ramped-up covert action program and limited air strikes to press Baghdad and possibly to create the circumstances in which Saddam might be overthrown."[35] Actively confronting Iraq did not especially fit into the Clintonesque view of pursuing engagement in a world of interdependence which required it.[36] So as was the case in the 1991 war, U.S. policy in the Middle East would contrast sharply with U.S. policy in a globalizing, post–Cold War world at the international level. Thus, dual containment took on a harsher tone on the surface than it did on the ground.

Nonetheless, dual containment represented a change. The United States did pursue a stronger approach against Iraq, more zealously exploring how the Iraqi opposition might overthrow Saddam, and especially against Iran. In fact, as one official points out, Brent Scowcroft was trying to create better relations with Iran in the early 1990s, but the Clinton administration dropped that approach rather clearly.[37]

Dual containment had several goals. First, it aimed not only to impede the ability of Iran and Iraq to threaten neighbors but also to undermine their ability to build conventional and unconventional military capabilities. This approach, unlike deterrence, would cripple their ability to be aggressive in the first place, rather than deterring already capable states from being aggressive. Second, the United States, along with all GCC states and members of the European Union, aimed to force Iraq to comply with all UN resolutions, in particular with those aimed at disarming it, and to stand "firmly behind the security and the integrity of the states in the area against any future aggression."[38]

The administration also aimed to increase the pressure on Iran, albeit chiefly through American, rather than international, sanctions. In April 1995, the United States announced a ban on all U.S. trade and investment with Iran after Clinton signed two executive orders that prohibited U.S. companies and their foreign subsidiaries from conducting business with Iran. This action reversed the trade relationship that had existed under the Bush administration.

In August 1996, the House of Representatives approved a broader sanctions bill, which Clinton signed into law. It extended pressures on Iran by ordering sanctions against foreign companies that invest in Iran, an act that Germany and France denounced as a barrier to international trade. The Iran and Libya Sanctions Act aimed to reduce Iran's income and to weaken its ability to support terrorism and acquire WMD. The law called for sanctions on foreign companies that invest more than $40 million in Iran's oil and gas sectors. Under the law, the president would be required to impose at least two of the following sanctions: import and export bans; embargoes on lending by U.S. banks; a ban on U.S. procurement of goods and services from sanctioned companies; and a denial of U.S. export financing.[39]

Third, at the political level, the United States and other actors, especially the Saudis, worked to isolate Baghdad. Iraq sought to break this isolation by re-establishing relations with its archrival Iran—which, despite its purchases of Iraqi oil, rebuffed Iraq—and with other Gulf states.[40] Iraq had limited success with Oman, the only GCC state to maintain relations with Iraq after the Persian Gulf War, and Qatar. Riyadh criticized these two states for their attempted rapprochement with Iraq, arguing that Iraq was "working to divide the GCC."[41]

Fourth, dual containment rejected the European approach called "critical dialogue," which consisted of encouraging trade and other interactions with Iran for purposes of generating interdependence and giving Iran a vested interest in the status quo while promoting dialogue over Iran's problematic behavior. The Europeans, including the British, thought that "critical dialogue" with Iran could bring about change better than other, stronger approaches. Thus, when asked in 1998 if France shared the view that Iran continued to pose a threat to its Arab neighbors, French defense minister Alain Richard referred to the need to combat terrorism, adding, "Political dialogue is possible and useful with Iran."[42]

Washington tended to see critical dialogue as wrongheaded and as a failed policy. Placating Iran and Iraq in the 1980s in the effort to moderate their behavior had revealed them to be implacable. Iraq invaded Kuwait on the heels of constructive engagement, which was a major embarrassment to the administration of George H. W. Bush, and Iran manipulated the arms-for-hostages fiasco without moving any closer to Washington, which was a major embarrassment to the Reagan administration.

In addition, dual containment played well to the domestic audience in the United States, although not in Europe. The American experience with both Iran and Iraq was etched on the public mind. Although they meant little to Americans in the 1970s, by the time of the Iran hostage crisis and the Iran-Iraq War, not to mention the 1991 war, both states were increasingly viewed as exporters of terrorism, war, anti-Americanism, and anti-Zionism. Based on domestic factors, the European approach would not make much sense, but strong-arming Middle East dictators certainly could.

There was a fifth aspect to American policy which was exercised concomitantly with dual containment but which extended beyond basic containment.

Washington also aimed to undermine the regimes in Iran and Iraq. In the popular mind, the notion of regime change emerged only in the period preceding the American invasion of Iraq in 2003, when the Bush administration referred to it repeatedly and then practiced it. But regime change had been in the air for some time.

The United States had decided not to march on Baghdad in 1991 or even to help the Kurds and Shiites overthrow Saddam when they rebelled in the immediate postwar period. This decision was made partly because the United States believed that the rebels would succeed in undermining Saddam. When they failed, the United States began to take measures to unseat the dictator. The CIA tried, beginning shortly after the 1991 war, to overthrow Saddam by cooperating with Iraqi exiles who had contacts within the regime and possibly others who wanted Saddam gone.[43] In 1996, the CIA mounted an even more serious effort to overthrow Saddam in cooperation with the Iraq National Congress and the Iraq National Accord, two major opposition groups, but Saddam defeated them in August 1996 when the United States proved incapable of protecting anti-Saddam forces against his military attack.[44] Moreover, as I discuss later in this chapter, President Clinton signed the Iraq Liberation Act of 1998 into law.

American policy toward Iran was much less openly hostile, but it was also based on the notion that its regime needed to be changed. In 1994, Clinton signed an intelligence order in which he outlined a strategy of covert action based on an aggressive antiregime propaganda effort. And in 1996, bowing to pressures from the Republican leadership in Congress, President Clinton authorized the CIA to mount a covert operation to "change the nature of the Government of Iran."[45] Of course, such an effort was largely theoretical. Any Iranian that supported U.S. efforts to overthrow the regime would likely be shot, arrested, or shunned even by antiregime proponents — less because the Iranian regime was well liked than because of an almost universal aversion to outside interference in Iran's affairs.

Dual Containment versus Balance-of-Power Policy

Sometimes containment and balance-of-power policy are conflated, but the Clinton administration's policy of dual containment differed significantly from balance-of-power policy.[46] First, dual containment did not seek to strengthen Iran to balance Iraq or vice versa. As national security adviser Anthony Lake observed, through dual containment the United States rejected the past approach of "building up" Iran to check Iraq and vice versa and sought, with its regional allies, "to maintain a favorable balance without depending on either Iraq or Iran."[47] Martin Indyk, the special assistant to the president for Near East and South Asian Affairs, who devised the policy of dual containment, argued that previous "balance of power policies that depended on either Iran or Iraq were less than good, to put it mildly. One might say disastrous in terms of what followed, both in terms of the revolution, in terms of the Iran-Iraq war, and then of course in terms of the invasion of Kuwait."[48]

For Indyk, dual containment was based fundamentally on the view that the United States should not "continue the old balance of power game, building up one to balance the other," for a few reasons: "We reject that approach not only because its bankruptcy was demonstrated in Iraq's invasion of Kuwait. We reject it because of a clear-headed assessment of the antagonism that both regimes harbor towards the United States and its allies in the region. And we reject because we don't need to rely on one to balance the other."[49]

Second, balance-of-power approaches do not aim to change the politics of states. They treat states as unitary actors and do not make assumptions about what does or should take place within them. The key goal is to check the strongest actor and not to change the nature of its regime or worldview. Yet, as Lake asserted, America aimed to "neutralize, contain, and, through selective pressure, perhaps eventually transform these backlash states into constructive members of the international community."[50] Dual containment "rejected balance of power approaches and instead aimed to place pressure on both Iran and Iraq in the hope that they would eventually collapse internally due to their ineffective political and economic systems, somewhat akin in this regard to containment of the Soviet Union."[51]

Third, balance-of-power approaches also are not motivated by ideological concerns. States will balance against the strongest state, even if they favor its ideology, and they will not balance against weaker states, even if their ideologies are obnoxious.

In the context of dual containment, however, Iran and Iraq were viewed as incorrigible in the absence of external pressure because of their ideology and historical background. As Indyk stated, "The current regime in Iraq is a criminal regime, beyond the pale of international society and, in our judgment, irredeemable."[52] Lake was more optimistic about Iran but still asserted that its "revolutionary and militant messages" were "openly hostile to the United States and its core interests." He believed that "this basic political reality" would shape relations "for the foreseeable future."[53]

Under dual containment, the U.S. approach toward Iran and Iraq would not change if either state developed prevailing power or threat. It would continue to contain them both, with no real hope that either would be reintegrated into the regional or global realm, in contrast to balance-of-power or balance-of-threat policy, which posit flexible shifts in alignment. As one scholar asserted, dual containment "explicitly disavows the need for any kind of political relationship with Iran or Iraq and rejects the idea that a rough military equivalence between them is an important element of gulf stability."[54] That is a major shift from the Bush administration approach. As Scowcroft put it, "We were not containing Iran but were trying to deal with Iran periodically through diplomats and businessmen. Iran wanted to meet but would back away, even in our private meetings. We searched for ways to penetrate the Iranian structure. Clinton won't do that under dual containment."[55]

Dual containment, furthermore, risked pushing Iran and Iraq closer together. Balance-of-power policy would seek to avoid precisely such a power combination. Even balance of threat would focus on prevailing power and threat, rather than on the full range of threats, unless they were projected by a coalition. Iran and Iraq obviously were not a coalition. Balancing would also mandate checking Saddam but leaving him in power to balance Iran, on the presumption that his ouster would weaken Iraq's ability to balance Iranian power and threat. Balancing was one motive for the Bush administration at the Persian Gulf War's end, but the Clinton administration preferred to remove Saddam under dual containment as well.

Dual containment was motivated, in part, by domestic concerns and individual factors, which balance-of-power policy ignores as a motivation. President Clinton's policy options on Iran "were constrained by the 1994 mid-term elections, when Congress became more hawkish on terrorism in particular, and by his Secretary of State, Warren Christopher, who did not want to give the Iranians any breaks, based on his experience negotiating the hostage release in 1980–81."[56] The Israelis also wanted to pressure Iran more seriously, which added to the American interest in doing so in Congress and in the executive branch.[57]

The Middle East peace process could have benefited from pressure on Iran. It has been an axiom of Middle East politics, although one not well acted upon by Arab states, that Israel will not make peace concessions if it feels insecure. Saddam's survival after the Iraq war was disconcerting to Israel because even if he was boxed in, he could still develop WMD. Meanwhile, Israeli leaders from Yitzhak Rabin to Benjamin Netanyahu had stressed to the Clinton administration that the United States would have to limit Iran's ability to attack Israel if it expected Israel to take risks for peace.[58] From Israel's perspective, Iran was problematic because it pursued WMD, supported terrorist groups such as Hizballah and Islamic Jihad, opposed the Middle East peace process, and rejected Israel's right to resist.

Conclusion

For the most part, dual containment is not balance-of-power policy. The latter is fundamentally concerned with the relative position of states and assumes that the stronger actor will be balanced against. Dual containment aims to contain both states, irrespective of which one is stronger. The weaker state may still be the target of containment and may be contained for reasons that have little to do with systemic realities. This principle also holds true for balance-of-threat policy, although dual containment was motivated by an effort to balance against threat—not prevailing threat from one country but threats from both Iran and Iraq. As Peter Tarnoff, undersecretary of political affairs, put it: "We designed this strategy to counter, in the ways most appropriate for each specific threat, the set of challenges presented by Baghdad and the set of challenges posed by Tehran."[59]

CHAPTER SEVEN

Containment-Plus and Regime Change in Iraq

Containing Iran and Iraq proved to be a major challenge for the United States and its allies. Over time, dual containment became less tenable as a strategy, owing to international criticism, global noncooperation with Washington's approach, enduring Iraqi intransigence, and Iran's resurgence in the region.[1] Iran and Iraq defied sanctions with some efficacy, but partly because Iraq was viewed as a greater threat, its case gained more public and official attention in Washington, raising the prospect for regime change one more notch in decision-making circles.[2]

The notion of regime change had a pedigree in American foreign policy long before Saddam Hussein ever became a problem. After World War II, the Roosevelt administration decided to deal with the problem of Germany and Japan not by simply destroying their ability to wage war and placing sanctions on their war-making capacities but rather by changing their regimes and remaking them as democracies and free-market economies in the American image.

In the 1990s, the United States could have decided to continue to contain Iraq, but its view of the Iraqi problem slowly shifted. Although the idea of eliminating Iraq's regime did not take hold over night, it started to gain ground after it became apparent that Saddam would not only survive the 1991 war but would reconsolidate his power domestically and sometimes successfully flout the international community. As one official put it in 1994, "As long as Saddam survived, he paralyzed our policy."[3]

However, it took some time for regime change to become official American policy. By 1998, the United States started to see Saddam's removal as a more pressing necessity for generating stability in the Persian Gulf. That type of thinking emerged slowly and represented a shift in previous policies. Indeed, during the Iran-Iraq War the United States bolstered Iraq; after the war, it placated Saddam; in the 1991 Gulf war, it hoped to kill him but would not venture into Iraq to do so; and then in the 1990s, it decided to contain him in every manner possible, but its official policy was not regime change. The shift to regime change would occur in earnest in 1998.

Events Leading to the Policy of Regime Change

It is unclear how history would have changed if Saddam Hussein had acceded to UN Security Council resolutions and created a different future for his country. We do know the path he chose, a path to ruination. The policy of regime change was a response in part to Iraq's noncooperation and to the threat that Iraq projected.

Saddam became more adept at using sanctions to his advantage at home. Sanctioned items were hard to obtain at reasonable prices, so they became very valuable to the Iraqi people. Saddam and his henchmen profited by exploiting Iraq's burgeoning black market, either by skimming profits from the marketeers or by rewarding his supporters with access to this market. Honing his gangsterism, Saddam also learned to manipulate the UN oil-for-food program, which gave out contracts for oil sales and goods purchases. The committee to review the UN oil-for-food program, headed by former Federal Reserve chairman Paul Volcker, found that Baghdad earned $11 billion by smuggling oil to neighboring countries in violation of UN sanctions and that Saddam demanded kickbacks in exchange for selling oil and buying food, medicine, and other humanitarian goods from other countries.

The oil-for-food scandal underscored the difficulties of using economic sanctions to pressure regimes. Sanctions hurt the Iraqi economy and its people but may have helped the regime preserve its power. Meanwhile, global sympathy for the plight of the Iraqi people began to mount. They were increasingly seen as innocent victims of UN sanctions, dying by the tens of thousands, while Saddam built one palace after another and the United States ignored their problems.

International cooperation on sanctions began to falter. France and Russia did not agree with Washington's economic sanctions policy. They did not cooperate with the Iran and Libya Sanctions Act, barely hiding their contempt for it as an example of American unilateralism. Moreover, they sought to ease UN sanctions on Iraq by moving to assert that Saddam had, in fact, complied with them. France sympathized with Baghdad's cause, perhaps because it wanted to benefit from postsanctions business in Iraq, improve its position in the Arab world, mollify its own Muslim population, and tweak the nose of the United States in the process. Indeed, as Richard Butler, chairman of the United Nations Special Commission (UNSCOM), described it, France was "edging toward a position where it assessed Iraq as having been substantially disarmed and certainly posing no threat to France," and Russia was hoping that the work of testing Iraq's position would end soon so that a comprehensive review could be conducted, which would have cleared Iraq and lifted UN sanctions against it.[4]

Russia was Saddam's best bet for having sanctions lifted and also for impeding the American use of force against Iraq.[5] Iraq remained an important state in Moscow's Middle East strategy, albeit one diminished by its own travails associated with the failed invasion of Kuwait.

Like France, Russia was motivated in no small measure by economics. In the fall of 2002, Russia and Iraq signed a new five-year economic cooperation agreement worth $40 billion over a ten-year period. The agreement was problematic and angered Bush administration officials, chiefly because it signaled Moscow's intent to nurture or improve relations with a state that Washington had quite visibly labeled as part of the axis of evil, in a period when it was trying to garner international support for a potential war against Iraq. Russia, which had complained that it lost more than $30 billion as a result of the sanctions on Iraq, emphasized that the agreement did not violate UN resolutions against Iraq and did not involve arms sales.[6] Secretary of Defense Donald Rumsfeld, the first official to address the deal, asserted that the Russian administration was "fairly pragmatic at this stage" and that its interest in the United States was greater than its interest in Iraq; in his view, even a U.S. attack on Iraq would not damage relations because of Russia's view of the longer-term benefits of economic ties to the West.[7] Washington was troubled by the potential that Iraq could wiggle out of UN sanctions by dividing the UN Security Council.

Sanctions were accomplishing less than the United Nations intended, and

UN inspections also ran into trouble. The United States and its allies sought to enforce UN resolutions against Iraq, especially Resolution 687, throughout the 1990s. But Iraq used various methods of deception to complicate efforts by UN inspectors to assess to what extent it had destroyed its stockpile of biological and chemical weapons and ceased its programs to develop weapons of mass destruction (WMD). This deception once again raised suspicions that Iraq had the capability to produce weapons of mass destruction and that it might use them; it also created the opportunity for the Bush administration to push for the ouster of Saddam's regime by force in 2003.

Perhaps bolstered by support from France and Russia, Iraq appeared brazen enough to reject the UN sanctions regime altogether. In mid-1995, Iraq asserted that it had met all the disarmament obligations contained in Resolution 687 and expected UNSCOM to end its operations in Iraq, thus effectively allowing for sanctions to be lifted on Iraq and for Iraq to resume WMD programs in earnest and unfettered. Iraq's action precipitated a minor crisis that might have become full blown had Saddam's sons-in-law not defected to Jordan with significant evidence of Iraqi noncompliance and cheating. This development subdued Saddam's bravado and forced Iraq to explain the revelations, but Iraq continued to defy UN inspectors.

Its defiance peaked in 1998. In mid-January, Baghdad blocked a series of planned inspections of presidential sites, which it believed should be off-limits. It then demanded a three-month moratorium on inspections and a six-month deadline for lifting sanctions altogether, irrespective of its disarmament status and in violation of the basic thrust of Resolution 687 and subsequent UN resolutions requiring that the United Nations give Iraq a clean bill of health before sanctions were lifted. Such conflicts with Iraq continued throughout the year, forcing the United States to try to shore up its support in Europe and the Persian Gulf.[8]

In August 1998, angry that UNSCOM would not clear Iraq, Saddam stopped cooperating with UN inspectors, although he did allow some monitoring activities to proceed. He was not yet ready to make a complete break with the United Nations, but he was headed in that direction. Russia and France continued to intercede on Iraq's behalf, arguing that it would cooperate if it knew exactly what it needed to do to have sanctions lifted. The United Nations responded to Iraq's defiance in a reasonable, even cooperative manner by preparing to offer Baghdad a comprehensive review of its case if Iraq allowed UNSCOM inspections to proceed.

Saddam could have seized this opportunity and split the Security Council, with some members — Russia and France in particular — arguing that Iraq should pass the comprehensive review and that the United Nations should lift sanctions. Instead, he took an unpredictable step. On October 31, 1998, Iraq shut down completely all international inspection and monitoring activities. If Baghdad's strategy had been to try to divide the Security Council in order to have UN sanctions lifted, Iraq now appeared to jettison even semblances of cooperation with the United Nations — an affront that surprised even France. On December 16, 1998, UNSCOM withdrew its staff from Iraq.

The Clinton administration viewed Iraq's noncooperation as serious enough to launch Operation Desert Fox in December 1998. A total of forty ships participated, with ten of them firing more than three hundred Tomahawk missiles and ninety cruise missiles over a period of several days. This operation demonstrated that the United States was willing to use force to check WMD, but such strikes could have only so much effect.

Saddam was now free of UN inspectors and was perceived in Washington as more able to pursue his WMD programs than he had been before. He could always rebuild destroyed sites and restart his biological and chemical weapons programs. In fact, he began more assiduously to harass American and British aircraft protecting the no-fly zones over Iraq. No aircraft were shot down, but the pilots were in jeopardy, and the costs of enforcing the no-fly zones were high.

Overall, the United States found this state of affairs to be unacceptable. It had grown tired of playing games with Saddam, trying to contain him, enforcing no-fly zones, and trying to keep the international coalition intact. The time for change had come. As U.S. secretary of state Madeleine Albright pointed out, the United Nations had been "given the job of doing something never before done — disarming a country without militarily occupying it."[9] That very fact allowed Iraq to try to elude sanctions and presented Washington with a significant problem.

Episode 9: Containment Plus Regime Change as Official Policy, 1998–2001

The departure of international inspectors put greater pressure on the United States to think outside the box regarding the Saddam problem. After nearly two years of dramatic crises with Iraq, culminating with Operation Desert Fox, America decided to change its official policy toward Iraq. As Secretary Albright recalled, "[With] UNSCOM and the IAEA no longer in Iraq, we shifted our policy toward Baghdad from containment with inspections to an approach we called containment plus."[10] Containment-plus included several actions. Washington practiced stricter enforcement of the no-fly zones over northern and southern Iraq; took stronger military actions against Iraq's radar and antiaircraft facilities; backed further expansion of the oil-for-food program; developed smart sanctions; strengthened the Iraqi people's opposition to Saddam's rule; and, most important, adopted regime change as an explicit goal in U.S. policy.

On December 19, 1998, the day Operation Desert Fox ended, President Clinton made a radio address in which he announced that American policy was now to replace the regime of Saddam Hussein, which was incorrigible and which could not be dealt with in another manner.[11] In October, Clinton had signed the Iraq Liberation Act of 1998, at which time he had asserted that the Iraqi leader threatened "the security of the world" and that the best way to end that threat once and for all was with a new Iraqi government."[12] This act authorized up to $97 million in military assistance to the Iraqi opposition forces to eliminate Saddam Hussein's regime and to usher in democratic practices in Iraq. Although the Iraq Liberation Act was a statement of congressional sentiment on the importance of regime change in Iraq, by mid-November 1998 President Clinton began to assert publicly that it was official U.S. policy, as well.

Thus the United States sought officially to remove Saddam from power well before September 11, 1991, although that goal was pursued zealously only after September 11.[13] National security adviser Samuel Berger asserted in a private meeting with National Security Council official Kenneth Pollack in early 1999 that the administration had concluded that it "could not keep playing cat-and-mouse games with Saddam" and that it had "decided that the only solution was to topple" Saddam's regime, and so in this period the administration started to develop options to do just that.[14] As Pollack describes it, there was a broad consensus in the administration "that containment was failing and that the only way to get rid of Saddam was to mount an invasion of Iraq."[15] This consensus about Iraq, however, did not translate into serious action partly because the domestic and international support for such action did not really exist. Clinton believed that the Iraqi people would benefit from Saddam's elimination but also understood that the United Nations had not authorized such action.[16]

The fact that the administration could not really execute forceful regime change, combined with the need to continue to contain Saddam, created a split policy on Iraq: seek regime change but, while doing so, also continue UN sanctions and containment. Testimony by Secretary of State Colin Powell in a 2002 congressional hearing reflected this position: "We continue to develop sanctions, improve our sanctions regime toward Iraq to make sure that they [*sic*] do not succeed in their horrible quest to develop weapons of mass destruction. And we are also examining options with respect to regime change."[17]

In the summer and fall of 1999, Washington had negotiated UN Resolution 1284, which reorganized the inspections program. Passed in December 1999, this resolution called on Iraq to allow the reentry of the UN inspection teams, which it had earlier ejected from the country, and it reinforced the system of monitoring, inspection, and verification. The resolution gave inspectors six months to reach preliminary conclusions about whether Iraq was developing prohibited weapons, and it held out the prospect that economic sanctions could be lifted if inspection teams believed that Iraq had cooperated fully. The United States had wanted a tougher resolution, but as Thomas Pickering, ambassador to the United Nation, recalls, Washington had negotiated hard and long with other Security Council members and ultimately achieved Resolution 1284 with language that leaned toward what it wanted.[18]

Russia had wanted to veto the resolution but sought to avoid a confrontation in the Security Council, chiefly with the United States, and thus the most it was willing to do, along with France and China, was to abstain.[19] It is important to note that the State Duma (the lower house of the Russian legislature) in February 2001 pressured the government to withdraw unilaterally from the UN sanctions regime against Iraq. For its part, Iraq did not even recognize Resolution 1284; nor did it pay heed to subsequent resolutions. Rather, it made it clear that it was not ready to accept the reentry of the UN inspection teams.

In early 2001, the United States sought to strengthen UN sanctions against Iraq by replacing the existing sanctions with "smart sanctions." Instead of letting Iraq off the hook, the United States aimed to ease economic sanctions, which had drawn international rebuke for their impact on the Iraqi people, while tightening sanctions against military and dual-use goods. Colin Powell asserted that through smart sanctions the United States was able to keep Saddam "in a box."[20]

Regime Change in 1998 versus Regime Change after September 11

The policy of regime change that developed in 1998 and 1999, under the broader approach called containment-plus, was not the same as the policy of regime change that was part of the overall thrust of the Iraq war of 2003.[21]

First, the policy of regime change under containment-plus was nonmilitary in nature. No invasion of Iraq was seriously planned. No armies would march on Baghdad and seize the reins of control. No Saddam statues would fall to occupying American forces. The administration planned to overthrow Saddam chiefly through political means and subterfuge, in cooperation with his internal and external enemies.

Second, regime change under containment-plus was not a top priority for the administration, compared with other pressing concerns around the world. That can help explain why it was to be conducted politically and not militarily. A military approach would have reflected greater urgency and importance. Of course, the situation would change dramatically after September 11, which, for the Bush administration, made regime change in Iraq a priority.

Third, the containment-plus policy was a recognition that dual containment was not working but that invading Iraq to overthrow Saddam was too dramatic and would lack support. The attack on September 11 provided some of this support domestically and internationally, although invading Iraq remained controversial at home, abroad, and, to some extent, in President Bush's cabinet even after September 11. For instance, Secretary Powell still believed that containment was the better option in Iraq to make sure it did not develop weapons of mass destruction.[22]

Fourth, regime change by political means ran fewer risks than regime change by invasion. The latter not only put human lives at risk but also increased the chance that Iraq would be ripped apart into its three historical parts, that it would gain more power in the region, that American and other forces would be bogged down in Iraq, and that Washington would have to undertake a massive nation-building enterprise. These risks also attended in eliminating Saddam's regime politically, but more of the government and military would have remained intact in that scenario as compared with the case of a full-scale invasion and occupation.

Fifth, the broader policy thrust of the 2003 war was to eliminate the WMD and terrorist threat in Iraq and democratize Iraq and the Middle East. Regime change was the vehicle through which these other goals could be accomplished. In contrast, although the containment-plus policy included regime change, it did not have the seemingly urgent goal of dealing with a terrorist threat or the longer-run goal of democratizing the Middle East.

Regime Change and Balance-of-Power Policy

Regime change, even when pursued in a nonmilitary manner, is not a balance-of-power technique. In fact, the two policies differ quite markedly in their motivations, approach, and end goals.

In balance-of-power policy, states are treated as unitary actors with a permanent presence. In contrast, regime change aims to take one of the actors out of play and replace it with another. Regime change in Iraq ran the risk of tearing the country asunder partly because Saddam, through his brutality, may have helped keep it together. Balance-of-power policy, then, is based on working with existing states, rather than taking actions that might eliminate them. This has been the case for centuries. Thus, in the nineteenth-century balance-of-power system, which differed radically from twentieth-century politics but nonetheless involved conscious balancing efforts among the great powers, France was allowed to reenter the system and was not eliminated, despite the objections of Prussia, which saw France as inherently wicked.[23]

The Iraq war of 2003, of course, raised the acceptability of intervening in the affairs of other states to a quintessential level. But elements of such thinking can be discerned even in Clinton's administration, indicating the further evolution of American foreign policy away from realpolitik and balance-of-power realism. Indeed, in April 1993, Clinton asserted that balance-of-power politics was no longer sufficient for keeping the peace: "American policies must also focus on relations within nations, on a nation's form of governance, on its economic structure, on its ethnic tolerance. These are of concern to us for they shape how these nations treat their neighbors."[24]

Regime change policy also conflicts with the notion of sovereignty, which has become enshrined in international law, especially in the second half of the twentieth century. Balance-of-power policy is based on the notion that the state actor is sovereign and represents the fundamental unit of world politics, whereas regime change is driven by the notion that one state can enter into another and enhance stability by changing its regime.

Regime change policy also aims, in addition to eliminating the regime, to reshape society, to alter the ideological foundation and orientation of people. Balance of power does not include these motivations. Indeed, it does not allow for balancing behavior that is motivated by ideological preferences or by disdain for the government and leaders of other states.[25] These are subsystemic concerns, or those that lie within states. If realism and balance of power stand for anything, it is not to meddle in the internal affairs of other states. Regime change, especially when achieved through a military invasion, blatantly violates that core notion.

Finally, pursuing regime change in Iraq ran the risk of making Iran far stronger than Iraq in the Persian Gulf by leaving Iraq weak militarily and subject to Iran's opportunism politically. This risk was made more acute in the Iraq war of 2003, which I elaborate upon in the next chapter.

Conclusion

Regime change emerged as official policy long before September 11, 2001, although popular accounts would suggest otherwise. Most Americans and others around the world may well have believed that the Bush administration developed and executed regime change on its watch. That is only half true. It didn't develop it, but it did execute it in a forceful manner, unlike the Clinton administration.

By the time the administration of George W. Bush took the helm, containment in any form was widely viewed as a failing policy. In the first weeks of President Bush's administration, his key advisers had conceded that Saddam had won the public relations argument that international sanctions were hurting his people and not undermining his rule.[26]

The United States had become increasingly more aggressive against Iraq, but, though successful in some ways, its policies did not seem to accomplish enough. Dual containment sought to contain Iraq and Iran simultaneously as a way of protecting and advancing American interests in the region; containment-plus added regime change as official American policy. But the events of September 11 changed the way Washington thought of the world and the Persian Gulf and heralded a new world in which neither containment nor regime change through political means was viewed as sufficient to protect American security.

In reacting to unfolding events, Washington escalated its policies. It had preferred to support Saddam Hussein during most of the Iran-Iraq War and then placated him after the war, despite his predominant threat and power. But Iraq's invasion of Kuwait forced the United States to shift course radically. After the war, it increased the pressure on Iraq and Iran, as well. Washington began with containment, but when that policy did not prove to be effective enough in its view, it moved to the more aggressive policy of dual containment. The United States' next policy, regime change through political means under containment-plus, was more powerful than containment alone; regime change by use of force under the administration of George W. Bush, however, would be the most muscular policy of all. Saddam would no longer be supported, placated, simply contained, or considered a target for regime change by political means. He would be eliminated altogether as a leader by force of arms.

CHAPTER EIGHT

The Iraq War of 2003

The Iraq war was launched in March 2003, but U.S.-Iraqi tensions had been building throughout the 1990s. Although the 1991 war had severely weakened Iraq, not only did the wily dictator from Takrit fail to cooperate with UN inspectors as mandated by UN Resolution 687, but he acted as if he had weapons of mass destruction (WMD), which he evidently did not. The great irony was that he may well have thought that this pretense would send a signal to his real and imagined adversaries at both the domestic and international level that he was strong, that he could deter their attacks, even punish them with retaliation if needed.[1] Yet, by creating this impression, he constructed himself as the very threat that the administration of George W. Bush would want to check and then eliminate after September 11. In this sense, unbeknownst to himself, Saddam was once again acting as his own worst enemy.

As we shall see, the American approach toward Iraq after September 11 deviated significantly from balance-of-power policy, although to some extent it did reflect balance-of-threat policy. These points are supported in sketching the motivations for war. After providing a brief backdrop to this conflict, this chapter seeks to identify the key motivations that led the United States to invade Iraq, as well as possible secondary motivations. It then analyzes the extent to which American motivations and actions conformed with balancing policy.

Episode 10: The Iraq War of 2003, 2003–2005

Iraq's record of defiance was not in doubt among many nations of the world, although the decision to go to war against Iraq was controversial. Iraq had defied sixteen UN resolutions passed between 1991 and 2002, starting with Resolution 687, which was the most important (see Chapter 6).

In his speech to the United Nations on September 12, 2002, President Bush demanded that Iraq comply immediately with the sixteen UN resolutions. He claimed that because Iraq was continuing to pursue the acquisition of WMD and missile delivery systems, it represented a "grave and gathering danger" to American and global security. And he pointed out that the United Nations had struggled with Iraq for a dozen years to ensure its compliance with the demands of UN Resolution 687 and that Iraq had defied its wishes, thus creating a credibility crisis regarding UN resolve.[2] He held out the prospect that UN inspectors could find Saddam's WMD, but he also asserted that the United States was willing to act unilaterally, observing that it was not possible to "stand by and do nothing while dangers gather."[3]

Washington pushed hard to pass the seventeenth resolution against Iraq. Resolution 1441, as it was called, required Baghdad to admit inspectors from the UN Monitoring, Verification, and Inspection Commission and the International Atomic Energy Agency and to comply fully with all foregoing resolutions.[4] Passed unanimously by the UN Security Council on November 8, 2002, the resolution stated that Iraq "has been and remains in material breach" of its obligations under previous UN resolutions; it gave Iraq thirty days to declare its WMD to the Security Council and underscored that false statements would constitute a further "material breach," for which Iraq could face serious consequences.

However, the consequences of committing another "material breach" were interpreted differently by the various Security Council members. France, Russia, and China preferred to avoid war, and certainly opposed one on Washington's and London's terms and timetable, but none of them threatened to veto Resolution 1441. However, France, with support from Russia, worked hard to change some of the resolution's language in order to put brakes on a move toward war, leaving such authorization until after the arms inspectors reported very serious violations by Baghdad.[5]

For its part, Iraq moved to comply with Resolution 1441 by allowing UN inspectors back into the country and by submitting twelve thousand pages and several compact discs containing information that supposedly described its capabilities. Baghdad asserted that it had no WMD programs and no WMD in storage. Unfortunately, these disclosures were not viewed as complete.

Chief UN weapons inspector Hans Blix issued a report in January 2003 which was critical of Iraq's efforts to disarm or cooperate with UN inspectors.[6] He observed that serious questions remained about Iraq's chemical and biological weapons capability, some of which he believed was unaccounted for in Iraq's disclosures to the United Nations. Not surprisingly, the Bush administration found Iraq's cooperation highly problematic. Secretary of State Colin Powell asserted that American experts found the Iraqi declaration to the United Nations to "be anything but currently accurate, full, or complete" and that the declaration "totally" failed to meet the resolution's requirements.[7] As Powell explained to the United Nations in his famous appearance on February 5, 2003, "We haven't accounted for the anthrax, we haven't accounted for the botulinum, VX, both biological agents, growth media, 30,000 chemical and biological munitions."[8] Perhaps feeling at increasingly greater risk, Saddam moved to offer more support to UN inspectors in Iraq. He may have thought that he could complicate U.S. efforts to invade Iraq without revealing the fact that he had very few or no WMD.

On February 10, 2003, Blix offered a more optimistic account of Iraq's cooperation, seeing a new "positive attitude" on the part of the Iraqi regime, and asked for more time for inspections.[9] Although Russia, Germany, and France in particular seized on Blix's report to try to impede the American and British drive toward war, Washington and London proved recalcitrant. They may well have concluded that Saddam was simply engaging in more games with UN inspectors, that his track record suggested no real interest in changing his attitude completely, and, that, as a result, inspections were doomed to fail. From their perspective, if Saddam did have WMD, he would not help UN inspectors find them, and without his help, they could remain hidden. Meanwhile, even if the inspectors did find WMD, they could not be sure that they had uncovered them all or that, after they left, Saddam would not resume some of these programs.

Partly because of these reasons and partly because Iraq, especially in the view of the United States and Britain, did not appear to meet the conditions of UN Resolution 1441 or previous UN resolutions, the United States and Britain moved to present the eighteenth resolution against Iraq, which, in essence, called for war. To pass this resolution, the United States needed the support of nine of the fifteen Security Council members while avoiding a veto by any of the four other permanent members. The Security Council had unanimously supported the seventeenth resolution, but the underlying differences on going to war complicated U.S. efforts to pass the eighteenth resolution. Russia threatened to veto it, though Moscow avoided an open breach with Washington. Russian president Vladimir Putin supported earlier U.S. efforts to contain and defang Iraq and possibly to go to war on a much slower timetable, but he could not do so for a war that was viewed worldwide and in Russia as rushed or outright ill advised.[10]

France in particular viewed the seventeenth resolution differently. It saw the resolution as a warning to Iraq to comply more fully with UN inspectors but not as a casus belli. After France threatened to veto the eighteenth resolution outright, possibly with backing from China and Russia, the United States and Britain altered strategies, especially when they learned that even some of the smaller countries on the UN Security Council would not support their action.

The United States and Britain offered somewhat different justifications for war but argued that Iraq's violations of the previous seventeen UN resolutions gave them sufficient basis for using force.[11] As a result, they gave Saddam, his sons, and key elites the opportunity to leave the country within forty-eight hours or face war. Saddam rejected the ultimatum, perhaps fearing that the United States would eventually track him down if he left Iraq or that he could survive the American-led onslaught to fight another day. Some strong evidence also suggests that he did not expect a massive American onslaught but rather a more limited attack and preferred to maintain the myth of his WMD potential as a deterrent chiefly against Iran but also against a broader American invasion.[12] In another interpretation, it may be possible that he and his generals had plans to stand down and disperse into a guerrilla movement, with greater chances of evicting American forces from Iraq through a war of attrition. Minutes of a meeting of his top commanders chaired by Saddam underscored this interpretation.[13]

Operation Iraqi Freedom was launched on March 19 with a massive air attack on Iraq, an assault referred to with overcharged bravado as "Operation Shock and Awe." Bombs hailed down precisely on their targets. Saddam fell to this massive onslaught, and his regime came crashing down with him, but the security and political debris that he left in his wake would continue to bedevil the United States and its allies, who were bent on rebuilding Iraq in the Western image.

The Key Motivations for Going to War

It will take years and perhaps decades for the declassification of documents that will allow a clearer picture of exactly why the United States invaded Iraq, but it is possible at this time to offer educated conjecture on the broad sweep of motivations. The United States gave three key reasons for going to war.[14] They do not likely capture the full story of American motivations but do appear to be central.

First, the United States was concerned about Iraqi WMD programs. On August 14, 2002, national security adviser Condoleezza Rice chaired a principals meeting that laid out U.S. goals in Iraq in a draft of a National Security Presidential Directive entitled "Iraq: Goals, Objectives and Strategy," which the president signed into effect on August 29. It emphasized the desire to free Iraq in order to eliminate WMD, end its regional threat, create democracy in Iraq, and limit the chance of a WMD attack on the United States or its friends and allies.[15]

In June 2001, the CIA asserted that, though the evidence was not fully clear, it appeared likely, especially given its past actions, that Iraq used the period between 1998 and 2001 to rebuild prohibited WMD programs.[16] The intelligence to which the Bush administration was privy was contained chiefly in a top-secret document that was made available to all members of Congress in October 2002, days before the House and Senate voted to authorize Bush to use force in Iraq. This National Intelligence Estimate (NIE), titled "Iraq's Continuing Programs for Weapons of Mass Destruction," reflected the combined U.S. intelligence community's most authoritative judgments. It asserted: "Iraq has continued its weapons of mass destruction programs in defiance of UN resolutions and restrictions. Baghdad has chemical and biological weapons as well as missiles with ranges in excess of UN restrictions; if left unchecked, it probably will have a nuclear weapon during this decade."[17]

In one key document, President Bush noted that if the Iraqi regime was "able to produce, buy, or steal an amount of highly enriched uranium a little larger than a single softball, it could have a nuclear weapon in less than a year."[18] In September 2002, he cited a British intelligence report indicating that Iraq could launch a chemical or biological attack forty-five minutes after the order was given to do so.[19] The administration also described Iraq as capable of using WMD against the United States, a position that was not shared by the intelligence analysts who wrote the NIE.[20]

For their part, senior U.S. officials repeatedly asserted that Iraq sought to rebuild its nuclear program and to hide its facilities by placing some underground or camouflaging them. In this view, inspections could not stop these activities, and even if they could, Iraq would resume them once the inspectors left the country.[21] In the event that Iraq did not possess actual capabilities, the administration believed that it had the intellectual infrastructure and intent to produce them. That alone was enough of a threat after 9/11 to motivate U.S. action against Iraq. The administration did not trumpet this argument because it was less marketable than other arguments for war.[22]

The attacks of September 11 raised the stakes so high that the administration had a low level of tolerance for WMD in a dictator's hands, especially one with Saddam's record of aggression.[23] Vice President Richard Cheney asserted in August 2002, "If the United States could have preempted 9/11, we would have, no question. Should we be able to prevent another, much more devastating attack, we will, no question."[24] From this perspective, emphasis was not placed on having irrefutable facts about Iraq's capabilities and intentions. Rather, Saddam had given the administration enough reason to have serious doubts about his intentions in a post–9/11 environment. As Bush declared in his January 28, 2003, State of the Union speech, "[A] brutal dictator, with a history of reckless aggression, with ties to terrorism, with great potential wealth, will not be permitted to dominate a vital region and threaten the United States."[25]

President Bush had described Iraq, Iran, and North Korea in his now famous January 29, 2002, State of the Union message as part of an "axis of evil" against which preemptive force might have to be used. Later, on September 28, 2002, Bush elaborated on the Iraq problem: "[The] danger to our country is grave and growing. The Iraqi regime possesses biological and chemical weapons, is rebuilding facilities to make more and . . . is seeking a nuclear bomb, and with fissile material could build one within a year."[26] As former CIA director George Tenet describes it, policymakers "seized on the emotional impact of 9/11 and created a psychological connection between the failure to act decisively against al-Qa'ida and the danger posed by Iraq's WMD program."[27]

The second motivation for the invasion, as asserted by the administration, was Iraq's ties to terrorism. This concern was played to or was buoyed by the fact that a majority of Americans (53 to 64 percent in an August 2002 Gallup poll) mistakenly believed that Saddam was directly involved in the 9/11 attacks.[28]

Prior to September 11, the administration was not especially concerned about Al Qaeda. It tended to follow in the direction of the Clinton administration, which aimed to eliminate the Al Qaeda threat not by physical deployment of forces or extensive pressure on the Taliban but rather through the use of domestic law enforcement bodies (though it did make one effort to assassinate bin Laden with a missile strike on his training camp in Afghanistan). The Bush administration was more fixed on the Al Qaeda threat than the Clinton administration, but it was not so concerned that it took speedy action to address it. The broader tenor among high-level Bush administration officials was reflected in Rice's slow response to suggestions made in a key memo by counter-terrorism coordinator Richard Clarke to take action against Al Qaeda; Rice was subsequently accused of ignoring the threat prior to September 11.[29] Ironically, on September 10, she was in the process of preparing a National Security Directive on how to eliminate Al Qaeda.[30] For his part, President Bush did not receive even one brief from his chief counter-terrorism expert prior to 9/11.[31] In Clarke's account, the administration was stuck in bureaucratic inertia and politics and unable to make sensible adjustments regarding the Al Qaeda threat until the 9/11 shock wave.[32]

After September 11, the administration appeared to be concerned about, even obsessed with, the connection between WMD and terrorist organizations, as suggested in many speeches by top American officials, including Vice President Richard Cheney.[33] Rumsfeld successfully encouraged his deputy, Paul Wolfowitz, to push the issue of confronting Iraq at a two-day Camp David war council meeting on September 15, which was aimed at fashioning an American response to the September 11 attacks. For his part, Bush had Iraq on his radar screen but wanted to wait for the right time to get him, although he did order the creation of contingency plans for forceful regime change.[34]

Exactly how much the administration manipulated intelligence to support the war may not be fully known for some time. However, it seems clear that the administration was concerned that Iraq could conceivably support transnational terrorists. Evidence for this interpretation came in the now famous Downing Street Memo, which summarizes a July 23, 2002, meeting of British prime minister Tony Blair with his top security advisers. In the memo, which is actually minutes of the meeting, the head of Britain's M1–6 intelligence service reports on his high-level visit to Washington that "Bush wanted to remove Saddam through military action, justified by the conjunction of terrorism and WMD. But the intelligence and facts were being fixed around the policy."[35]

Even though the link to Al Qaeda proved very dubious,[36] it was Saddam's misfortune that Iraq represented precisely what the Bush administration feared after September 11: a dictator developing WMD with connections to terrorist groups. In describing Saddam after 9/11, Bush said that "all his terrible features became much more threatening. Keeping Saddam in a box looked less and less feasible" to him.[37] In Rumsfeld's words, "We acted because we saw the existing evidence in a new light, through the prism of our experience on September 11th," which highlighted America's vulnerability to states with WMD and connections to terrorists.[38]

Even Secretary Powell appeared persuaded to some extent by Iraq's threat, although he may have also been playing a role as obedient soldier to the president and vice president. In his critical speech to the United Nations on September 12, 2002, he stated that terrorism had been a "tool" used by Saddam for decades: "Saddam was a supporter of terrorism long before these terrorist networks had a name, and this support continues. The nexus of poisons and terror is new. The nexus of Iraq and terror is old. The combination is lethal."[39]

Some scholars have argued that the administration used the WMD threat to justify a war that it had already decided to launch even before 9/11. That does not seem likely. September 11 not only gave the administration a basis for garnering public support for war, which it had lacked, but also affected its strategic calculations decisively, animating it to take major actions against the chance that terrorists could obtain WMD.[40] This strategy included a democratization effort in Iraq and in the Middle East, which had been viewed skeptically by high-level Bush administration officials prior to September 11 but which slowly gained traction after the attacks.[41]

Having been advised that Al Qaeda may well have planned the 9/11 attack, Donald Rumsfeld reportedly asked for plans to invade Iraq in the hours following the attacks, while Wolfowitz pushed for an invasion of Iraq ahead of an attack on Afghanistan.[42] Meanwhile, the president asked for contingency plans to attack Iraq if it was shown that Al Qaeda was involved in the attacks or sought to exploit the crisis for its own gain.[43] Like Wolfowitz, Bush made it known early on that he thought Iraq was involved in the 9/11 attacks, and he reiterated the concern that Iraq had long-standing ties to terrorist groups capable of and willing to deliver weapons of mass death.[44]

The United States gave a third reason for going to war: it hoped to democratize Iraq and to see whether, if that effort was successful, it could sow the seeds of democracy more broadly in the Middle East. The United States did not fixate on democratization initially as a motivation, but it would be a mistake to consider it simply an afterthought.

President George H. W. Bush was criticized for lacking vision, but his son developed a major vision, whatever one thinks of its merits, in the post–9/11 period. His vision adhered (though perhaps not knowingly on Bush's part) to a view of history that is unilinear rather than cyclical. Bush's vision was unilinear in its belief in human progress, in this case the democratization of a challenging region, rather than cyclical and realist in assuming that the afflictions of international relations would simply repeat themselves over time.[45]

In response to September 11, and well before the United States ran into trouble in Iraq, Bush stated in an address to the nation on 9/11 that the United States "would go forward to defend freedom and all that is good and just in our world."[46] Thereafter, he emphasized how the United States would reinforce and spread democratic ideas.

The objective of democratizing Iraq and the Middle East gained currency as time wore on, especially after WMD were not found in Iraq and the Al Qaeda connection to Saddam proved dubious. This approach broke with past U.S. foreign policy in the region. Even the Clinton administration, which prided itself on respect for human rights abroad, did not launch a democratization drive in the Middle East. As former secretary of state Madeleine Albright describes the situation, "We have been afraid to push too hard for democracy, especially in Arab countries. We worry, perhaps with reason, that if radical Islamists obtain power through an election, there would be no more elections . . . and instability might be created."[47] In 2005, however, Secretary of State Rice asserted, that "[For] 60 years, my country, the United States, pursued stability at the expense of democracy in this region here in the Middle East, and we achieved neither. Now we are taking a different course. We are supporting the democratic aspirations of all people."[48]

In the administration's view, democratization could undermine the demons that drive transnational terrorism,[49] a theme that dominated the administration's list of priorities by 2004. In his State of the Union address on February 2, 2004, Bush urged Saudi Arabia and Egypt to "show the way toward democracy in the region."[50]

The Conceptual Motivation for War: Preemption and Prevention versus Containment

The motivations for war discussed above are not sufficient to explain the decision to go to war. After all, if the concern about WMD was so vital, why didn't the administration attack North Korea, which was more of a threat with regard to WMD than Iraq even in the prewar period when Iraq was believed to have some WMD programs? As Tenet recalls, it is possible that "WMD was emphasized as a cause because it was the issue that everyone could agree on."[51] If fighting terrorism was key, the administration could just as easily have decided to focus on strangulating Al Qaeda globally rather than executing regime change in Iraq, even if it saw a Saddam–Al Qaeda connection. If it was concerned about WMD and terrorism, the administration might also have decided to ratchet up its containment of Iraq with increased military, political, and economic pressures in lieu of invasion and occupation. Why war?

Simply put, after 9/11, the administration did not believe that containment would work. That was not an overnight epiphany. Even the Clinton administration started to doubt the benefits of containment and moved to dual containment before adopting the policy of containment plus regime change. However, Iraq's perceived WMD and connections to terrorism further drove a change in American policy away from containment and toward preemption, and preemption became the conceptual basis for invading Iraq.

Of course, American action appeared to be prevention more than preemption, and the administration apparently understood this distinction.[52] Preventive war assumes that military conflict, while not imminent, is probably inevitable and that delay would be risky, whereas preemption is acting defensively in response to fear of imminent attack. Prevention can be used more easily, as it may well have been in the Iraq war, but it is harder to sell to the public and justify internationally because the urgency of preventive war is not clear. If we conceive of the Iraq war as prevention, then it differs even more starkly from balance-of-power policy, which does not aim to anticipate threats and then to use force to prevent their manifestation.

In any case, prior to 9/11, the administration viewed the policy of containment as problematic. Bush stated that he was "not happy" with that policy because it was not toppling Saddam or changing his behavior, but he also pointed out that, prior to September 11, a "president could see a threat and contain it or deal with it in a variety of ways without fear of that threat materializing on our own soil."[53] These words roughly describe the disposition of the Clinton and Bush administrations. The latter was content with strengthening the containment effort against Saddam Hussein through "smart sanctions," which aimed to prevent Iraq from obtaining military goods while relaxing the embargo on trade items that Iraq's people needed. Prior to 9/11, Iraq was barely mentioned by top officials, except as a possible longer-term threat,[54] even though consensus had developed among them that Saddam's regime needed to be removed and regime change had become official American policy in 1998. Some Bush administration officials such as Colin Powell believed that Saddam was largely contained by allied forces and by smart sanctions. And even Bush, while running for the presidency, asserted several times that while Al Gore believed in using troops for nation building, Bush himself would be "very careful" about doing so.[55]

After September 11, U.S. policy toward Iraq changed notably from regime change by use of political means to regime change by use of force.[56] The Bush doctrine of preemption was articulated in the president's State of the Union address on January 29, 2002, and then formally encapsulated in the National Security Strategy of September 2002.[57] It was based partly on the notion that deterrence and containment may not succeed, placing emphasis on the need to resort in appropriate cases to preemptive measures.[58] For Paul Wolfowitz, 9/11 was the "most significant thing" that generated a change in U.S. foreign policy and may go down as one of the top ten events, if not *the* top event, of the "last one hundred years."[59]

The United States had always practiced preemption when necessary, but preemption had never before been openly presented as a strategy and then used so brazenly to justify war on another country. The September 11 attack, however, altered the stakes. As President Bush put it, September 11 made it such that after 9/11 the "doctrine of containment just doesn't hold any water."[60] Bush asserted in a speech in Cincinnati in October 2002 that the United States had to take preemptive action because, after September 11, it could not "wait for the final proof — the smoking gun," which would come in the "form of a mushroom cloud."[61] America's threshold level for terrorism had been lowered enough that Iraq became a key target for vigorous American action. Containment was a passive approach; now, the United States would become much more active.

Regime change by use of force was one key element of the broader policy of preemption, but preemption also sought to stop terrorist attacks before they occurred by other measures. Regime change was the most visible and riskiest of these measures and provoked controversy, even across the American political spectrum. Richard Haass, a former high-level official in the administration of George W. Bush, even referred to it as a "fantasy of a quick fix."[62]

Faulty and Selective Intelligence

Wars in history have often been started because of miscalculations about the strength of other actors or the threats they pose. The Bush administration's conceptual shift toward preemption and war in Iraq was driven partly by faulty intelligence regarding Iraq's WMD, its connections to Al Qaeda, and possibly the ease of postwar nation building.[63] The administration failed to understand that Iraq lacked such weapons and connections to terrorism, and it clearly over-estimated its ability to rebuild Iraq after war.

The declassified NIE essentially asserted that Iraq was continuing its WMD programs in defiance of UN resolutions and restrictions, had chemical and bio-logical weapons as well as missiles with ranges in excess of UN restrictions, and, if left unchecked, would have a nuclear weapon within this decade. The NIE, however, expressed doubt that Saddam would give chemical or biological weap-ons to terrorists for use against America, unless he was attacked by the United States, in which case he might turn to Al Qaeda to conduct such attacks.

It is fair to conclude that faulty intelligence was important in the decision to go to war. Poor intelligence had created a specter of a much greater Iraqi threat than existed; it had facilitated the administration's efforts to gain public and, in some quarters, international support for war; and it had predisposed key officials to believe that Iraq could be rebuilt and refashioned without the extraordinary challenges that would arise in the postwar period. If we reverse these conse-quences of faulty intelligence, the decision to go to war becomes less palatable and marketable.

For its part, the administration held fast to the notion that it had made good decisions for war based on the evidence at hand, faulty as it was, and challenged criticisms that it had cooked the books for war. In comments that reflected the administration's position, Powell stated that he was "disappointed" that the intel-ligence was not on target but that the administration did not mislead because it believed what it said about Iraq. "We thought Iraq had stockpiles of WMD."[64]

It may never be fully evident to what extent the administration, or particular members within it, also manipulated intelligence to justify war, in a misleading manner to boot.[65] Nor is it the goal here to provide a speculative analysis on that count. It is only important to raise the issue as one key factor to consider in explaining the American approach toward war.

Two major official inquiries by the Senate Intelligence Committee in 2004 and the Robb-Silberman Commission in March 2005 found no evidence that political pressure by the Bush administration had contributed to these intel-ligence failures.[66] The inquiries did find that Vice President Cheney and others had encouraged analysts to rethink their findings but that this did not lead to different conclusions. The inquiries, however, did not have access to White

House documents. Moreover, although they found that political pressure by the administration did not contribute to intelligence failures, they left open the question of the extent to which the administration exaggerated the threat from Iraq and, in particular, the Al Qaeda threat to justify war.[67]

In fact, one February 2002 declassified document from the Defense Intelligence Agency asserted that Ibn al-Shaykh al-Libi, a top member of Al Qaeda in American custody, was intentionally misleading American debriefers about Iraq's support for Al Qaeda with illicit weapons.[68] The administration repeatedly drew on his testimony, as did Colin Powell in his February 2003 UN speech. Libi withdrew his story in 2004, and the CIA withdrew all claims based on it, but his input raised questions about the extent to which the administration dramatized, fabricated, and/or misunderstood the Saddam connection to Al Qaeda.[69] For his part, CIA director George Tenet asserted in his 2007 book that the CIA had found no link between Iraq and terrorism prior to the U.S. invasion and that the White House pressured the CIA to revise a report on that issue.[70]

Other Possible Motivations for War

In addition to the motivations for war discussed in the previous pages, we should consider several others. Many people around the world viewed the war as unnecessary. If the war was not really intended to address some imminent and fanciful threat from Iraq, they thought, then what were its real aims?[71] The following possible motivations clash strongly with balancing policy.

Oil Security and Alternatives to Saudi Energy

Many people in the Middle East and around the world believed that the war was about oil. According to a Pew Research Center opinion poll, 76 percent of Russians, 75 percent of French, 54 percent of Germans, and 44 percent of British believed that the war was driven by a desire to control Iraq's oil.[72] Most Iraqis, it is fair to say, held this view, which was prominent among moderate and radical Islamists around the world. As Shibley Telhami points out, although "most Arabs" attributed American behavior in Iraq to traditional American interests, primarily oil and Israel, "the aim of weakening the Muslim world was later seen as almost the equal of those interests."[73] For his part, Osama bin Laden asserted in a 1998 interview that the Muslim world and Islam are under assault: "[Others] rob us of our wealth and of our resources and of our oil. Our religion is under attack."[74] This view of oil-stealing Americans stayed fairly constant in statements by Al Qaeda and its affiliates.[75]

Although it is obvious that the United States views access to Persian Gulf oil as vital to U.S. and global security,[76] little evidence exists that it has sought to steal this oil. For instance, it did not seize Iraqi oil fields or monies from oil sales. Rather, oil may very well have been one of the motivating factors for the invasion of Iraq for other reasons.

First, September 11 raised issues about Saudi stability, some sensible and some not but all carrying some influence on elite and public opinion in the United States. The fact that fifteen of nineteen hijackers came from Saudi Arabia raised questions about whether their hatred for the United States was more endemic in the kingdom than previously believed. It also raised questions about whether they attacked the United States to create a schism in U.S.-Saudi relations, thus hurting the legitimacy of the Saudi regime, which, after all, was one of their primary targets.

Of course, concerns also arose about whether elements in the Saudi regime actually supported the terrorists, suggesting a radical element within the royal family itself. Another possibility was that the regime turned a blind eye to the terrorists either because it did not want to confront them or because its own religious system had hatched them. In any of these explanations, the future of U.S.-Saudi relations were in potential jeopardy.

With Saudi Arabia and the U.S.-Saudi relationship less stable, securing Iraq's vast oil resources made more sense. If Iraq's oil production were in friendlier Iraqi hands, the West would have greater leverage for obtaining oil in the event of political or security problems in Saudi Arabia. Even if the Saudi regime was initially stable, U.S.-Saudi tensions might mount over time, thus making Iraq more important as a way of diversifying oil supply.

Second, regime change could allow for higher Iraqi oil production. It is believed that Iraq has 112.5 billion barrels of known reserves, which places it second only to Saudi Arabia's 262 billion. Iraq's proven reserves are found in seventy-three fields, only one-quarter of which have been developed to any degree.[77] Other Middle East states such as Iran and Kuwait hold approximately 90 to 120 billion barrels, but those fields do not have the upward potential of Iraq's because they are already producing at a high rate. Iraq possesses 11 percent of the world's proven oil reserves, yet even at its peak production in 1979, it was producing only 5.5 percent of world supply. Iraq's potential could have been viewed as enormous precisely because it has been hamstrung over the past twenty-five years. The Iran-Iraq War (1980–1988), the 1991 Gulf war, subsequent UN sanctions, periodic American military attacks, and Saddam's own mismanagement and corruption further curtailed Iraq's potential and left its oil infrastructure in disarray.

Iraq's various conflicts with the United Nations resulted in a drop in production from an average of 2.0 million to 2.6 million barrels per day (mb/d) from 1999 to 2001, under UN Resolution 986. It hit a high of 2.6 mb/d in 2000 (equal to 3.4 percent of world supply) and dropped to 1.7 mb/d by August–September 2002.[78] Some analysts believed that, with a totally rebuilt oil infrastructure, Iraq could have increased oil production to an estimated 6 to 12 mb/d within a decade, partly because Iraq's oil was relatively underexplored and underdeveloped.[79] In early 1990, prior to the invasion of Kuwait, Baghdad had planned to raise production and export capacity to 6 mb/d by 1996.[80] Since May 1997, Iraq's oil ministry worked assiduously in producing a postsanctions oil development plan, the latest version of which preceded the Iraq war of 2003 and had a goal of producing 6 mb/d within six years.[81]

Third, eliminating Iraq's regime could have ended Iraq's threat to regional oil fields, at least in the near term. After all, Iraq's invasion of Kuwait had demonstrated that Saddam might be inclined once again to invade Kuwait or even to invade Saudi Arabia. Eliminating Iraq's regime, and thus its threat to regional oil fields, would be particularly important if the UN sanctions and international pressure began to wane and left Saddam greater room to maneuver in the region.[82]

These three reasons may very well have added to the Bush administration's interest in invading Iraq. Administration officials could not have underestimated the importance of oil to the American and global economy and potential problems with Saudi Arabia. Nor could they overlook the fact that Persian Gulf oil would only become more important as other sources of oil around the world began to dry up.[83]

The Military-Industrial Complex

Some observers, especially those prone to conspiracy theories, might say that the so-called military-industrial complex, which President Eisenhower famously warned about, also had a role in driving the United States to war, despite the fact that many military leaders were against the invasion.[84] According to some thinkers, going to war would be in the interests of this "complex" of military and business organizations because of the prestige and money to be gained. Wars result in bigger military sales, military research budgets, and influence.[85]

Invading Iraq could benefit the military-industrial complex. It could produce and sell more and better weapons. The influence of the Department of Defense could rise if the armed forces performed well, and the military might stave off budget cuts and base closings and gain support for weapons programs that it sought. And the much maligned CIA could have a mission in the post–Cold War era.

As a twist on the military-industrial complex explanation, some might argue that a potential oil explanation for invading Iraq is that Vice President Cheney, and his contacts in the oil world, could benefit. They could gain potentially large oil contracts after Iraq was liberated by American forces.[86] With America dominating or influencing Iraq, the United States could vie for such contracts much more effectively with countries such as France, Russia, and China, which already had a foothold in the region. Not only would the United States get a bigger piece of the existing pie, but the size of the pie itself would expand because Iraq could produce far more oil with Saddam gone, UN sanctions lifted, and foreign investment revitalizing its oil sector.

This view of American motivations is cynical and may have been originated by the administration's detractors to embarrass it, but Cheney's previous role as CEO of Halliburton, along with the oil background of President Bush, was identified as supporting this view.[87] The Bush administration's Energy Task Force, which was headed by Cheney, presented a draft report in April 2001 saying that the United States should reconsider sanctions against Iran, Iraq, and Libya which prohibited U.S. oil companies from "some of the most important existing and prospective petroleum-producing countries in the world."[88] Moreover, immediately prior to the attack on Iraq in early 2003, Halliburton's subsidiary, Kellogg, Brown and Root, received a multi-billion-dollar contract from the Defense Department to repair oil fields in and import consumer fuels into Iraq.[89] Halliburton itself was given a $15 billion monopolistic contract by the army to provide services such as delivering food and fuel to American troops, a contract that was controversial partly because its critics associated it with cronyism in the Bush White House.[90]

It is not very likely that Cheney would risk a national and global scandal to help a company for which he no longer worked, especially since he likely would have known that he would be suspect. Some people have argued that he still had

Halliburton stock from which he could benefit, but it is not clear that he would risk a high-profile scandal for money, especially given the fact that Halliburton was under much scrutiny and government investigations at the time.[91]

It is likely that most oil companies saw a potential benefit in the invasion of Iraq in that they would be able to exploit the vast business deals that could arise from a successful venture. Mining Iraq's energy resources could benefit companies like Halliburton which support the infrastructure for oil production, although an invasion of Iraq could have affected big oil producers both positively and negatively: as more oil flowed from Iraq, the price of oil would likely decrease based on simple dynamics of supply and demand. Big oil companies could realize profits only if the benefits that accrued to them from additional contracts in Iraq outweighed the losses they would face from decreased oil prices. Nonetheless, the factor of domestic oil and oil services companies needs to be considered.

Whether big oil saw an invasion of Iraq as in its basic interest and, if it did, to what extent it pushed the administration directly or indirectly to invade Iraq is conjecture at this point. But these issues would be worth exploring in much greater detail.

Father and Son: Personal Reasons

We can speculate that President Bush was affected by the fact that his father evicted Saddam Hussein from Kuwait in 1991 but left him in power. In this scenario, George W. Bush invaded Iraq to finish his father's work. Saddam's longevity proved to be a source of embarrassment to the elder Bush, not just because he survived the 1991 war, when many thought he would fall, but because he continued to be perceived as a major threat.

An invasion of Iraq might result in Saddam's death or capture or at least eliminate his regime. In the process, the legacy of President Bush's father would benefit. George W. Bush could also preempt the possibility of Saddam's supporting a future terrorist attack on America by taking the matter into his own hands, thus also helping secure the United States and his own legacy to boot. Indeed, Bush repeatedly asserted that he would have been held accountable if the United States did not do anything to undermine Iraq's threat and Iraq was involved in a major WMD attack on American interests.[92]

Bush may have also sought to avenge Saddam's effort to assassinate his father in Kuwait in 1993, while he was on a visit there. His reference to Saddam Hussein as "a guy that tried to kill my dad" suggested a less-than-veiled hostility toward the dictator.[93] We do know that loyalty runs strong in the Bush family and that

Bush was actually an enforcer of loyalty in his father's administration, which may at least suggest a personality characteristic that was at play in how he viewed Saddam Hussein in 2003.

Carving his Own Path

President Bush may have also sought to set his own independent course as a determined leader rather than as a reputed follower of others. This motivation may have been reinforced by criticisms that it was really Richard Cheney, one of his father's closest advisers, who ran the administration. This criticism could not have been lost on Bush and certainly not on his handlers, who may have seen a side benefit of the Iraq war in the opportunity to establish the president's credentials. Interestingly, when asked by Bob Woodward if he had consulted with his father about going to war in 2002, President Bush asserted famously, "There is a higher father that I appeal to," diminishing his father's role in rather unambiguous terms.

Moreover, Brent Scowcroft, his father's influential national security adviser and close friend, argued in the *Wall Street Journal* that Iraq should not be invaded, that doing so would impede the war on terrorism, that containment was working quite well, and that an invasion would destabilize the region.[94] This view may have also reflected the views of the elder Bush, whose administration did not seriously consider invading Baghdad in 1991. Whatever the case, ignoring the advice of his father's key adviser, and possibly that of his father, may have also suggested that he was determined to chart his own course.

Bush, God, and Religion

If Bush's father played a limited role in shaping his decisions, that was not the case with respect to God. President Bush raised the issue of God and religion in his speeches more than most presidents. From the day after 9/11 when he asserted that he was in the "Lord's hands" to his rhetoric about evil and good and his reference to the war on terrorism as a crusade, Bush was prone to a religious interpretation of events.[95] His notion of "crusade" was quite different from that of many Muslims, based on different perspectives of understanding.[96] He saw it as an effort to confront evil terrorists and individuals and groups that supported them, whereas Muslims interpreted it in terms of their difficult historical experience with the Christian crusades.

Bush referred several times in the spring of 2004 to the notion that a higher source was driving his behavior. The United States, of course, had been promoting the liberal tradition as a transnational set of ideas but largely kept religion out of politics. Indeed, it differed fundamentally from Islamists on that score. President Bush was not deviating significantly from that tradition; nor did the president speak for all Americans or officials. But his words were enough to raise questions in the Muslim world about a Judeo-Christian showdown with Islam. The notion that the war on terrorism was really a U.S.-led war on Islam had wide circulation and acceptance in the Muslim world, beyond the confines of Islamic radicalism.[97] In fact, in a 2004 poll in Egypt, Jordan, Saudi Arabia, Morocco, Lebanon, and the United Arab Emirates, political scientist Shibley Telhami along with Zogby International discovered that more than three-fourths of the respondents believed that American aims in Iraq are intended in part "to weaken the Muslim world."[98] That President Bush embraced Israel's Prime Minister Ariel Sharon added to this perception because it fed into conspiratorial thinking about a Zionist-Crusader conspiracy.

One might surmise that Bush would be heavily criticized for copious religious imagery, and to some extent he was. But even during the presidential election, the campaign of Senator John Kerry veered away from open criticism. Bush's religious imagery may have struck a chord not only among Christian conservatives and evangelicals who had a biblical interpretation of world events but also among Americans who held negative views of Muslims even prior to September 11.[99]

It is possible that Bush saw Iraq partly through the prism of religion. The United States was a God-fearing Christian nation, and Iraq was fit for transformation. Of course, Iraq could not be Christianized, but the messianic impulse may have been part of what bolstered Bush's determination, an impulse that also meshed well with his brand of American exceptionalism.

Exceptionalism

Unlike empires and great powers of the past, America has not desired to spread a settler population in order to mark its acquisitions and expand its citizenry. Far from it. It has shied away from commitments of this kind. American administrators, moreover, have not run other countries, except on a temporary basis, such as in Iraq on the presumption that U.S. forces would depart when Iraqis could assume sovereign control on their own.

However, one imperial aspect of American foreign policy derives from exceptionalism.[100] Exceptionalism was first evidenced perhaps when John Winthrop proclaimed that the Puritan settlement on the Atlantic's western shore represented a model for the rest of the world.[101] Since then, American leaders have often held the luxuriant notion that others would do well to be more like the United States, which sees itself as an exceptional country endowed with a special mission, a providence to export its superior values and to transform countries such as Iraq into its own image.[102]

President Wilson exported American exceptionalism in such an obvious way that the prime minister of Britain, Lloyd George, remarked that Wilson came to the Peace Conference of 1919 like a missionary to the rescue, with his "little sermonettes full of rather obvious remarks."[103] In more recent times, President Ronald Reagan famously referred to the United States as a "city on a hill," harking back to the descriptions made by the first European settlers. This city was above others, on the commanding heights, with vision, and serving as a model that others could emulate.

Exceptionalism has assumed two forms in history. Exemplarism has argued that the United States should promote democracy by offering a shining example of its successes, while vindicationism has argued that it must move beyond example and actively push its model around the world, through intervention and even force if necessary. The Bush administration pursued the latter form of exceptionalism.[104]

After 9/11, President Bush elevated exceptionalism, intentionally or unintentionally, in promoting Iran, Iraq, and North Korea from the Clintonian status of rogue states to an outright "axis of evil." If America could label them as evil, it followed that it considered itself good. In this sense, a cosmic struggle was under way. Good was fighting evil. And good, presumably, would prevail and carry its values to the world. Changing Iraq, and perhaps the broader Middle East, for the better reflected one of the most profound manifestations of exceptionalism.

Analyzing U.S. Strategy

To what extent was the United States practicing balance-of-power policy? We can explore several factors pertaining to U.S. policy, along with the extent to which America's different motivations for going to war were related to balance-of-power policy.

Iraq: Not the Stronger Actor

Iraq was not the stronger actor in the region in 2003. In fact, it was economically supine and militarily weakened by wars and UN sanctions. To be sure, the United States did see Iraq as a threat, but not because of Iraq's capability relative to Iran or even relative to other regional actors. Iraq was fairly well contained at the conventional level. The United States' view of Iraq as a threat was due to Iraq's potential to develop WMD and to provide them to terrorists. That is a different type of threat than an imbalance of power. Balancing against capability is fundamentally about a response to current realities rather than future threats. Yet a central notion driving the war on terrorism and the war in Iraq has been that it is not possible to respond simply to current conditions because the United States cannot, as President Bush put it colorfully, "wait for the final proof — the smoking gun — that could come in the form of a mushroom cloud."[105]

Regime Change: Not a Balancing Technique

In any case, while we can determine whether the United States balanced against the stronger actor, we can also judge to what extent the mechanics of its actions conformed with balance of power. As laid out earlier in the book, prior to 9/11 the administration viewed the policy of containment as problematic, but Iraq was not viewed as an urgent threat, even though consensus had developed even during Clinton's administration that Saddam's regime needed to be removed.[106] After September 11, U.S. policy toward Iraq changed notably from regime change by use of political means under containment-plus to containment toward regime change by use of force.[107]

The previous chapter laid out why regime change is very much not a balance-of-power technique. But since the Iraq war represented a more aggressive pursuit of regime change than existed under the Clinton administration, we can add one more point.

As I touched upon in the previous chapter, regime change, particularly if conducted by use of force, ran the risk of strengthening Iran. Yet in the administration's top-secret document on objectives to be achieved in the Iraq war, as well as in one presentation to top officials titled "Examining Things That Could Go Wrong: Strategic Risks," Iran was absent as a balance-of-power concern and barely mentioned at all. The concern, inasmuch as Iran was relevant, was that Tehran might help Iraq or that it might exploit the chaos created by the Iraq war to advance its own interest.[108] In a memo from Rumsfeld to the president, Rumsfeld identified the types of problems that could result from a conflict with Iraq, and again there was no mention of balance of power, although one of the concerns was that "another state could try to take advantage of the U.S. involvement or preoccupation with Iraq."[109] That item probably did refer to Iran but did not necessarily reflect concern that it would become the stronger power in the region.

For his part, Colin Powell offered a list of warnings about going to war against Iraq when he met with President Bush, but he did not mention the notion of balance of power or the fear that Iran could emerge from the war a much more powerful actor.[110] If he intended to put his best case forward, we might guess that he would have included the Iran factor if it were a serious concern.

Of course, some might say that the United States had not expected Iran to become stronger as a result of the Iraq invasion. In this view, the potential that Iran would be strengthened was not given short shrift by the United States, relative to other goals and concerns, but rather was not anticipated at all. That, however, is hard to believe. Indeed, at least three major concerns were quite public and bandied about by scholars and political pundits, which suggests that the administration was aware of this potential problem but downplayed it.

The first was that Iraq's military would be undermined in war and nearly destroyed outright. Even before the war, Iran had rebuilt its military capabilities and economy to the point where they were stronger than Iraq's, which suffered near economic collapse. A devastating defeat in war would set back Iraq's military capabilities even further. Rebuilding them would take much time, during which Iran could become even stronger.

Second, Iran's Shia clerics, and others in Iran's political spectrum, could gain influence over Iraq's Shia power bases or part of the Shia movement. This concern was heightened by the fact that Iran and Iraq had the two largest Shia populations in the world. The natural assumption, though not one necessarily accurate, is that religious kinship would be a force for alliances and shared political outlooks among the Shia from Iran and Iraq.[111] This concern continued well after Saddam's demise and was substantially heightened by the insurgency that raged for years following Saddam's downfall.

Even after Iraq assumed semblances of democracy, presuming that occurred, Iran could still influence the new government or its constituencies in profound ways. Time proved this concern to be a realistic one. Indeed, in July 2005, Rumsfeld delivered a blunt message to Iraqi leaders that they needed to be more aggressive in opposing the meddling of Iran in Iraq's affairs if they expected the United States to withdraw its forces — a message that was sent to leaders who increasingly had been strengthening their co-religionists in Tehran.[112] Iran's influence increased as the struggle between Shiites and Sunnis within Iraq mounted because this struggle increased the importance of religious affiliation among Shiites in Iran and Iraq relative to the importance of nationalism shared by Shiites and Sunnis within Iraq.

Third, the war could produce a major outcome: Iraq could collapse into its three historical parts, Basra, Baghdad, and Mosul, which would surely strengthen Iran's position in the regional balance of power. With Saddam at the helm in the Iraqi state, the state, though potentially threatening, had much more capability than a dismembered Iraq.

It is possible that the administration preferred not to air these balance-of-power risks because it was trying to sell the war to the public and world. Displaying the concern that war against Iraq could strengthen Iran would not have served this goal. In any case, the United States appeared willing to tolerate this potential balance-of-power problem in pursuit of its other goals, including eliminating Saddam Hussein. Interestingly, even the Saudis were not especially concerned about the balance of power because they apparently urged the United States to get rid of Saddam.[113]

All this does not mean that balance-of-power concerns were irrelevant or that the United States did not care if Iran became stronger. It does suggest that balancing was not a priority or even a secondary concern.

One might say as a counterpoint that the administration sought to balance against Iraq because it was a gathering threat. Yet balance of power assumes that states will balance against real and not emerging capability, and it does not presume that they will do so through regime change.

We might also counterargue that the Bush administration believed that it would leave Iraq stronger by refashioning and rebuilding it under the banner of democracy, market economics, and respect in the international community. But while that is certainly true, the administration said little or nothing about doing so either to balance against Iran or to maintain a balance of power in the region.

Overall, the U.S.-led war on Iraq created the potential for a militarily weaker Iraq to become politically vulnerable to its chief rival and former nemesis. The implication for balance of power was vast in this sense. In fact, there was no parallel for such an outcome in the modern history of the Persian Gulf, where Iran and Iraq had always checked each other.

American Goals and Balance-of-Power Policy

Another angle to take in examining the role of balancing in U.S. policy is to ask to what extent its other officially stated objectives reflected balance-of-power policy. The first one was to rid Iraq of WMD. Invading Iraq for this reason might be consonant with balance-of-power policy if Iraq were the stronger actor and if the United States did so to reestablish the balance of power rather than to occupy and remake Iraq. Even so, invasion of another country is not a typical balance-of-power policy technique.

The second objective was to eliminate the possibility that Iraq could provide terrorists with WMD. Invading Iraq for this purpose is not consonant with balance-of-power policy because this objective is concerned with domestic issues. The concern was not that Iraq was too powerful but that it might support terrorists who could then wreak havoc on the United States and its allies.

The third stated objective in invading Iraq was to democratize it as well as the broader Middle East. Democratization, which is a centerpiece of liberal thought and practice, has nothing to do with balance-of-power policy. Indeed, realism not only counsels against using force to spread democracy but also does not assume it is the best form of government. As Francis Fukuyama put it, "realists by and large do not believe that liberal democracy is a potentially universal form of government or that the human values underlying it are necessarily superior to those underlying non-democratic societies."[114] Oddly, the Bush administration's push toward democratization contrasted sharply with its initial image as a caretaker of realpolitik and did not reflect the hardcore realist approach to Middle East politics whereby states are the fundamental actors and the support of corrupt autocrats is sensible, even if amoral or immoral.

Democratization, in fact, threatened to weaken the very monarchies on which the United States would depend for a robust balance-of-power approach in the region. They could be overthrown by popular movements triggered by liberalization; they could be thrown out of office in future voting; or their power could slowly diminish as more individuals and groups that did not want them in power became enfranchised. They could also become more anti-American, thus making it harder for the United States to count on their strategic and political support for purposes of balancing.

The case of Saudi Arabia was telling insofar as the Saudi public was more anti-American than the regime itself. A Saudi intelligence survey purportedly revealed that 95 percent of educated Saudis between the ages of twenty-five and forty-one supported bin Laden.[115] *USA Today* discovered that during the summer of 2002 nearly four of five hits on a secret Al Qaeda Web site were made from within Saudi Arabia.[116] A nine-nation poll of Muslim countries, released on February 27, 2002, showed that only 16 percent of Saudis had a positive view of the United States; 64 percent viewed it negatively, and only 3 percent saw it as trustworthy.[117] Meanwhile, another poll, conducted by Shibley Telhami, found that in

2000 more than 60 percent of Saudi citizens expressed confidence in the United States whereas by 2004 less than 4 percent had a favorable view.[118]

It follows from this polling information that a democratic Saudi Arabia would be far less inclined to support American efforts to balance against Iraq or Iran in the future. It is hard to see how weakening the Al Saud could be consistent with balance-of-power politics. Rather, democratization represents a different approach toward generating stability — one that is based on spreading a particular set of ideas or ideology within borders rather than checking power between borders and states. Democratization does not emphasize the cultivating of ties among states but rather puts greater emphasis on preventing terrorism by altering the ideology and context in which it arises, even if that threatens the type of interstate relations that facilitate balancing. It is not easy to see how a mix of strategies toward the region could easily contain balance-of-power policy and democratization when one challenged the goals and techniques of the other.[119]

A number of nonofficial motivations were also broached earlier in the chapter. It is worth assessing them in terms of balance-of-power policy.

American Exceptionalism and the Balance of Power

The notion of exceptionalism clashes with balance-of-power politics. Exceptionalism is based on the idea of American moral superiority, of the preeminence of American values. This type of concept is not what drives balance of power, a clearly amoral approach to world politics which focuses on capability, not ideology and ethics. If anything, pursuing American exceptionalism can impede balancing by alienating the very states that are needed for balancing purposes, although successful balancing can create conditions that facilitate the exportation of American values.

The Military-Industrial Complex

Obviously, military-industrial complex explanations are fundamentally different from balance of power for numerous reasons. Most important, they assume that foreign policy is driven by domestic concerns, rather than international ones, and that decisions are made to protect domestic constituencies rather than national interest.

In particular, invading Iraq for the purpose of advancing the interest of American oil corporations such as Halliburton was not balance-of-power policy at play. Generating U.S. security with respect to energy, however, might be consistent with balance-of-power policy if it aimed to protect oil security by balancing against the stronger actor. One might argue that the United States invaded Iraq in order to prevent it from invading Persian Gulf oil fields in the future, which would have increased Iraq's relative power in the region. But not much evidence suggests that this concern was a key motivation. Nor would a future concern about the balance of power necessarily confirm that balance-of-power policy was at play. An invasion of Iraq on the basis of a future concern would do more to confirm that balance-of-threat policy was at play because it asserts that threat perception is a product partly of how actors view the intentions of others rather than their capability. Of course, even if we assume that the United States was partly motivated by oil, it was also motivated by oil issues that had little to do with balancing, such as liberating Iraqi oil fields for higher oil production or creating an alternative to heavy reliance on Saudi oil.

Faulty Intelligence

Although faulty intelligence is not a motivation, it certainly can affect foreign policy actions, and when it is present, it makes it harder to conclude that any conscious design such as balancing policy is at play. Faulty intelligence predisposes states to stumble into foreign policy actions, rather than to manage them deftly in balance-of-power machinations. Even if faulty intelligence leads to actions that conform with balancing, these actions would be taken for nonbalancing reasons. And in the case of the 2003 war, faulty intelligence led to actions that were quite significantly different from what we would expect from balancing considerations.

Balance-of-Threat Policy

If the United States did not balance much against power, how about against threat? The case of the Iraq war does offer some support for balance-of-threat policy, but not unambiguously. As laid out early in this chapter, the Bush administration asserted that it was concerned about Iraq's aggressive intentions and believed that Iraq intended to harm American interests. In this view, even if Iraq did not pose an immediate threat, it could develop into one over time. Its track record suggested that someday it would once again attack its neighbors, threaten global oil supplies, and even use WMD outside the region, possibly on the American mainland. But there are four problems with this explanation.

First, balance-of-threat policy is aimed mainly at existing threats, rather than just anticipated ones. President Bush asserted, "If we wait for the threat to fully materialize, we will have waited too long."[120]

Second, the United States was likely motivated by more than just threat perception in invading Iraq. For instance, a slew of domestic- and personal-level motivations may have played a role in the decision to go to war, as considered earlier in this chapter. The more the United States was motivated by such factors, the less it was engaging in balance against threat.

Third, and perhaps most significant, in order to say that balancing against threat was in play, it is important to show that Iraq was viewed as a greater threat to American interests than Iran was, but whether Iraq was viewed as the greater threat is not entirely clear. Some evidence would support this interpretation. After all, Iraq had invaded Iran and Kuwait, gassed its own people, and was involved in two major conflicts with the United States and its allies. These things cannot be said of Iran. Iran, moreover, was not in breach of seventeen UN resolutions. North Korea and Iran appeared to be treated as secondary threats to Iraq, on which the administration focused primary attention in the period following September 11.[121]

At the same time, it is possible to argue that the Iraq threat was exaggerated in order to support the case for war. The Downing Street Memo notes that British foreign secretary Jack Straw, a close colleague of Colin Powell's, believed that "Bush had made up his mind to take military action, even if the timing was not yet decided. But the case was thin. Saddam was not threatening his neighbors, and his WMD capability was less than that of Libya, North Korea, or Iran."[122] This memo did not represent a criticism of the United States but rather the sincere interpretation of America's best ally in the conflict.

Some would argue that neoconservatives who saw Saddam as incorrigible and wanted to democratize Iraq and the Middle East duped key administration officials into viewing Iraq as connected to Al Qaeda. In this view, U.S. policy toward Iraq was not driven necessarily by national security concerns. It may have been driven by a particular ideology about how to govern the world,[123] which was related to but different from concerns about Iraq's threat to American security.

Fourth, Iran was also viewed as a significant threat. Indeed, it was ranked as one of the most dangerous supporters of terrorism and was listed as part of the "axis of evil." According to one account based on declassified documents and interviews with former high-level sources in the American and Iranian governments, Iran, in fact, was known to have been much closer to developing nuclear weapons than the Bush administration let on; it had much stronger ties to terrorism than Iraq did; and it even sheltered Al Qaeda officials, including Osama bin Laden.[124]

One could argue that the United States attacked Iraq rather than Iran not because Iraq was the greater threat but rather for other reasons. One is that Iraq was an easier target than Iran and even North Korea for that matter.[125] The United Nations had a long-standing record against Iraq, making it easier to gain international support against Iraq than Iran. Moreover, Iraq's smaller population could be expected to want Saddam gone much more than Iran's much larger population would accept having the revolutionary regime eliminated. If American forces faced an insurgency in Iraq, they might face a nightmare in Iran. In addition, if the United States did want to democratize the Arab world, Persian Iran was not the right model. Arab Iraq would be far better.

Conclusion

The story of why the United States invaded Iraq and to what extent balancing strategies were at play is complex. It is worth repeating that divining American motivations for war represents academic conjecture. Still, it appears that the United States invaded Iraq chiefly because it feared WMD in the hands of a dictator and assumed the worst about his connections to terrorism. These concerns were significantly piqued and reframed by the attack on September 11. That tectonic event altered the prism through which Bush administration officials saw the world and Iraq's threat. This event can help explain why the United States saw Iraq so differently than did many other countries around the world.

American fears and concerns after 9/11 were heightened by poor intelligence, which, when seen through the "9/11 prism," took on new meaning. Most likely, this intelligence was also used selectively or outright manipulated by some officials to justify a war that the administration thought was necessary. While 9/11 created a potential strategic rationale for going to war against Iraq, it also allowed the administration to garner public support for war, which had been lacking even after the United States made regime change in Iraq its official policy in 1998.

By eliminating Saddam's regime and refashioning Iraq, the administration could also advance democratization in the Middle East. If terrorists were hatched partly because they lived in repressive societies, democratic "shock therapy" to the region might ameliorate this problem. In the process, the United States could help secure Iraq as a hedge against post–September 11 instability in oil-rich Saudi Arabia.

Of course, we cannot rule out domestic and personal motivations for war, but they do not appear to be as important as the other motivations explored herein. After all, they had not motivated war earlier, in the absence of these other motivations.

The story of balance-of-power strategy in the Persian Gulf is that it was often interrupted by one or more priorities. Over time, the United States tended to drift farther from a balance-of-power approach in the Gulf. The case of the Iraq war of 2003 supports this point. Balance-of-power policies were not in evidence in U.S. foreign policy in this case. Some evidence could be interpreted to support the notion that the United States balanced against threat, but even in this respect the picture is mixed.

CHAPTER NINE

The Decline of
Balance-of-Power Policy

So far, this book has shown that the United States did not behave much as an active balancer in the Gulf region, although when it did balance, it did so more often against the most threatening state in the region than the strongest one. This chapter introduces a temporal dimension to this analysis. It first draws on the foregoing chapters to show that balance-of-power policy declined in America's approach to the region over time, as did balance-against-threat policy, albeit to a lesser extent. More important, it then proceeds to explain the decline in balancing over time.

Evidence of Decline

Much evidence supports the notion that balance-of-power policy declined in U.S. foreign policy toward the region. In the 1970s, the notion of balance of power was prominent in the realist approach to world politics pursued by President Nixon and Henry Kissinger. America's quasi alliance with Iran was an effort to balance against Moscow at the global level, partly by checking Iraq at the regional level.

In the early 1980s, the United States tilted in Iraq's direction so as to balance against Iran. But as the decade wore on, American behavior clashed rather strongly with balancing. Indeed, the Iran-Contra and constructive engagement episodes ran fundamentally counter to both balance-of-power and balance-of-threat policy. Instead of balancing against power and threat, the United States took actions that actually increased power and threat.

In the 1990s, the United States adopted a policy of dual containment. It sought to constrain any actor from gaining hegemony in the Gulf region. On the surface, that policy seemed to smack of elements of balance of power because it also aimed to prevent predominant power from developing in any one state. Containment, however, is not the same as balance of power. Balance-of-power policy is fundamentally concerned with the relative position of states and requires that the stronger actor be balanced against. In contrast, containment is not necessarily about the relative position of states because the weaker state in a region can still be the target of containment or may be contained for reasons that have little to do with systemic realities. Containment may also be practiced against more than one state, as in the dual containment of Iran and Iraq. This is not how balance-of-power policy works, unless it aims to check an alliance. That was not the case in the Gulf, since Iran and Iraq were not in alliance and, in fact, were adversaries.

The policy of containment-plus moved even further away from balance-of-power policies. It deviated in the ways described above but also added an important element: regime change. Although regime change under containment-plus was to be conducted politically rather than through an invasion of Iraq, the policy itself did not resemble balance-of-power approaches, since these approaches do not aim at removing a regime within a state.

Some decision makers and scholars argued that containment should continue to be the primary U.S. approach toward Iraq, but the Bush administration had a different view after September 11.[1] It heralded in an aggressive form of preemption and prevention. If U.S. policy had moved from a strong inclination to balance in the early 1980s toward a mixed set of strategies in the mid- to late 1980s and toward dual containment in the 1990s and then containment-plus, it now took yet another step further in its movement away from balancing.

Preemption and balance-of-power policy are not outright contradictory. If preemption deliberately aims to weaken a state in order to re-create a balance of power or to check that state's outsized capability relative to other states, it could fall under balance of power. But that is not the case with regime change in Iraq. Washington did not pursue regime change because it was concerned about Iraq's capability relative to Iran; it did so for a variety of other reasons, including mistaken concerns about weapons of mass destruction (WMD) and Iraq's connection to terrorists. This point is fundamental in considering the role of balance of power in American policy.

The shift away from balance-of-power policy could be seen in the extent to which the United States was willing to take the risk of Iraq being dismembered or of Iran emerging the much stronger power in the region. In 1982, the United States was not willing to tolerate such an outcome, and it tilted in Iraq's favor. By 1991, Washington was to some extent concerned about Iraq falling apart if the United States invaded Baghdad at the end of the Gulf war, although this concern was not a primary consideration. Under containment-plus, the United States was much more willing to risk Iraq's dismemberment, as it planned politically to remove Saddam Hussein from power. By the war of 2003, the United States took an even greater risk of dismembering Iraq because it now would use force to eliminate Saddam's regime, creating the potential of sending Iraq into chaos or at least of leaving Iran the much stronger regional actor.

Why Balance-of-Power Policy Declined

The following sections identify and elucidate the four developments that explain the decline of American balancing. In brief, the end of the Cold War facilitated efforts by the United States to adopt nonbalancing strategies that would otherwise have threatened Moscow, such as invading its ally, Iraq. The rise of American global power, important in its own right even before the end of the Cold War, provided the United States with the capability to apply nonbalancing and more aggressive approaches in the region. The September 11 attacks highlighted the risks of transnational terrorism, which generated security challenges at the domestic and transnational level against which balance-of-power policy was not effective. Meanwhile, domestic politics in the United States were also salient. Indeed, the rise of neoconservatism meant that balancing would lose whatever luster it had as an idea and practice in U.S. foreign policy. All these developments reinforced one another at different times and decreased the prominence of balance-of-power policy in U.S. foreign policy in the Persian Gulf.

The End of the Cold War

The end of the Cold War left Washington without a significant global rival in the region. Washington's attention shifted from jockeying for influence against the Soviets to focusing more on regional threats such as Iraq and Iran.

The end of the Cold War created an environment in which the United States was more likely to deviate from balance-of-power policy. First, balancing strategies were more useful during the Cold War because they tend to be less provocative than other forms of statecraft and thus less likely to spark confrontation between superpowers. Nonbalancing strategies such as dual containment, military preemption, and efforts to contain an "axis of evil" that included Iran, Iraq, and North Korea are usually more provocative than balancing approaches, and these nonbalancing strategies became easier after the fall of the Soviet Union.

During the Cold War, the United States was also hampered in how it could treat Iraq. The 1991 war is a case in point. Moscow had long-standing relations with Iraq and did not want to see it attacked by U.S.-led forces in 1991, but Soviet leader Mikhail Gorbachev believed, as one high-level insider noted, that cooperation with the United States in a period of improving relations was critical.[2]

Even with superpower relations warming, Moscow was still split on the issue of how to approach Iraq. Foreign Minister (until January 1991) Eduard Shevardnadze represented one side as the sole spokesperson for closer cooperation with the United States; the Arabists, who were led by Yevgeny Primakov, promoted a more traditional role in the Middle East.[3] Primakov, who was close to Iraq's elites, including Saddam Hussein, did not want to see Iraq undermined.[4] The internal power struggle in Moscow remained intense, and it was not clear that the United States understood the opposition that Shevardnadze and Gorbachev faced from the military, the Arabists, and others who resented U.S. power in the Middle East and globally, opposition that in fact influenced Gorbachev to turn to the right in the political spectrum.[5] To entice Gorbachev into further cooperation against Iraq at a Helsinki summit meeting, Bush offered significant economic incentives. Gorbachev denied a quid pro quo, but the record revealed otherwise. Indeed, Bush even asserted that Moscow's "convincing cooperation" made him "inclined to recommend as close cooperation in the economic field as possible."[6]

Moscow supported U.S.-led sanctions against Baghdad during the conflict and UN Resolution 687 at the end of it. Debates continued about how to approach relations with Iraq, with some calling for their termination and others calling for them to be nurtured, but Moscow was not reluctant to take a tough line against Baghdad. Thus, it condemned Iraq in June 1992 when it was revealed that Iraq was hiding nuclear weapons research material and later that year when it endorsed a U.S.-led resolution calling on Iraq to meet all its obligations under UN Resolution 687.[7]

During the Cold War, Moscow clearly would have vigorously opposed an attack on Iraq on the order of the war of 2003. Partly because of this opposition, America would have been less likely to launch it and to pursue a policy of pre-emption, which went against the grain of balancing strategies. As the rules of the game changed with the end of the Cold War, so did the range of actions that Washington could take in the region. The more nuanced and less threatening balance-of-power approach could be jettisoned for more aggressive strategies.

Second, with the Cold War over, the United States did not have to be nearly as concerned that its foreign policy in the region would leave Moscow with the potential to create political inroads with Iran and Arab Gulf states. That was not the case in the late 1970s when Moscow sought to capitalize on the Iranian revolution or in the 1980s when a strong-armed American approach toward Iran allowed Moscow to cast itself as the noninterventionist power and to paint Washington as imperialistic. For example, the U.S. bombing of an Iranian oil platform in April 1988 was described in *Pravda* as "primitive," and the shooting down of the Iranian airbus by the USS *Vincennes* on July 3, 1988, was described by *Tass* as "by no means accidental" but rather "a direct result of a policy of force by the U.S."[8] Iran expressed its gratitude for the Soviet position on this tragedy and stepped up its high-level visits to the Soviet Union.[9] First Deputy Minister of Affairs Yu M. Vorontsov was invited to Iran, where both sides agreed that the enormous U.S. military presence in the region remained "the principal destabilizing factor there."[10]

Moscow's efforts to exploit American foreign policy toward the region yielded it some gains that concerned Washington. Soviet-Iranian relations continued to improve in 1989. A February communiqué from Khomeini confirmed Iran's commitment to Soviet-Iranian friendship.[11] Shevardnadze's trip to Iran in the following month was viewed in Moscow as marking "a new and higher level" of bilateral relations.[12] In June, significant bilateral agreements were signed; among other things, Moscow agreed to "cooperate with the Iranian side in strengthening its defense capabilities," which included a major arms sale to Iran.[13] Thereafter, Iran expressed its satisfaction with Moscow on several occasions.[14]

Third, during the Cold War, states were more willing to support American balancing efforts in the Gulf than they would be after the Cold War ended. The fear of Moscow was never as strong in the Gulf as the United States might have wanted, but it was a concern. The United States focused more on Moscow than on regional threats, while regional actors focused more on regional threats than on Moscow.[15] But they were all concerned about threats at the global and regional level, which helped strengthen their cooperation in ways that made balancing more possible when it did occur.

Fourth, the extent to which balancing was prominent in the overall mix of American approaches depended in part on the origin of the threats to American interests. During the Cold War, the major threats came from states — namely, the Soviet Union, Iran, and sometimes Iraq. As time progressed, these threats decreased. Iran and Iraq were weakened by the Iran-Iraq War; Iran's revolution mellowed over time; the Soviet Union fell; and Saddam Hussein's regime was removed in 2003. Since balancing approaches focused at the state level, as concern about states decreased, so did the relative importance of balancing approaches.

Although the level of threats from states diminished over time, the same cannot be said about threats to U.S. interests from within states in the region. After the Cold War, the United States faced an array of domestic-level threats. They included home-grown terrorism and domestic actors that support it, as well as the sometimes connected problem of dealing with failed states and nation building. The latter was true in Bosnia in 1995 and Kosovo in 1999, and in Afghanistan in 2001 following the 9/11 attacks. The elimination of Saddam Hussein's regime highlighted this shift most dramatically. Iraq's regime had posed a threat to other states in the region, but after the fall of Saddam, the real threat emerged from within Iraq as a virulent anti-American insurgency.

In the post–Cold War and post–9/11 world, the term *balance* took on new meanings. In Iraq, the United States sought a balance of tribes and ethnic groups so that a representative government could form and endure, rather than one that was imbalanced to the point that it sowed the seeds for its future demise. In Iran, the United States was at least as concerned with the balance of factions at the domestic level as it was with abstract notions of the balance of power at the interstate level. It clearly wanted the more moderate factions to prevail over the mullahs, with the support of a liberalizing population.

And in the broader region, it sought "a balance of power for freedom" — a mantra that Bush administration officials repeated numerous times after the Iraq war of 2003, following its enshrinement in the U.S. National Security Strategy of September 2002.[16] Although this verbal concoction was interesting, it oddly combined the realist term "balance of power" with the liberal notion of "freedom." As Rice asserted, "Our goal today, then, is not just a favorable balance of power, but what President Bush has called a balance of power that favors freedom."[17] It is not fully clear what the concept means, but one can interpret it to mean that an imbalance of power in favor of the United States mattered insofar as it promoted democratization. Interpreting it that way is something like sub-contracting realism to serve liberalism. Balance of power would serve a new goal and not one subscribed to it in theory. It would now generate freedom rather than stability. In this sense, it would have a moral purpose and not just serve the benefits of amoral stability, the likes of which balance-of-power policies were intended to create.

Perhaps these new incarnations of "balance" were a way to salvage or reinvent a venerable concept at a time when the world had become a bit too messy for it to operate easily. Traditional balancing approaches were not intended to deal with ethnic strife, religious radicalism, inflamed insurgents, dysfunctional parliaments, maximalist terrorists, and the breakdown of central state functions.

Fifth, during the Cold War, the ends often justified the means, and thus Washington could not push its values if doing so would harm its chances for success in the Cold War. Quite the contrary, it often overlooked the abuses of dictators and autocrats so as to gain their support against Moscow.[18] Indeed, even thinkers who believed that America had a mission to spread its views around the world always recognized, as one scholar put it, the "necessity of keeping America's powder dry."[19] Washington could pontificate, even huff and puff, but it could not take exceptionalism to the point that it threatened to antagonize Moscow and trigger serious confrontation. That situation changed with the end of the Cold War.

The Rise of American Power

The end of the Cold War contributed to another development that was important in its own right: the rise of American power. As suggested earlier in the book, the rise in American power in the Persian Gulf region took place over four decades. At the global level, this development was stunning. In 1980, America was in recession, and Ronald Reagan was elected by the American people with what appeared to be a mandate to shore up American power and pride. At the time, the Soviet Union appeared to be ascendant in global political rivalry, and Japan seemed to be eclipsing the United States on the global economic stage. Yet it would not be long before the Japanese bubble would burst and the Japanese miracle would turn into the Japanese economic debacle. Not much later, the Soviet Union would disintegrate.

American dominance was certainly aided by these tectonic events as well as by its own military, technological, and economic improvements. Reagan, capitalizing on public concerns about America's role in the world, launched a massive defense-spending spree and assumed a more stern and anticommunist approach at the global level. By the 1990s, the United States had emerged as a colossus, a powerhouse in world politics.[20] In the words of political scientist G. John Ikenberry, it had "no serious competitor in sight."[21] Just a few short years before the 1991 Gulf war, the big debate revolved around whether the United States was in decline, but after it the debate turned to whether any state in history was as powerful as America.[22]

The rise in American power reinforced an effect of the end of the Cold War analyzed earlier in this chapter: Washington could pursue more aggressive foreign policy strategies in lieu of balancing. It could practice a strategy of unilateralism and enforce its interests with less support from others. Thus, a strategy based on using local powers, which it practiced in the 1970s, was not nearly as necessary. The caution of the post-Vietnam Nixon Doctrine could be replaced with the assertiveness of war, containment, regime change, and finally outright invasion. Collective security as well was less important because Washington had greater capability to bring about outcomes on its own. It did not need to use the auspices of the United Nations as much or a coalition that could increase its capability and legitimacy outside UN action. This development might help explain why the elder Bush was much more multilateral in his approach toward Iraq in 1990–91 than his son was in 2003.

The rise of American power also allowed Washington to strong-arm potential adversaries that it had placated in the past, such as Iran in the Iran-Contra affair or Iraq during constructive engagement. The rise of American power even led some actors, including Saddam Hussein in his famous speech of February 24, 1990, to refer to the United States as a regional hegemon.[23] In fact, although the United States became a regional powerhouse, it never regulated regional economic, political, and security dimensions to the extent characteristic of the British era, but it developed enough power to be able to pursue more aggressive strategies.

The United States, for instance, could never have reversed Iraq's invasion of Kuwait were it not for the development of its rapid deployment forces capability, of access to regional facilities, and of the massive infrastructure in Saudi Arabia for the deployment of American forces and for the coordination of U.S. air force attacks. All these assets were developed in the late 1970s and especially in the 1980s in response to fears about a Soviet invasion of the Gulf region from Afghanistan and concerns that Iran might win the Iran-Iraq War and dominate the region.[24] In Desert Storm, the United States for the first time actually utilized in a full-scale manner the major capabilities it had been developing, especially in the 1980s.

Nor could the United States as easily have made the decision to launch the even more aggressive Iraq war of 2003, which involved preemption and provoked global controversy and much opposition, had its capabilities not risen in the region and globally. In fact, this capability was critical in allowing for such a powerful foreign policy in the beating heart of the Arab world. Because the invasion of Iraq was so controversial, we can only imagine that a weaker United States would have faced an even more difficult time executing it. In contrast, a globally dominant United States had greater freedom to pursue this approach because it could expect to be in a better position to eliminate Saddam's regime while still protecting its other interests around the world. In a more dangerous world where the United States lacked predominant power, it could not have expected such an outcome. Thus, we could surmise that it would have been less likely to resort to force compared with other alternatives.

The fact that the Cold War tied down American forces in Europe and elsewhere is also important. Many of the troops for Desert Storm came from the European theater, where their role was to deter a Soviet invasion of Western Europe. Obviously, these forces could not have been withdrawn from Europe had the Cold War not ended. That Moscow no longer viewed Iraq as its regional ally in the post–Cold War era also made the invasion of Iraq easier to undertake.

In a way, then, the United States invaded Iraq partly because it could, because it had the capability to do so. Without such preponderance, its freedom of action in the foreign policy realm would have likely been curtailed.

The rise of American capability was important both in quantity and in quality. As Paul Kennedy chronicles, great powers in history husbanded their economic power but were also able to make breakthroughs in military capability. Their eminence was aided by qualitative military breakthroughs. Hence, armed with the new weapons, the musket and cannon, Russia could expand and establish itself as one the "gunpowder empires."[25]

In modern times, precision bombing made it easier to take the country to war. It created the temptation of demonstrating American technological wizardry and prowess. Thus, the "Shock and Awe" campaign that touched off the Iraq war of 2003 employed an array of precision weapons that enabled Washington to flex its muscles and to send messages to would-be aggressors that they would be punished. Presumably, it was also easier to launch a seemingly antiseptic military campaign than one of anticipated death and destruction.

In addition, precision bombing decreased the likelihood of American casualties and collateral damage, which presumably made the use of force more publicly acceptable. The armed forces used also did not have to be as large and certainly were less likely to be drawn from a national draft. Thus the public was less involved directly in the use of force by the military, which meant that it would be less likely to put the brakes on the use of force than would be the case otherwise.

America's power also allowed it to pursue grand visions that required significant capability, such as the spread of democracy, even if this vision required the use of force to establish Iraq as a model for the rest of the region to follow. As the 2002 National Security Strategy stated, American global preeminence allows for the United States to "extend the benefits of freedom across the globe."[26] In this sense, America's power has been a fundamental determinant of its foreign policy.[27]

After 9/11, Washington was more likely to seek predominance in world affairs.[28] The end of the Cold War, combined with its own rise in capability, predisposed it to such ambitions. Meanwhile, September 11 stirred its worst fears and pushed it to try to realize these ambitions. Aiming for predominance in world politics ran counter to the fundamental elements of balancing policy.

All this is not to say that the rise of American capability actually gave the United States more influence or success. That is a different question, as the Iraq occupation underscored. But Washington's behavior was affected by the capabilities at its disposal. Overall, the weaker it was in the region, the more it needed to rely on balancing strategy because it lacked the ability to deter, mitigate, and contain threats through its own capability. As U.S. capability in the region increased, Washington could be more aggressive or resort to force either in an alliance or unilaterally.

Transnational Terrorism and Balance-of-Power Strategies

The rise of transnational terrorism, especially after 9/11, made it harder for the United States to balance against threat and power. The war on terrorism clashed with balance-of-power approaches in fundamental ways.

First, balancing approaches treat states as unitary actors, whereas the war on terrorism treats states as open systems penetrated by terrorists. Fighting terrorism requires penetrating societies in order to attack terrorist groups directly and the broad infrastructure of financing and training that supports them. Neither balance-of-power policy nor containment, nor deterrence for that matter, would eliminate terrorist threats. These strategies could not eliminate the leaders who could transfer WMD materials, technology, and knowledge to terrorists. Quite the contrary, these strategies could provoke states to support terrorism. They might do so out of revenge or as a way of competing in a manner that was not possible on the battlefield.

The shift toward a focus on domestic threats was tied to a broader move in world politics. As two high-level officials in the administration of George W. Bush put it, in "today's interconnected world, weak and failed states pose an acute risk to U.S. and global security. Indeed, they present one of the most important foreign policy challenges of the contemporary era."[29] It is hard to imagine those words uttered by top officials in previous eras, but the question of failed states, though important for decades, if not longer, became linked to transnational terrorism, especially after 9/11, and thus assumed much greater salience. In this sense, the contrast between the period of the 1991 war and that of the 2003 war was stark. As Fouad Ajami put it, after Desert Storm, Iraq was defeated, and the "internal order of the Arab states did not concern George H. W. Bush."[30] In contrast, after September 11, the administration was fundamentally concerned with the internal order of Arab states, with democratization, with attacking terrorists holed up inside states, and with changing the domestic environment in which terrorism is hatched.

Second, the war on terrorism is focused not only on threats that arise domestically but also on those that are transnational, which also does not fall neatly into the balance-of-power model. The terrorist threat exists at once below the level of the state, in the stealthy ether of societal penetration, and above the level of the state, in the transnational space of ideology and group interaction. Indeed, as the quintessential extremists, jihadists seek a universal, unified *umma*, or religious community in transnational space, rather than its division within and into nation-states.[31] And they see the struggle with the West as implacable and transnational and one requiring violence.[32] Balance-of-power policy does not work well with such threats. As Raju Thomas points out, "balance of power politics face an uncertain future at the onset of the 21st century," in part because of the rise of nonstate terrorist organizations against which traditional forms of statecraft do not work well.[33]

Third, balancing approaches also seek to address imbalances of capability at the systemic level. The war on terrorism, in contrast, is not focused on relative capability. It is clear that in terms of capability the United States is far stronger than terrorist groups. If anything, what is relevant is not the balance of capability but the balance of resolve and strategy.

Fourth, if the end of the Cold War created greater opportunities for the United States to pursue an aggressive regional approach to security, September 11 gave it significant impetus to do so. One of the reasons the United States did not practice balance-of-power policy in the Iraq war was that this approach clashed with the strategies that were used in the global war on terrorism. In fact, balancing strategies may redress imbalances at the systemic level while worsening opportunities to fight the war on terrorism because they train our eyes on the wrong level of analysis, divert resources there, and motivate the types of policies that cause resentment. Thus, coddling dictators may serve to keep a rising power in check, but it may well anger jihadists who loathe repressive and secular autocrats.

The following strategies were adopted in the war on terrorism but are largely or totally inconsistent with balance-of-power policy: regime change and preemption or prevention; democratization; and the use of soft power. They are analyzed in the following pages.

Regime change is not a balance-of-power technique, as discussed earlier in the book. Nor could it be expected to achieve a greater likelihood of balance of power in the region than would be the case if Saddam were left in power. Regime change is one form of preemption.

The Bush administration believed that preemption was critical against terrorists because they use asymmetric warfare, an approach that exploits vulnerable nodes in an unexpected manner that is hard to detect and defend against. Once the stealth attack is in motion, it is difficult to stop. We can contrast fighting against asymmetric warfare with balancing against threat or power. The latter can be done more slowly because threats often gather more gradually at the interstate level, as do changes in the distribution of capability. Moreover, the targets of balancing are clearer. The target is the strongest or most threatening state, and its address is known. In contrast, terrorists represent more elusive targets, even if they can be identified.

Fighting asymmetric warfare requires focusing on particular individuals and groups, which is about as far from balance of power in practice as one can imagine. The rise of asymmetrical warfare generated a shift in Pentagon doctrine. The transformation of the military aimed to make its forces lighter, smaller, and more agile for the purpose of fighting terrorism, even at the individual level. The

United States was successful in deterring major global war during the Cold War, or at least the record would suggest so, but asymmetrical warfare poses a very different fight. As a former Pentagon official points out, "History was telling us that we were moving progressively away from warfare against states or even blocs of states and toward a new era of warfare against individuals."[34] Osama bin Laden and his coterie became serious targets whose assassination or capture could improve American security as much as winning some small wars in past eras.

The rise of liberal notions in American foreign policy, culminating with the democratization drive in the Middle East, also contrasts with balancing approaches. In the 1980s, liberal notions of democratization and a new world order were inapplicable to the Middle East. In the 1990–91 Gulf crisis, the notion of a new world order was bandied about genuinely and also for purposes of selling the war and wrapping it in the garb of morality.[35] The Clinton administration dropped the notion of a new world order but did push human rights at the global level. This type of liberal internationalism played itself out in Somalia, Haiti, and Bosnia and in the U.S.-led NATO war against Serbia over Kosovo.

President George W. Bush introduced a different component of liberal internationalism — not on the human rights front but rather in pushing democratization in the Middle East. Under this motivation, invading Iraq made sense because people would be liberated to adopt American-style government, even if mixed with strong elements of political Islam and nurtured in a different cultural context.

Balance-of-power policy gets lost in some of these notions, as it did under the administration of Woodrow Wilson. It is not that liberal internationalism and balance-of-power policy are mutually exclusive always, but often they are.

Democratization might be viewed as a type of soft-power strategy, but soft power is a broader notion. Soft power, a concept coined by international relations professor Joseph Nye, is "the ability to get what you want through attraction rather than coercion or payments."[36] In contrast to the hard power of economic and military might, it refers to the "ability to shape the preferences of others," which involves "leading by example and attracting others to do what you want" through things such as attractiveness of political institutions, culture, values, and policies that exude moral authority.[37]

As many observers have noted, the war on terrorism is more than a war of hardware. It is a software war in which ideas are competing for attention and in which the ability to co-opt others is important in preventing Al Qaeda from gaining more adherents and sympathizers, and in gaining supporters in the fight against terrorism who will speak out against it, cut off its finances, legislate against it, share intelligence about it, and ultimately crack down on terrorist cells. One former CIA analyst asserted that bin Laden was "the most respected, loved, romantic, charismatic, and perhaps able figure in the last 150 years of Islamic history . . . a practical warrior, not an apocalyptic terrorist in search of Armageddon."[38] That characterization is doubtful but contains kernels of truth, as suggested by polls of Muslims worldwide. In this sense, transnational liberalism, which is the strongest global ideology, is confronted by a primordial brew of political and religious ideas that are sometimes carried under the terrorist banner. Most of the audience will not emulate Al Qaeda, but it would be a mistake simply to confine Al Qaeda to the lunatic fringe of global Islam.[39] Jihadists see a profound incompatibility between the Islamic and Western worlds and desire to bring about a confrontation between Islamic and Western civilization.[40] Al Qaeda's actions suggest that it is trying to fuel a war of ideas, to agitate the audience to its cause, to win the hearts and minds of the Muslims.

For his part, President Bush became increasingly sensitized to the notion of transnational conflict but seemed to dismiss its importance. As he pointed out in his September 22, 2004, address to the UN General Assembly, "When it comes to the desire for liberty and justice, there is no clash of civilizations."[41] However, over time, the Bush administration increasingly recognized that the war on terrorism is a war on ideas as well. In pushing for funding for State Department initiatives, Secretary Powell asserted that it has become much more urgent since 9/11 to "teach the world about America, about our values system, what we believe in," through an active public diplomacy program.[42] In the summer of 2005, the president appointed his longtime confidante, Karen Hughes, as undersecretary of state for public diplomacy and public affairs. The post clearly was aimed at fighting a global war of ideas against a shadowy enemy that had no zip code but did have admirers worldwide.

Fifth, the war on terrorism also complicates the ability to gain the support of states for balancing efforts. The war on terrorism requires the cooperation of other states. They are needed to stem terrorist financing, to allow basing rights and access to attack terrorists, and to crack down at home in ways that weaken terrorism. Policies that are necessary to obtain such cooperation may make balancing strategies more difficult. The United States might very well placate the most threatening or powerful regional state if doing so means that it will obtain important support in the war on terrorism. The war on terrorism also sometimes places greater priority on fighting terrorism even if that runs counter to creating the potential to balance or to balancing itself.

Saudi Arabia is a case in point. It has played a pivotal role in American security. Anytime Washington has balanced since 1980, the Saudis have played a role. Yet the war on terrorism has altered the U.S.-Saudi relationship.

The war on terrorism made Saudi Arabia a greater concern for American strategists. Since it was viewed by many as an exporter of terrorism, it became more important for the United States to try to alter the Saudi domestic milieu, pressure the Saudi regime to reform its education and religious system, and liberalize, with the hope that angry young men, once given a voice in the affairs of the state, would be less likely to support or engage in terrorism. But such an approach also threatened to undermine the Al Saud and to harm the U.S.-Saudi strategic relationship, which was important to balancing approaches.

Sixth, while the United States faced a shift toward greater domestic-level threats in the region and less serious interstate threats, so did key Arab Gulf states. They faced a trade-off. Supporting the United States was positive for their security from external threats but often posed the risk of alienating or angering important domestic constituencies that resented the connection to America. It is fair to say that the greater the level of external threat, the more likely the Arab monarchies would tolerate the costs of their strategic relationship with Washington. It is also fair to say that the lower the level of domestic threat to their regimes, the more likely they would accept the U.S. connection, thus making it easier for the United States to balance with their support.

Events at the global and regional level, however, affected this calculus. Because the Soviet Union fell and because Iran and Iraq were weakened by war, interstate threats to the stability of Gulf states diminished. At the same time, the various wars in the Gulf brought American forces into the heart of Arab world politics, into the land of Mecca and Medina; they heightened sensitivities to U.S. involvement in the region; and they may have contributed to terrorism.

Al Qaeda is a case in point. The fact that the Saudi regime allowed U.S. forces entry in 1991 and let some forces stay thereafter strongly motivated Bin Laden and other Saudis who opposed the regime and hated Americans.[43] Bin Laden offered the services of his Afghan Arabs in the effort to protect the kingdom against Saddam Hussein but was rebuffed by defense minister Prince Sultan. Sultan replied, "There are no caves in Kuwait," and Bin Laden responded, "We will fight them with our faith."[44] Since at least 1992, Bin Laden singled out the

United States for attack, suggesting a direct time line to the 1991 Gulf war. In his August 1996 Declaration of Jihad against the Americans Occupying the Land of the Two Holy Places, he asserted, in fact, that to "push the enemy — the greatest *kufr* [infidel] — out of the country is a prime duty. No other duty after Belief is more important than [this] duty. Utmost effort should be made to prepare and instigate the *umma* against the enemy, the American-Israeli alliance."[45] In his second paragraph, following typical praises for Allah, he asserted that the "Arabian peninsula has never — since Allah made it flat, created its desert, and encircled its seas — been stormed by any forces like the crusader armies spreading in it like locusts, eating its riches."[46] After describing a variety of aggressions against the Muslim world by the Zionist-Crusader alliance, the declaration referred to the occupation of the two holy places, Mecca and Medina, as the most serious transgressions of all.[47]

The specter of transnational terrorism and of terrorist cells seeking to overthrow Gulf monarchies also increased or seemed to increase the perception of domestic threats. Bin Laden had his sights on more than American power. In fact, it is probable that his main target was the Al Saud. This slowly became clear to the Saudi regime. In May 2003, Al Qaeda bombed Western residential compounds in Riyadh, killing thirty-five people, inaugurating a string of similar attacks. The Saudis had been slow to realize the extent of their problems. Prior to the May 2003 crisis, threats to the kingdom either were external or could be viewed as aimed at foreign forces, and the sentiment, as encapsulated by Prince Nayef, was that the Al Qaeda presence in Saudi Arabia was "weak and almost non-existent."[48]

Events in the kingdom made the regime more serious about confronting its own profound and, to some extent, self-inflicted problems of extremism.[49] It cracked down on militants and more zealously sought a dozen prominent Saudis suspected of giving Al Qaeda millions of dollars.[50] Sixteen Al Qaeda-linked suspects were arrested; authorities uncovered a network of Islamic extremists so large that it surprised Saudi officials.[51] These efforts were further energized when investigations revealed that Al Qaeda was effectively organized within Saudi Arabia, that it clearly sought to overthrow the regime, and that it even targeted senior Saudi officials, including interior minister Prince Nayef.[52]

Partly as a result of terrorist threats, the Saudis were more concerned with internal rather than external threats, although they certainly remained concerned about both. Faced with external threats, the Arab Gulf states were more likely to support efforts that could facilitate American balancing. However, faced with internal threats, these same efforts posed a risk to their domestic stability and position and could even exacerbate the internal threats they faced by energizing jihadists or even moderate opposition to their rule. As time wore on, they were less inclined to offer the support that made balancing easier to manage, if that made internal stability harder to maintain. This was a continuum of concerns, but it shifted in favor of addressing domestic threats, and the shift had implications for the United States. Thus, Saudi Arabia proved reluctant to host U.S. forces in the invasion of Iraq, and ultimately American forces left the kingdom altogether in 2003, perhaps because the political costs domestically in Saudi Arabia of keeping them there had begun to outweigh their strategic benefits. The U.S.-Saudi military infrastructure stayed in place for any emergencies, but the United States moved key operations to Qatar and, in fact, established the headquarters of U.S. Central Command (USCENTCOM) there.

The Rise of Neoconservatism

This chapter has focused so far on critical developments in global and Middle East politics which can explain the decline of balance-of-power policy, but one key domestic-level change is also salient. Balance-of-power policy increasingly fell by the wayside partly because neoconservatives gained influence in Washington.[53] Their ideology clashed with balance of power, which they saw as backward and ineffective, and sprouted wings after September 11.[54]

We might have expected the United States to eschew balance-of-power policy in earlier eras. It was far less accepted by American elites than by their European counterparts, who elevated it to the point that "pamphleteers and historians were agreed" that it outright safeguarded the "peace and freedom of Europe in the 18th century."[55] It reached almost God-like political stature in the nineteenth-century European balance-of-power system inaugurated at the Congress of Vienna in 1815, which established a balancing mechanism against any future Napoleons.

Moreover, the United States did not need to practice balance-of-power politics as much, given its geography. The Founding Fathers understood the European balance of power and manipulated it first to generate American independence and then to preserve it, but in the decades thereafter the United States enjoyed a secure existence, remote from the dangers that affected and shaped other areas of the world, and did not partake in balance-of-power politics.[56] By the end of World War I, the notion of balance-of-power policy was relegated to the dustbin of history when President Woodrow Wilson cast it aside in favor of the ill-fated collective security mechanism of the League of Nations and the romance of democratization, human rights, and American providence to change the world in its image.

In contrast, the intellectual thought underlying neoconservatism was as old as the Republic. However, neoconservatism as an actual movement emerged in the mid-1970s driven partly by anticommunism, a distrust of détente, and a belief that American strategic superiority could win the Cold War, a view held strongly by President Ronald Reagan, who was influenced by neoconservative thought.[57]

In representing aspects of the older traditions in American foreign policy,[58] the neoconservatives exhibited a Wilsonian skepticism about, even hostility toward, balance-of-power politics. Unlike Wilson, however, they did not promote collective security as an alternative to balancing; rather, they promoted a foreign policy that was not averse to the use of force to bring about democratization and other outcomes in world politics.[59] It is not exactly clear how they came to the conclusion that balance-of-power politics were ineffective or immoral, but it is possible that they believed that President Reagan held this position, which may be quite mistaken,[60] or that their optimism in human progress and democracy led them there.

It is also the case that the changes in world politics explored in this chapter shaped their views or helped them exercise them more effectively. For instance, the rise of American power inspired neoconservatives to push for a stronger foreign policy. As Halper and Clarke put it, for the younger neoconservatives, the "unipolar landscape after Soviet collapse was to be combined with America's surgical and specialized weapon-capabilities to define a new agenda of the possible for U.S. foreign policy."[61] In this way, the neoconservatives, "seduced by the power of U.S. precision weapons," have attempted to make balance of power "yesteryear's phrase."[62] America's power could be applied in the service of democratization, and other states would bandwagon with the United States or join its cause, rather than balance against it, thus creating an imbalance of power in favor of the United States and liberal change.[63]

American power allowed for neoconservatist views to be applied, but neoconservatism also altered how the United States used its own power. As America's power grew in the twentieth century, the United States also proved reluctant to use it easily, thus gaining the label of "reluctant superpower."[64] Even after the end of the Cold War, Richard Haass described the United States as a "Reluctant Sheriff."[65] Neoconservative ideology, however, featured not just a powerful United States but one that would actually use that capability with some zeal.

For their part, William Kristol and Robert Kagan captured the neoconservative mood in asserting that the United States should not be merely an "offshore balancer, a savior of last resort, as many recommend. . . . American pre-eminence cannot be maintained from a distance, by means of some post–Cold War version of the Nixon doctrine, whereby the United States hangs back and keeps its powder dry."[66] This prevailing view among neoconservatives not only downplayed balance-of-power policy but also mocked its easy machinations and goals of creating stability without expending much energy. For the neoconservatives, that goal was not possible and, with the rise of American power, no longer necessary to consider because the United States had the ability to be altogether present in regions, rather than on standby. The rise of American power alone would not necessarily translate into a change in foreign policy. After all, the United States was relatively powerful in the interwar years, but it was also isolationist. The combination of the rise of American power and the ideology of neoconservatism made a more aggressive American foreign policy far more likely.[67]

For the neoconservatives, even the elder Bush was off track. In fact, before affecting the nature of U.S. foreign policy under George W. Bush, they attacked his father's Middle East policy prior to Iraq's invasion of Kuwait. To them, he was a conservative of the old stripe. Capturing their sentiment, Joshua Muravchik asserted, "Bush's courtship of Iraq was justified in part by the need to counterbalance Iran; but we have learned that we also courted Iran. . . . Bush calls this foreign policy realism. But since both of these regimes remain bloodily repressive, internationally mischievous, and implacably hostile to America, just what is realist about it?"[68]

In 1998, the vanguard of the neoconservative movement created the Project for the New American Century. On January 26, 1998, the key members of this movement, including Donald Rumsfeld and Paul Wolfowitz, sent President Clinton a letter, which asserted that the "only acceptable strategy is one that eliminates the possibility that Iraq will be able to use or threaten to use weapons of mass destruction. In the near term, this means the willingness to undertake military action as diplomacy is clearly failing. In the long term, it means removing Saddam Hussein and his regime from power."[69] Many of the signers of this letter would become influential in the administration of George W. Bush, although it should be pointed out that, in contrast to Donald Rumsfeld, the president, vice president, secretary of state, and the national security adviser could not be classified as neoconservatives.[70]

Inasmuch as neoconservatives influenced American foreign policy, they certainly pushed it away from balance of power toward other strategies. Their rise in influence was slow and built over decades, taking some effect at least as early as the 1970s for the purposes of this book. Indeed, as Francis Fukuyama put it, given the "origins of the movement in left-wing anti-communism, it is not surprising that neoconservatives would for the most part end up opposing the realist foreign policy of Henry Kissinger during the 1970s."[71] But although their influence built slowly, it culminated perhaps with the Bush presidency.[72] Halper and Clarke suggest that after 9/11 the neoconservatives were able to seize the reins of U.S. national security policy by capitalizing on the fear and confusion besetting the nation.[73]

While the neoconservatives believed in unrivaled American power, in Washington's ability to use its resources for a vast foreign policy agenda, their detractors cautioned that America could not easily bring about the outcomes it desired, some even referring to the superpower myth.[74] For them, the way for the United States was not to use force in order to reshape the Middle East. That effort had a seductive appeal but was too romantic for the region, and the United States was not the right actor to carry this banner. Nor was it safe to reject the warnings about imperial overstretch, as neoconservatives tended to do.[75]

Conclusion

It is useful to close this chapter with two brief comparisons that underscore how U.S. foreign policy changed in the region and how external and offshore balancing became less prominent. These two comparisons are of the administrations of Richard Nixon and George W. Bush.

President Nixon sought to avoid involvement in the Persian Gulf region in the post-Vietnam period. President George W. Bush launched a massive invasion and occupation of Iraq, generating heavy American casualties in an unpopular war abroad.

The Nixon administration sought to protect American interests in the region through proxies, relying on Iran chiefly but also on Saudi Arabia. The Bush administration did so mainly with American armed forces, and in a much more unilateral manner.

In contrast to the Nixon administration's hands-off foreign policy, the Bush administration adopted a policy of prevention or preemption. It counted on a forward military presence that had been developed over two decades to support its foreign policy, whereas the Nixon administration completely lacked such a presence.

The Nixon administration could not imagine a foreign policy of overthrowing regimes and engaging in nation building in the Middle East. That was not a sensible way to approach a state-centric world, in line with the mandates of realpolitik. The Bush administration did so fundamentally in Iraq.

The Nixon administration did not have an ideological agenda for the region but rather simply wanted to manage its security at the least cost. Ideology was central in the Bush administration policy, which aimed to bring democracy to the Middle East, partly as an antidote to transnational terrorism.

As we can see, balance-of-power policy became increasingly less prominent in American approaches. The central tenets of Nixon's foreign policy were roughly consonant with realism and active balancing. In sharp contrast, the central tenets of Bush's foreign policy did not reflect the approach of an external or offshore balancer. Moreover, America did not pursue a grand strategy that was consistent across this period. Indeed, its policies changed throughout this period and sometimes radically, as the Nixon-Bush comparison should make obvious.

CHAPTER TEN

The Balance Sheet, So to Speak

This chapter cycles back on the book and summarizes and elaborates upon its findings and arguments. It begins by evaluating balance-of-power and balance-of-threat policies and then draws on this analysis for an examination of the grand strategy of balance of power (active and offshore balancing) versus the grand strategy of hegemony. A broad examination is fitting in this chapter because, now that the various policies of the United States have been examined, it is possible to take the long view and to see to what extent we can discern grand strategies at play over time. All the separate episodes examined add up to one long case for this purpose.

A Look Back

This book has explored ten episodes:

1. The Nixon administration's twin pillar policy (1972–79)
2. The Reagan administration's tilt toward Iraq during the Iran-Iraq War (1982–85)
3. The Iran-Contra affair (1985–86)

4. The U.S.-led reflagging of Kuwaiti oil tankers (1986–87)
5. The Bush administration's constructive engagement toward Iraq (1988–90)
6. Iraq's invasion of Kuwait (1990–91)
7. Washington's war-termination strategy (1991)
8. The Clinton administration's policy of dual containment of Iran and Iraq (1992–98)
9. The Clinton administration's policy of containment-plus (1998–2001)
10. The Iraq war of 2003 (2003–5)

In examining these episodes, I laid out three initial propositions to test, which I discuss in the following three sections of this chapter:

P1: The United States would balance against the strongest state in the region.

P2: The United States would balance against the most threatening state in the region.

P3: The United States would balance against the power or threat (or both) of Iraq (Moscow's client state) even if Iran was more powerful or threatening at the regional level.

In assessing these propositions, I offer gradations of confirmation in the discussion and in table 5: strongly confirmed; confirmed; weakly confirmed, meaning that only minor evidence confirms the proposition; disconfirmed; strongly disconfirmed; and unclear or not applicable when the extant conditions do not provide a clear and fair test.

Balancing against Power

To what extent did the United States balance against power? Except for the Nixon administration's twin pillar policy, which receives a weak confirmation, proposition 1 received no strong confirmations or even confirmations. Indeed, when we look back on the episodes, the United States did strengthen Iran in the 1970s by selling it arms and providing other forms of military and economic support. However, this action did not really reflect balancing against the strongest actor in the region, since Iran was for the most part stronger than Iraq in 1972 and throughout the rest of the 1970s. However, the case for balancing is partly salvaged in that America's connection to Iran reflected primarily an effort

Table 5. Findings of the Book (1972–2005)

Episode	Propositions		
	1	2	3
1	Weakly confirmed	Strongly confirmed	Confirmed
2	Disconfirmed	Strongly confirmed	Strongly disconfirmed
3	Unclear	Disconfirmed	Disconfirmed
4	Disconfirmed	Strongly confirmed	Strongly disconfirmed
5	Strongly disconfirmed	Strongly disconfirmed	Strongly disconfirmed
6	Weakly confirmed	Strongly confirmed	Strongly disconfirmed
7	Weakly confirmed	Unclear	Not applicable
8	Strongly disconfirmed	Disconfirmed	Not applicable
9	Strongly disconfirmed	Disconfirmed	Not applicable
10	Strongly disconfirmed	Weakly confirmed	Not applicable

Note: The findings do not rate balancing at the global and regional levels as separate episodes but reflect the overall outcome that those pressures generated.

to balance against Moscow at the global level by checking Iraq at the regional level. Moreover, it represented an effort to balance against Iraq's threat at the regional level, if not Iraq's prevailing power.

The United States strongly balanced against threat in Operation Staunch (1982–85) but not against power. In the Iran-Contra case (1985–86), Washington did not balance against the strongest state but rather engaged Iran. Even more problematic, from 1980 to 1988 the balance of power shifted unmistakably in Iraq's favor, but in 1988 the United States was accommodating and not balancing against Iraq—a fact that strongly disconfirms the notion that it balanced against power. The American-led response to Iraq's invasion of Kuwait did reflect balancing, although not strongly, because it was ensconced in a broader collective security effort. Meanwhile, the decisions to end the 1991 war included balance-of-power policy as a secondary or tertiary motivation. Although it was not clear after the U.S.-led victory in 1991 whether Iran or Iraq was the stronger or more threatening actor, it is clear that dual containment strongly disconfirms the first proposition, as does containment-plus and the invasion of Iraq. Indeed, Iraq was not stronger than Iran when the invasion was launched.

Balancing against Threat

As table 5 shows, the United States balanced against prevailing threat much more than against predominant power. It may have done so partly because, as one astute decision maker put it, balance of power "may be an end goal but we try to affect the behavior of the strongest and most aggressive state. The problem with balance of power is that it focuses on objective capabilities, thus ignoring the great role that perception of such capabilities has in affecting political-security dynamics."[1]

Balance-of-threat policy was strongly confirmed by the Nixon administration's twin pillar policy, which clearly represented an effort to balance against Iraq's threat at the regional level, if not Iraq's prevailing power. It was also strongly confirmed in the Operation Staunch case (1982–85), as well as in the reflagging and 1991 Gulf war episodes. However, balance-of-threat policy faced some not insignificant problems. Although it accurately reflected U.S. balancing against Iran from 1982 to 1985, it certainly did not predict U.S. appeasement of Iran in 1985–1986, since Iran, in fact, became a much bigger threat than Iraq after its victory at Fao in February 1986. If anything, we would have expected a much stronger balancing approach after Fao. Yet that did not take place until 1987. The balancing in 1987 does not salvage the case for balancing because of the blatant shift from balancing against Iran in the period from 1982 to 1985 to appeasing it in 1985 to 1986. Meanwhile, dual containment did involve balancing against threat, but against both Iran and Iraq rather than prevailing threat, a factor that would largely disconfirm balance against threat in this episode. In this regard, containment-plus moved even further away from balance against threat because it officially added a policy of regime change for Iraq and Iran. The invasion of Iraq did focus singly on Iraq, rather than on both Iran and Iraq, and thus did include elements of balancing against the greater threat, although not unambiguously because Iran was also viewed as a threat.

Balancing Given the Global-Regional Dynamic

On the whole, global imperatives had less of an impact on regional balancing than expected, with some notable exceptions. Thus, we could not say with confidence that the United States did not practice balance-of-power policy much because it was preempted by balancing concerns at the global level.

We would have expected that the United States would balance against Iraq's power or threat (or both) even if Iran was more powerful or threatening (or both) at the regional level (proposition 3). In particular, Stephen Walt finds that the history of the Middle East shows that the superpowers act primarily to balance one another in the region.[2] However, proposition 3 receives mixed results at best.

Global-level concerns cannot explain why the United States tilted toward Iraq beginning in the 1982–83 period. Iran was not disposed toward Moscow, whereas Iraq was close to the Soviet Union, even in a quasi alliance. Thus, balancing against Iraq at the regional level would have made more sense if Washington sought to balance Moscow at the global level. Rather, the United States balanced against Iran in the Operation Staunch and reflagging episodes. Even more problematic, the United States appeased Iraq from 1983 through 1990, with only sporadic shifts in policy. In this sense, it not only failed to balance against Iraq but actually strengthened it, sometimes when Iran was far more threatening.

Three episodes do represent exceptions. The twin pillar policy clearly was motivated in no small measure by U.S. concerns about Moscow. Thus, by strengthening Iran against Iraq, Washington also balanced against Moscow, which was aligned with Iraq. The twin pillar policy also was an effort to balance against Iraq's threat at the regional level, if not Iraq's prevailing power.

For its part, the Iran-Contra affair threatened to do the exact opposite of balance-of-power or balance-of-threat policy. However, the United States was partly motivated by a desire to prevent Moscow from gaining a foothold in Iran and capitalizing on its perceived internal turmoil. In this sense, the United States was balancing against Moscow's threat at the global level, albeit this was a tertiary motive for the arms-for-hostages strategy.

In the reflagging case, the United States once again clearly did not balance against Iraq, which we would have expected if it was concerned about balancing against Moscow, even though it partly aimed to preempt Moscow from reflagging Kuwaiti tankers. The reflagging effort confirms balance-of-threat policy in action in that the United States balanced against Iran's threat at the regional level. However, it disconfirms balance of power because Iraq, the stronger regional actor and one aligned with Moscow, was helped by it.

In the episodes when the United States balanced at the regional rather than global level, it balanced against regional threat rather than power. The exception is the Iran-Contra case, in which the United States balanced against Iraq, but only as a tertiary motive at best. In no instance did balancing global power take precedence over balancing regional threat. Why? We can guess that failure to balance against intense and urgent regional threats poses a greater short-term risk to national security than failing to balance against power at the regional or global level. It may also be that balancing against power can be delayed without suffering near-term losses, whereas that is less true of failing to balance against threat. Threats are more immediate and dangerous in that sense.

The ending of the Cold War makes the 1991 war-termination and 1990s dual-containment episodes less of a fair test of proposition 3 (yielding "not applicable" designations in table 5). We would not expect the United States to balance against Iraq, in order to balance against Moscow, with relations improving at the global level. And this is even more true of containment-plus and the Iraq war of 2003.

However, we can point out that if global balancing concerns were really important in impeding regional balancing, we would expect the United States to balance more at the regional level after the end of the Cold War, since it would no longer be significantly motivated to balance at the global level at the expense of regional balancing. Yet what we find is that the United States balanced even less in the region after the end of the Cold War than during it. Although it balanced at times during the Iran-Iraq War, it balanced little after the 1991 war, either during the war-termination phase of that war or in the 1990s under dual containment.

Balancing Theory and the Role of Individuals

American foreign policy in the region was driven by numerous motivations, as this book has demonstrated. But one point is worth emphasizing in its own right. Individuals mattered in shaping outcomes, sometimes in fundamental ways, and the influence of individuals is not what balancing theory assumes. Accounting for the role of individuals helps explain when the United States deviated from balancing approaches and provides more insight into the problems of balance-of-power theory in particular.

The Iran-Contra affair underscored the extent to which individual actors affect foreign policy. President Reagan was essential to the development of the policy, even if he did not handle its day-to-day evolution. His devoted underlings in the basement of the National Security Council (NSC) followed his general lead and then produced the approach. Imbalances of power were not especially important to them.

Even in cases in which the behavior of the United States did support balance-of-power theory, sometimes its actions were not driven by the motivation to balance. For instance, the United States did appease Iran in the Iran-Contra episode, which is what we would have expected as a balance against Moscow at the global level. But the primary motivation for the Iran-Contra episode was the president's concern about hostages in Lebanon.

For its part, dual containment was motivated by domestic concerns, as well as by America's interest in Israel's security, and by the inklings of particular admin-istrators, such as Warren Christopher, whose experiences negotiating the Ameri-can hostage release left him more inclined to see Iran in negative terms.[3] Of course, over time, the influence of neoconservatives also rose as an ideological force at the domestic level. Future work may consider their impact on American foreign policy. This topic is especially interesting for the study of balancing in U.S. foreign policy because neoconservatives have held balance-of-power policy in disdain.[4]

President George W. Bush was critical, perhaps decisive, in the decision to invade Iraq in 2003. That decision was also affected by a small cadre of neo-conservatives. Their ideological positions could not be accounted for in balanc-ing theory.

In other cases, domestic- and individual-level factors did not impede balanc-ing but were important in policy making in a way that balancing theory would not account for. Thus, Washington's tilt in favor of Iraq beginning in 1982–83 was affected by struggles in the United States between Soviet-, Israeli-, and Arab-centric decision makers. The tilt toward Iraq was related to the increasing effec-tiveness of the last group, largely with State Department links.[5] In contrast, Israeli- and Soviet-centric decision makers played a more significant role in motivating the approach toward Iran in 1985–86, dominated by the NSC.[6]

During the 1990–91 crisis, President George H. W. Bush drove American foreign policy. He was a critical, even decisive actor.[7] The United States did balance against Iraq's threat and to some extent against power as well in this case, but the greater the president's role as an individual actor, the less stock we can put in balancing theory as a very strong explanation.[8]

Evaluating Grand Strategies

We have examined various episodes to determine whether, in each, the United States practiced balance-of-power policy or balance-of-threat policy. In order to explore the question of grand strategy, however, it is vital to look at all the episodes taken together — as one long case of American foreign policy — because grand strategy, insofar as it can be discerned, becomes apparent only over a broader period of time.

Scholars sometimes seek to categorize and explain the behavior of states using different grand strategies. Thus, as noted earlier in the book, Layne believes that the United States has acted as an "extraregional hegemon."[9] At other times, scholars prescribe grand strategies for states to pursue. As Posen sees it, the major debate in the post–Cold War period was about which variant of hegemonic strategy the United States should pursue.[10] Whereas some scholars have promoted hegemony, offshore balancing, or some other nonhegemonic strategy, Robert Art developed and prescribed selective engagement as the best strategy for the United States to follow, which some scholars considered to be a preferred approach.[11]

This book does not prescribe a grand strategy. Rather, it examines to what extent the United States practiced grand strategy in the Persian Gulf context.

To reiterate a key point made in the Introduction, scholars differ on the number of different grand strategies available to states. Robert Art identifies eight, while Christopher Layne suggests that great powers can pursue either extraregional hegemony or balance of power, although he also considers the extent to which isolationism and selective engagement are distinct grand strategies in relation to hegemony and balance of power.[12]

This book examines balance of power and hegemony as grand strategies. It breaks down balance of power into active and offshore balancing. The bulk of the book showed that, from 1972 through 2005, the United States infrequently behaved as an active balancer and that it was even less likely to act in this manner in the region as time progressed. But these points raise this question: To what extent did the United States pursue a strategy of offshore balancing (as opposed to active balancing) or a hegemonic grand strategy? The evidence presented in this book and summarized above offers a clear answer: not much. The discussion below draws partly on the distinctions between offshore balancing and hegemony seeking, as discussed in the Introduction (see table 1, for easy reference).

The Offshore Balancer?

The United States did not act as an offshore balancer, but that is not to say that its behavior never resembled offshore balancing. In the 1970s, for instance, it displayed elements of being an offshore balancer insofar as it sought proxies to protect its interests in the Gulf region, and it showed much concern about Moscow's position in the global balance of power. However, it lacked any real ability to act as an offshore balancer to prevent imminent hegemony by Iran, Iraq, or the Soviet Union. It could not deploy to the region with even minimal force. That capability developed only over time.

Moreover, instead of giving allies the responsibility for regional security, as it had done in the Nixon administration's twin pillar policy, it moved in precisely the opposite direction. It assumed increasingly greater responsibility for the region's security until it had committed itself to the profound and daunting tasks of containing both Iran and Iraq, then to officially removing Iraq's regime, and finally to executing this official goal in the war of 2003. Rather than retracting its security umbrella in the region, which is what we would have expected of an offshore balancer,[13] the United States took actions in line with presidential doctrines to erect a larger security umbrella. Indeed, the Carter Doctrine pledged to protect the region from outside threats; the Reagan Doctrine asserted that the United States would also protect Saudi Arabia from internal threats; and the doctrine of George W. Bush committed the United States to preempt and even prevent rising threats and laid the basis for the Iraq war of 2003.

Nor could the United States get another great power to check the aggressor, a strategy that would have conformed with an offshore balancing approach. If the United States could have done so, it might have avoided the very difficult decisions of how to protect regional security and its own vital interests. But no other regional or global powers could play the role of regional gendarme at critical points such as in 1991 when U.S.-led forces evicted Iraq's army from Kuwait, although they did contribute in important ways to U.S.-led efforts. Thus the United States had to decide on what mix of strategies would best protect its interests at different junctures in history.

The U.S. eviction of Iraqi forces from Kuwait in 1991 partially reflected an offshore balancing approach. The United States ultimately did resort to massive force to achieve its ends to check Iraq, which had hegemonic ambitions in the region. In this sense, it acted as an offshore balancer. However, the United States had pursued a policy of constructive engagement with Iraq from 1988 until 1990 which actually strengthened the strongest and most threatening actor in the region. This approach is not especially what we would have expected of a great power that was concerned about balancing. Moreover, Washington did not sweep into the Gulf region when hegemony appeared to be imminent. Rather, it was already heavily involved and militarily present in the region. It had over the past decade assiduously built, with its local allies, a political and military infrastructure and a forward military presence. It is somewhat hard to describe the United States as intervening as a last resort, as it did, for instance, in World War II.

The 1990–91 crisis also had the trappings of a collective security operation, albeit an imperfect and American-dominated one. The offshore balancer is not viewed as acting under the umbrella of collective security, although one could imagine a hybrid approach that included a collective security mechanism.

Finally, the offshore balancer is concerned only with one key strategic interest: preventing hegemony in a region.[14] Yet the United States clearly had other strategic interests as well. These included releasing American hostages held in Lebanon by the radical Shiite group Hizballah — a goal that was not insignificant but, rather, largely drove the Iran-Contra policy toward Iran; securing Iraqi business for American farmers and the economy; democratizing the Middle East; dealing politically and strategically with transnational terrorism; and jockeying with Moscow in the region to prevent it from gaining an edge in global rivalry, even if it had very little chance of achieving hegemony in the distant Gulf, where Godless communism was viewed as anathema.

Globalization and economic and resource interdependence have made it harder for great powers to be offshore balancers. Global politics draw great powers into regions, as this book suggests about the United States in the Persian Gulf. As Josef Joffe has insightfully pointed out about the United States, "unlike Britain, it cannot withdraw from the game and return only fitfully to apply its might on the margin."[15] At a minimum, such an offshore balancing strategy would require a very sophisticated accompanying foreign policy to account for the interconnected nature of modern world politics. Such a foreign policy is not impossible but would require much thought and deft diplomacy.

The Extraregional Hegemon?

In contrast to the great powers of the past, the United States could not simply conquer and annex countries by use of force, even though some observers may have viewed the 2003 invasion of Iraq in that partial light.[16] In contrast, dictators long gone, and even polished statesmen of the great European powers of the nineteenth century, would have viewed such an imperial approach as not only sensible but perhaps necessary under the colonial regime of that century, a set of tacit rules and norms that governed the behavior of these great powers.[17] But if the United States could not be outright imperial, in the sense of being bent on territorial acquisition, did it behave as a modern extraregional hegemon? Contrary to the argument put forth by Christopher Layne and many others who would agree with at least some elements of his argument, this book holds that the United States did not pursue a strategy of hegemony, although it appeared more likely to do so by the time it invaded Iraq in 2003.

It is true that the United States recognized the importance of the region earlier in the twentieth century and that its interests there expanded over time.[18] However, expanding interests and hegemony are not the same thing. For all its expanding interests, by the 1970s the United States scarcely exhibited characteristics of extraregional hegemony. It preferred to rely on proxies to protect regional security and wanted, in the post-Vietnam era, to detach itself from the vagaries of regional politics. This approach was closer to the opposite of hegemony seeking. Washington did not even develop a forward military presence in or near the region until the events of 1979 forced its hand. Significantly, even then it preferred to stay out of the region and out of the Iran-Iraq War, which broke out in September 1980 when Iraq invaded Iran. Its official policy was that it wanted both sides to lose. Benign neglect, as some observers called the policy, was hardly the signature of a hegemony seeker.

In 1982, Washington was forced to move away from this rough neutrality to balancing against Iran. Even so, its involvement was largely unobtrusive. It did not send troops. It did not send arms to Iraq, except of a light variety. It did not ally with Iraq in any formal or even informal sense. It still hoped that its security in the region could be protected without much greater involvement, although the events of 1979 and the Iran-Iraq War had shocked it into creating a military infrastructure that could support greater intervention.

As time went on, the United States did begin to show some minor signs of extraregional hegemony. It had always sought to deny Moscow a role in the region, but in the 1980s it developed the military capability to deter and even repel an unlikely Soviet invasion of the Gulf or a hegemonic attempt by Iran or Iraq. Clearly, it was creating the potential for a much greater forward presence in the region. The most significant example of this effort is the sale of Airborne Warning and Control System (AWACS) aircraft to the Saudis in exchange for their promise to build huge underground strategic facilities,[19] which were intended to support a massive U.S. deployment of troops in the event of a major regional crisis. Oddly enough, such forces were used not against Iran or Moscow but against Iraq in 1990. They were a sine qua non for mounting Operations Desert Shield and Desert Storm in 1990–91.[20]

The reversal of Iraq's invasion of Kuwait in 1990 with massive military force might reflect aspects of a hegemonic strategy on the surface. But if the United States were acting as extraregional hegemon, it may well have continued to press its military advantage by invading Iraq, possibly to unseat the dictator that challenged its regional position. It certainly would not have ended the 1991 war earlier than its generals wanted or failed to support the Kurdish and Shia uprisings against Saddam, which it had encouraged. It is important to stress that a hegemon would not have retracted its forces from the region at the end of the 1991 war.[21] Yet the United States was eager to do so, for a plethora of reasons. Rather than acting like a hegemon, the United States chose not to use its vastly superior military position for the purpose of domination following the ignominious retreat of Saddam's forces.

In the 1990s, the United States pursued a more muscular approach toward the region than it had in the 1970s or 1980s. Dual containment of Iran and Iraq transformed into containment-plus an official policy of regime change in Iraq under Clinton. At the global level, the Clinton administration also flexed its rhetoric and perhaps its muscles. For instance, in 1995, it stated that the United States was the world's "only superpower."[22] The 1997 Quadrennial Defense Review, developed by the Pentagon, also asserted that the United States should aim to reduce the challenges to American dominance by checking rising new regional or global powers.[23]

The Bush administration's foreign policy elevated notions of American dominance to a still higher level and represented a fairly sharp break with past U.S. policies.[24] September 11 was of obvious importance, as discussed earlier in this book. Some scholars went so far as to argue that the Bush administration at first was "more realist than anything else" but after September 11 it "gravitated toward a new grand strategy, one of American primacy."[25] Such an interpretation is understandable in some measure. The National Security Strategy of September 2002 formally encapsulated the Bush doctrine of preemption and called for an American effort to maintain global dominance and prevent any serious challengers from arising.[26]

All these points having been made, it is fair to say that the National Security Strategy certainly did reflect a more muscular American foreign policy than had been practiced heretofore in the region. Moreover, the Iraq invasion and subsequent occupation of Iraq in 2003 reflected some elements of extraregional hegemony.[27] Following from the National Security Strategy, the United States executed a policy of regime change in Iraq. That approach was far more invasive than any other policy the United States pursued in the Persian Gulf and, in fact, in any region of the world.

Furthermore, American forces in massive numbers were used and remained in Iraq after the invasion. The long-term occupation of Iraq did not appear to be the intent of the Bush administration, but it could be construed to reflect a strain of hegemony in American foreign policy or at least a much more aggressive foreign policy than it pursued in the region in earlier periods.

American exceptionalism, which was a minor aspect of American behavior in the region in the past, also became more prominent and infused the discourse of U.S. foreign policy with concepts and terms that appeared to jibe with aspects of hegemony seeking. We could not blame many people around the world, and more than a few scholars, for describing the United States as a hegemon or hegemony seeker in this time period.

But although some elements of extraregional hegemony were at play in the 2003 war and subsequent occupation, and much more than in the past, several critical ingredients were missing from what could be called a hegemonic strategy. Most important, the United States, by and large, was not motivated to be a hegemon. Under President Clinton, the administration was more wedded to an internationalist foreign policy that respected the precepts of interdependence and multilateralism than to any notion of American preeminence, although that notion was more prominent within military circles.[28] Regarding the Bush administration, it is equally plausible that it sought to protect its security rather than seek hegemony. After the shocking attacks of September 11, it believed the best way to protect American security was through preemption and by checking rising powers.[29] After all, the National Security Strategy of 2002 also asserted with regard to weapons of mass destruction (WMD) that, "as a matter of sense and self-defense, America will act against such emerging threats before they are fully formed."[30] Protecting security and seeking expansionist hegemony are not the same, even though they may involve similar behaviors. Security-seeking is not offensive but tends toward protecting national interests.

It is also possible, though difficult to establish, that September 11 had a traumatic or at least psychological impact on some key officials. If so, it is harder to conclude that the American approach was to seek hegemony, much less by virtue of a carefully orchestrated grand or even nongrand strategy. Rather, it suggests that part of the narrative should include sensitivity to the immense pressures, including concerns about a WMD attack on a major American city, which contributed to official decisions. The inescapable sense of insecurity under these conditions may generate muscular behavior but not with the intent to dominate; more likely, the intention of such behavior would be to protect the United States against further threats to its security.

Chapter 8 underscored the multiple motivations underlying the U.S.-led invasion of Iraq, many of which were related to September 11. Washington was responding to threats that were italicized by the September 11 attacks; it was concerned about or took advantage of Iraq's record of defiance; and it was subject to faulty intelligence and likely manipulated some evidence as well in order to support a mission that was largely security-related. These motivations were different from hegemony seeking.

It is fair to argue that the United States was acting in Iraq to prevent serious losses more than to score gains. This is a central notion in prospect theory, and it may help explain some important foreign policy behaviors.[31] It also paints a different picture of the United States than its military adventures might suggest: it is a picture of a great power threatened by 9/11 and what it portended and motivated to act not for the purpose of hegemony but to protect itself from further losses of great magnitude.

It is also fair to say that even though the great power in pursuit of hegemony differs from the imperial actor, they both seek more power, usually much more power. Yet the United States could have sought greater power in the Gulf at earlier junctures and in the 2003 invasion. It could have, for instance, invaded Baghdad after the 1991 war when Saddam's forces were in retreat and in disarray. American generals wanted to crush Saddam's Republican Guards more effectively and believed that they could have easily pressed the advantage to Baghdad as well, though they did not push this approach and Washington rejected it, in any case.[32] It is clear that Washington saw access to Persian Gulf oil as vital to U.S. and global security,[33] but it did not seek to coopt Iraq's oil fields. It could have taken Iraq's oil and its oil revenues, and instead it put these resources under Iraqi control.

The United States at times looked reckless and overbearing. The "Shock and Awe" campaign sported a title that suggested a superpower on the loose, seeking to impress the global community with its military prowess. Yet, on the whole, the United States did not exercise its power to the extent possible, very much unlike great powers and empires of the past. This approach may have reflected a strain in American foreign policy. As Thomas Barnett points out, with a twist of hyperbole but also some truth, the United States has "willingly walked away from more global power than any empire in human history has ever achieved."[34] What is less dramatic to say is that its behavior, unlike that of true imperial powers of the past, did not seem, on the whole, to exceed by much its perceptions of its own national security requirements.[35]

Following from these points, it is a telltale sign that an actor pursuing hegemony does not withdraw its forces from a region. Yet it did not appear that the

United States intended to maintain a massive military force in Iraq. Rather, it intended to withdraw or at least significantly reduce this force once Iraq became more stable. No American leader could have sensibly said that the United States should occupy Iraq permanently with massive forces. In fact, serious plans for withdrawing American forces were unveiled in the national media by June 2006. They were premised on the notion that Iraqi security forces would be prepared to keep the order in Iraq, but they clearly signaled American intent to withdraw its forces from Iraq at some time.

Although Washington's foreign policy may have reflected elements of hegemonic strategy in 2003, that was not the case in the periods prior to it. Rather, its policies and approaches shifted and did not exhibit anything approaching the inexorable or unalterable underlying logic and rationale that is ascribed to hegemonic grand strategy.[36] Grand strategy is not something that becomes manifest in one short time period. It is discerned across a longer period of time. Of course, some scholars believe that grand strategies can change dramatically, but even then, they would tend to see the conduct of American foreign policy as being shaped, as Colin Dueck puts it, by "a set of beliefs," which, as he sees it, is liberal internationalism based on democratization chiefly and marketization, which America has pursued cautiously.[37]

It is possible to identify a shift in American foreign policy in the period after the Iraq war, as well. Even the elements of hegemony that were reflected in the Iraq invasion of 2003 started to be reversed when it became clear that Iraq lacked WMD and that rebuilding Iraq would be far harder than the Bush administration ever thought. Some observers even described this reckoning and aftershock as leading to the end of the Bush revolution.[38] By 2006, the administration appeared to take a step back from its effort to democratize the Middle East and to pursue a more muscular foreign policy. As one scholar described it, it "seems relatively clear that the Bush administration in its second term has itself sidelined regime change through war in its foreign policy."[39] And its approach to Iran and North Korea, both of which were viewed as serious WMD threats, was viewed as timid enough by some Republicans that they referred to it as Clintonian.[40]

American foreign policy, if anything, was reactive to events in the region. Even within single administrations, much less across a broader spectrum of time, Washington was far more likely to respond to crises and threats that arose than to to pursue an organized, longer-run approach to the region. That is true of many of its approaches, including to some extent the 2003 invasion of Iraq. It is hard to imagine such an invasion in the absence of the September 11 attack. As discussed earlier in the book, regime change was official American policy by 1998, but September 11 was critical in turning that abstract goal into an actual military invasion.

Conclusion

In brief, the notion that the United States balanced against power in the region is largely disconfirmed in evaluating U.S. behavior in the region.[41] In contrast, the United States was much more likely to balance against prevailing threat in the region. Moreover, global-level imperatives had less of an impact on regional balancing than expected — a surprising finding that deserves to be subjected to more tests in the future. However, in some measure, accounting for them yielded insights. Considering two-level imperatives helped explain, for instance, why behaviors that might contradict balancing at the regional level (such as in the Iran-Contra case) make more sense if we examine pressures at the global level. Exploring balance of power and balance of threat also allowed inquiry into how they were related at the regional and global level. It helped explain, for instance, how balancing against power at the global level did not affect regional balancing as much as balancing against threat did.

Not much evidence supports the notion that the United States pursued either balance-of-power (active or offshore balancing) or hegemonic grand strategies. However, it is worth emphasizing one point in comparing balance-of-power and hegemonic grand strategies over time. Although neither strategy seemed to be at play much, a more nuanced evaluation reveals that U.S. foreign policy in the immediate post-Vietnam 1970s was more reflective of offshore balancing than of extraregional hegemony. In contrast, by 2003 and owing to an evolution of American policies and to the impact of shocking events, American behavior reflected extraregional hegemony more than offshore balancing. Interestingly, the same reasons that made the United States increasingly less likely to act as an active balancer, which were discussed in the previous chapter, also explain why it was less likely to be an offshore balancer and more likely over time to exhibit some elements of extraregional hegemony.

CHAPTER ELEVEN

Theory, Strategy, and Realism

Like all great powers in history, the United States has sought to secure and advance its interests in faraway regions. It has been slowly drawn into these regions and particularly into Middle East politics in the past two decades. American security became inextricably linked to events in the Persian Gulf, largely because the United States and the entire global economy had become dependent on oil. And the United States and its role in the region morphed, as did our view of its role and of the region itself. In pursuing its interests in the region, Washington used a plethora of approaches that have changed over time as a result of domestic, regional, and international developments.

Exploring the American experience in the Persian Gulf offers a long and panoramic view that would not be apparent in examining just one case or time period. We can see not only that the United States did not practice balance-of-power policy much but that balance of power decreased in prominence in U.S. foreign policy. But these findings leave open broader questions. This chapter is devoted to three theory-oriented questions. If the United States did not engage much in balancing against power, either as an active or offshore balancer, and if it did so increasingly less over time, is this likely to be the case in other regions as well? Does this book suggest a problem with balance-of-power theory writ large? If the United States did balance against threat much more than against power but sometimes did not balance against threat, under what conditions did it balance or not balance against threat?

Broader Significance for Other Regions?

Regions are complex and varied, and it is challenging to treat them in similar ways. Yet the notion that the United States practiced balance-of-power policy less over time in the Persian Gulf is meaningful. It should lead us to wonder whether this outcome is also more broadly relevant.

The developments that contributed to the decline in American balancing in the Persian Gulf may not be limited to the U.S. role there. Transnational terrorism by nature affects and infects all regions, and neither the consequences of the end of the Cold War nor the rise of American power can be confined to one region. It follows that if these developments have made the United States less likely to act as an active balancer in the Persian Gulf, they may do so in other regions as well, although at varying levels as a function of regional politics and the extent to which these developments are salient in each region.

Of course, one could argue that these developments will be reversed over time. Such reversal is possible but does not seem likely in the near term at least. Moscow altogether cannot reconstitute the empire, even though President Vladimir Putin has displayed authoritarian tendencies, and U.S.-Russian tensions could arise again in serious ways. In the Middle East, the fall of the Soviet Union in 1991 altered Moscow's military and political role. Moscow no longer supports radical Arab states with military arms and economic aid. Russian advisers are not involved in the region's various conflicts. Moscow has become far less likely, willing, and able to engage in activity that could directly or indirectly challenge regional stability. Of course, important elements in Russia's foreign policy establishment have continued to view U.S.-Russian interaction as a power struggle, and President Vladimir Putin has shown some signs of reverting to Cold War behavior, but Moscow's tendency to rival the United States has been tempered and its inclination to cooperate increased.[1]

The rise of American capability can be reversed, although that does not appear likely in the near term. It takes time in world politics for a shift of that magnitude. Some scholars argue, in fact, that there are several facets of the American unipolar order, including technological dominance and democratic principles, which not only make it durable but even expansive.[2] Although this argument is not clear, the gap between the United States and its competitors is vast.

Transnational terrorism as well may ebb in importance, but for the foreseeable future it seems to be a significant fixture on the global landscape. Terrorists cannot be easily, if at all, reconciled, and the motivations that drive them are not only hard to understand but appear to be multiple. Even a small group of determined jihadists can carry out acts of anti-Western terrorism against a well-orchestrated campaign to destroy them and convert their supporters. And yet Al Qaeda may very well have millions of sympathizers and tens of thousands of willing supporters.

Even if the developments identified herein are reversed, it is doubtful that balance-of-power policy will become more predominant because it did not perform very well even before these developments took place. It is in particular trouble, however, because of the likely irreversibility of these developments.

However, this book also does not argue that balance-of-power policy is irrelevant in the broader mix of strategies adopted by great powers in regions. So long as states exist, and so long as world politics remains anarchical, states will be, at least to some extent, concerned about relative power in regions and about the potential that one state may become too strong. It would take an immense revolution in world affairs for this situation to change completely — for instance, a revolution that reverses the state-centric world into one of dukedoms, kingdoms, fiefdoms, and empires or one that replaces anarchy with some form of hierarchical governance above the state level.

Traditional Balance-of-Power Theory

As the quintessential state-centric theory, balance of power was a key target for attack by its critics, armed with the case of 9/11. September 11 seemed to herald in a world in which transnational actors would be more critical. Whether or not this is actually the case, the idea certainly raised the question about whether theories that were profoundly state-centric remained fully relevant, if relevant at all. How relevant could balance-of-power theory be in a world that seemed increasingly to include vital transnational actors and threats, as well as the daunting tasks of nation building and defusing civil wars?[3] Did Al Qaeda really fall into the balance-of-power paradigm? If transnational terrorist groups represented the biggest threat in the twenty-first century and balance-of-power theory could not explain their role, then how salient could it be?

This book makes two arguments about balance-of-power theory, but before laying them out, it is critical to make a few prefatory points. It is important to emphasize that this book seeks to test directly the external balancer aspect of balance-of-power theory. Balance-of-power theory does not really tell us how quickly an actor will respond to shifts in the balance of power, and we can debate what level of time must pass without balancing before the theory can be dis-confirmed in any one case. Yet although debate exists on this question, the question itself is much less problematic with regard to the external balancer version of balance-of-power theory. Indeed, in theory, and in terms of how it has behaved in history, the active balancer is clearly attuned to events and consciously alters its policy in response to them.[4]

While this book should be judged only in terms of the external balancer notion of balancing theory, readers may want to consider to what extent it sheds some light on, or at least provokes thought about, traditional and neorealist balance-of-power theories. It is possible, though it might be controversial, to present this book as a test of conceptions of balance-of-power theory which do not assume the intrinsic, automatic formation of balances. They include balance-of-threat theory, the strategic model of balance-of-power theory, and semiauto-matic conceptions of balance-of-power theory, which combine conscious and intrinsic balancing.[5] On that score, it would be controversial to present this work as a test of neorealism, but it would be neglectful not to discuss neorealism in the context of this book's goals. Kenneth Waltz observes that testing theories "always means inferring expectations, or hypotheses, from them and testing these expec-tations."[6] However, he does little to tell us how to test his theory beyond assert-ing that balances will recur under conditions of anarchy in which states want to survive, irrespective of whether individual states balance. Waltz stresses that neorealism is a theory of international relations and not one of foreign policy and that the behavior of states is thus indeterminate.[7] However, as Robert Keohane asserts, looking for balances to form and recur is not a test of the theory.[8] Only the rare event of the formation of empires, as David Lake points out, would disconfirm the theory on that basis.[9] Michael Mastanduno, for his part, argues that balancing does not occur if "states choose not to balance."[10] In fact, the notion that states will likely balance is an inference from neorealist theory which many scholars make.[11] Colin Elman, who argues that neorealism should be considered a theory of foreign policy, further asserts that Waltz, in fact, implicitly recognizes it as a theory of foreign policy when he draws on neorealism to try to predict, for instance, German and Japanese foreign policies in the post–Cold War world.[12]

On the whole, this book does not support the argument that balance-of-power theory is no longer relevant in explaining international relations. Not only is such a claim exceedingly strong given the great changes that take place in world politics, but this book is primarily designed to explore grand strategy and balancing as foreign policy approaches, rather than to test balance-of-power theory directly. As noted in the Introduction, realism is a structural theory. It explains systemic or global outcomes. We must make inferences from it about how great powers or specific states should behave, which is a common exercise.[13] Thus, the claims that I can make about balance-of-power theory writ large are circumscribed.

If the book does not support the notion that balance-of-power theory is dead, then what does it argue? First, the fact that the United States did not act much as an active or offshore balancer in the Persian Gulf region is important. The U.S. role in the Persian Gulf is a tough test case for balancing. It is a region in which international institutions and norms are far less developed, conflict is more prominent, and security concerns are more serious than in Western Europe or Latin America. The core premise of traditional balance-of-power theory is that actors will balance against the stronger actor. We should have expected the United States to be motivated by this notion and to act in line with it much more than it did in the Persian Gulf, notwithstanding the differences between balancing at the systemic level and as a great power involved in a region of the world. That outcome cannot be ignored by traditional balance-of-power theorists. Rather, it should be considered in broader questions about the theory's usefulness and the extent to which cases of great powers in regions reflect upon this usefulness. Second, some scholars argue that the United States, despite its preeminence in the post–Cold War period, has not been balanced against by other global powers and that this underscores that balance-of-power theory faces significant problems. Indeed, John Ikenberry in his valuable work *America Unrivaled* assembles an impressive array of scholars whose work raises profound doubts about balance-of-power theory. They believe that balancing against the United States has been impeded by a variety of factors including geography, international institutions, and the spread of transnational liberalism insofar as other states would not want to balance against a state with which they share transnational liberal views.[14]

This book is similar to Ikenberry's work inasmuch as it raises questions about balance-of-power policy and, depending on one's interpretation, in some measure traditional balance-of-power theory. But it differs from Ikenberry's work as well. His book focuses on why states are not balancing against preeminent American power at the global level, whereas this study examines why the United States itself has not balanced against preeminent power at the regional level. Moreover, the reasons that these works offer for nonbalancing differ markedly from the reasons advanced in this study for why the United States did not balance against power in the Gulf. For instance, it can hardly be said that balancing in the Gulf was not prominent because international institutions were developed in that region. Nor was balancing not prominent because the United States and the states of the region share transnational liberal principles that mitigate the pressures of anarchy and the propensity to engage in balancing.

In this sense, the absence of significant balancing in the Gulf region is all the more perplexing. The best reasons offered for nonbalancing at the global level cannot account for America's nonbalancing in the Gulf region. Rather, an array of other factors are at play, which may apply more to the role of great powers in regions than to the question of balancing at the global level. As suggested above, they include the end of the Cold War, the rise of American power, and the impact of transnational terrorism. Another variable, albeit one specific to the United States, is the rise of neoconservatism.

A Theory of External Balancing against Threat

The argument of this book that the United States balanced much more against threat than against power may be viewed as rough evidence in support of Walt's balance-of-threat theory, with two major provisos. Walt's theory, like traditional balance-of-power theory, is structural rather than directly a theory of foreign policy. If we interpret it as the latter, then this book offers a test of it, but if not, then the present work may or may not confirm Walt's theory. Moreover, Walt's theory is not designed to explain the role of outside powers in regions. That distinction, in particular, sets this work apart from Walt's.

In any case, a different theoretical question arises: As this book has argued, and as the previous chapter subsumed, balance-of-power approaches received much lower priority than theory would suggest, but this does not explain why the United States at times did balance, especially against threat. Although Walt does discuss conditions under which states balance rather than bandwagon and other scholars have introduced useful domestic variables to refine the theory, the question remains of when an external actor will balance against threat rather than pursue a nonbalancing approach other than bandwagoning.[15]

In Chapter 1, I presented three propositions that were worth examining in order to gain better insight into this key question of when external actors will balance:

> P1: The external actor believes that it is unlikely to engage the most threatening actor, through a variety of incentives, in lieu of tougher approaches such as balancing.

> P2: The outside state faces a regional military threat rather than a political or ideological threat.

> P3: Balancing against threat at the regional level does not contradict balancing against threat (not power) at the global level.

In comparing episodes of balancing and nonbalancing behavior explored in this book, the first two propositions are strongly confirmed, while the third is confirmed with qualification. Drawing on this approach, it is possible to identify three conditions under which an external actor will be much more likely to balance against the strongest threat in a region.

First, active balancing against threat is more likely when the balancer believes that it is unlikely to engage the most threatening actor, through a variety of incentives, in lieu of tougher approaches such as balancing. When Washington believed that engaging Iran and Iraq could contain them, it often pursued this approach as a distinct alternative to balancing.

The United States tried to moderate and co-opt Iran quietly at various junctures in the 1980s, but since the revolution Iran has been extremely reluctant to engage Washington. Mehdi Bazargan, the first prime minister of the Provisional Republic of Iran, and Foreign Minister Ibrahim Yazdi met with President Carter's national security adviser, Zbigniew Brzezinski, in Algiers in 1979; not much later the moderate Bazargan was ousted by Iran's more radical Islamists, who viewed him as weak on the "Great Satan" and who painted him successfully in those terms.[16] Both the Carter and Reagan administrations underestimated the influence of the more radical Islamists in Iran.

When Iran showed some potential to be engaged, the United States launched and pursued the arms-for-hostages approach — despite Iran's victory at Fao, the fact that Iran was the most threatening regional actor, and Iran's previous rejections of American overtures.

Similarly, Washington sought to engage and moderate Iraq from 1988 to 1990 with various incentives, despite recognizing that it was the most threatening and powerful state in the Gulf. It balanced against Iraq only when it was left with no choice after Iraq invaded Kuwait.

It is not clear why the United States preferred to engage rather than confront regional states. It may be that it is less costly to try to do so or that it is difficult to know when to balance rather than to engage and accommodate a threatening or powerful actor.[17]

Second, balancing against threat is more likely when the outside state faces a regional military threat rather than a political or ideological threat. Thus, in 1982, when Iran recaptured Khorramshahr and appeared to be gaining military momentum against Iraq, the United States began its tilt toward Iraq and against Iran in Operation Staunch in 1983. It is notable that the U.S. tilt did not occur in response to the Iranian revolution, which posed an ideological but not military threat at first.[18] Moreover, although the United States failed to balance after Iran's Fao victory in 1986, it did do so in 1987 when Iran was perceived as threatening Gulf shipping and Kuwait proper. Furthermore, Iraq's pan-Arab ideological and broader political threat, and even its implicit military threats, had not been sufficient to motivate U.S. balancing action from 1988 to early 1990, but they were in 1990 after the invasion. In fact, the United States engaged, even accommodated, both Iran and Iraq when they presented ideological and political, but not military, threats.

Third, it is true that global pressures did not play as great a role as expected in the United States' behavior in the Gulf. It is also true that the United States did balance against threat at the regional level even when that contradicted balancing against power at the global level. That is, it did balance against Iran's threat even if that strengthened Iraq, with which Moscow was aligned.

However, there was one type of situation in which global realities were important. We can extrapolate from the episodes that the external actor will be more likely to balance against threat at the regional level if that does not contradict balancing against threat (not power) at the global level. Thus, in the Iran-Contra case, the United States did not balance against threat as we might have expected, but partly because it was balancing against the threat that Moscow posed at the global level in its effort to lure Iran into its orbit. When that problem was not present, Washington did balance against Iran's threat, from 1982 to 1985. In the reflagging case as well, Washington could more easily balance against Iran's threat at the regional level because, by reflagging Kuwaiti tankers, it would also preempt a larger regional role by Moscow.

These three conditions pack independent explanatory power, but they work best in combination. We can see this clearly in the most extreme cases. From 1982 to 1985, and in 1987–88, when Washington strongly balanced against Iran's threat, these conditions were largely present. In contrast, from 1988 to 1990, when the United States clearly should have balanced against Iraq's threat, or at a minimum not appeased it, they were largely absent.

When considered together, these three conditions provide a more nuanced theory of when great powers will balance against threat in a region. As the stock of empirical tests grows, so will our confidence in this theory as compared with other possible explanations.

Conclusion

The school of realism has come under much attack, with some scholars considering it useful to write its epitaph.[19] It may, however, be too soon to do so. It is true that the results of this book do underscore how reality can clash with theoretical expectations. Ultimately, the real question is not whether the active balancer version of balance-of-power theory illuminates the behavior of states but whether states balance as much in the complex mix of strategies that they pursue, as the theory would have us believe.

The United States also did not behave much like an extraregional hegemon, which is what some would have expected. In fact, there appeared to be a disconnect between how people around the world saw the United States in the Persian Gulf and how it behaved. The United States, especially under George W. Bush, was viewed in many quarters as seeking to be a hegemon in the Gulf region. Certainly, some of its rhetoric fed into this perception, as did the invasion and subsequent occupation of Iraq in 2003. But, if we take the long view, it is hard to characterize the United States in this way across the period of time explored in this book. Although the United States did act much like an active or offshore balancer or an extraregional hegemon, it sometimes pursued balance-of-threat policy. This conclusion jibes with the general assumptions of at least some realist thinkers.

Realism and its many offshoots have competed with liberalism and its many offshoots for influence in the halls of academe, and though this book is not about liberalism, a few thoughts on the subject could not hurt. Liberalism, insofar as it constitutes a body of clear assumptions from which we can infer theories of grand strategy and foreign policy, would not have been a good guide in explaining American foreign policy in the Persian Gulf, largely because of the conflict-ridden nature of the region, one that seems to be a model for realist theory. Yet it is interesting to note that, over time, the United States did engage in policies that smacked of some liberal notions, perhaps in reaction to the prevailing realities of the Middle East. This behavior began partly with the notion of the new world order promulgated by the administration of the elder George Bush, which promoted some liberal notions within a broader context of realism in American foreign policy.[20] And it continued throughout the administration of George W. Bush, which sought to re-create Iraq with regime change and nation building and to spread democratic ideas in the Middle East, even at the risk of strategic upheaval.

Reactive Engagement

The United States, like other great powers in modern world politics or in history, could have pursued a grand strategy, but this book strongly suggests that it did not do so. The core of this book showed that the United States did not often act as an active balancer, carefully seeking to manage the regional balance of power and to apply balance-of-power policy. And it was even less likely to act in this manner over time from 1972 through 2005. Nor does the evidence in this book suggest that the United States was as an offshore balancer, involving itself in the region only as a last-resort strategy to prevent a major aggressor from gaining power. And contrary to the interesting case put forth by Christopher Layne, the United States also did not appear to pursue hegemonic strategy in the Persian Gulf, with the partial exception of the 2003 invasion of Iraq.

But all this leaves open a key question. If the United States did not behave much in line with these key strategies, how can we conceptualize its foreign policy in the region and what might this conceptualization suggest about foreign policy in more general terms?

I offer the concept of reactive engagement. Reactive engagement is not a conceptualization of how great powers develop or make foreign policy. That, of course, is a very complex subject area to which volumes and entire cottage industries are devoted.[1] Rather, it is a rough conceptualization of how the United States acted in a faraway place, a conceptualization that I believe explains American foreign policy in the Persian Gulf far better than can other conceptualizations and which may well apply beyond the Gulf context.

Several elements define what I mean by reactive engagement. First, reactive engagement does not reflect a grand strategy but rather no grand strategy. It challenges the notion that great powers have an organized, overarching strategy for dealing with world affairs. In this sense, it differs, for instance, from extraregional hegemony, which presumes that the United States pursued a strategy to dominate regions and the world, and from other grand strategies identified by various scholars.[2]

Second, the concept of grand strategy assumes that the foreign policy of great powers is consistent enough over time to lend itself to being described as a grand strategy. For instance, Layne notes that since "the early 1940s, the United States has pursued a grand strategy of extraregional hegemony," that it engaged in a "consistent" strategy to expand its power and hegemony.[3] For his part, Colin Dueck argues that "grand strategies persist until they have been proved a failure and are overturned in an election."[4]

Reactive engagement centrally underscores that foreign policy is often inconsistent over time. It assumes that it shifts, sometimes even rapidly and sometimes even in terms of the central approaches and beliefs that drive it. In the Persian Gulf, American policies did not fall easily or at all under one conceptual and organized roof. They sometimes were near opposites, based on different assumptions about and perceptions of Iran and Iraq, of the Middle East more broadly, and of America's role and capabilities in the region. Thus, constructive engagement toward Iraq was very much unlike balancing against Iran's threat, which was different from seeking to accommodate Iranian moderates or to engineer regime change in Iraq. Simply put, it is undeniable that the United States sometimes tried to placate or accommodate both Iran and Iraq and at other times it sought to undermine them, ultimately ousting Saddam Hussein.

In fact, the United States' goals shifted even at the most fundamental level. Basic elements of American political culture were deemphasized at certain points and emphasized at others. Thus, for most of the period covered in this book, democratizing the Middle East was subordinated to concerns about losing strategic allies, even if they were outright authoritarians of one stripe or another. For instance, Washington did not seek to push Saudi Arabia to democratize, partly because that could have weakened the royal family, which was more pro-American than the Saudi public. However, with the rise of the administration of George W. Bush, democratization became a more important motivation of U.S. foreign policy in the region, even if it ran the risk of alienating actors that many considered to be strategic allies.

Even the goal of protecting the region's oil supply shifted in importance from one case to another, though the tendency on the part of many observers was to see oil as consistently driving U.S. foreign policy. Thus oil was critical in pushing the United States to evict Iraq's forces from Kuwait, but it seemed to be at best a tertiary motivation in the invasion of Iraq in 2003 and in some previous cases as well, such as the Iran-Contra affair.

Third, reactive engagement posits that foreign policy is not consistent partly because great powers have so many goals across so many arenas. They sometimes conflict with one another and undermine the ability to develop grand strategy, even if that proclivity exists periodically in the minds of decision makers. The United States, for instance, had multiple goals at the domestic, regional, and global level which often precluded the pursuit of balance-of-power policy, insofar as it wanted to pursue it in the first place. Reactive engagement sees these multiple goals as expressing themselves in various parts in the content and nature of overall foreign policy, more like uncoordinated inputs than well-planned brushstrokes on a master painting.

Fourth, grand strategy tends to assume that the United States' behavior is similar in different regions. Otherwise we would not call it a grand strategy or at least would qualify grand strategy to be region- or time-specific. Reactive engagement asserts that even if grand strategy can be discerned in one region, it is not likely to be carried out in multiple regions. The concept of reactive engagement allows for the possibility that there are different strokes for different regions, insofar as we can discern such organized strokes on the complex tapestry of world affairs.

Fifth, reactive engagement recognizes that states formulate policies toward regions. But at its core, it posits that the foreign policies of great powers are often made in reaction to key events or are shaped by them. Reactivity is fundamentally different from grand strategy. Reactive behavior, by definition, is not planned but improvised. It is not governed by the motives and interests of great powers nearly as much as it is driven by events beyond their control. It sometimes results in changes in foreign policy that may throttle preexisting ideas and approaches. And it belies the image of control that great powers seek to project and which many people perceive in their behaviors.

American reactivity to unpredictable, surprising, and sometimes confounding events was plainly clear from the record. Thus, in the Persian Gulf, the Iranian revolution, which caught the United States by surprise, felled the twin pillar policy and inaugurated an era of greater American involvement in the region. The Iran-Iraq War, produced by Iraq's decision to invade Iran in 1980 and Iran's refusal to end the war with Saddam still in power, forced Washington to balance against Iran's threat in ways that it did not anticipate and did not manage well. High-level concern about American hostages seized in Lebanon, reflected in President Reagan's immense attention to their plight, played an important role in generating the Iran-Contra approach. The shocking invasion of Kuwait, which few predicted around the world, moved Washington from constructive engagement to war and containment. And the horrible attacks of September 11 contributed to an effort to launch regime change in Iraq by use of military force and in earnest.

The United States certainly did not predict these events. Nor did its existing policies offer the scaffolding necessary to deal with them. Nor, in fact, could it possibly understand how these events would independently and in toto alter history. Rather, it reacted to them, sometimes under time pressure and often with an exaggerated sense of its ability to effect outcomes. That was certainly true of the Iranian revolution, the Iran-Contra affair, efforts to accommodate Saddam Hussein in the late 1980s, and the 2003 invasion of Iraq. We might even say that, rather than pursuing a grand strategy, Washington pursued grand overoptimism.

Of course, it is possible to be reactive and still pursue a grand strategy, but that is difficult because policies shaped in reaction to various events are not likely to fall under one grand strategy and be consistent but will tend to be tailored to the time, event, and place. Thus, taken as a whole, they are likely to be different from one another, as our tale of U.S. foreign policy clearly shows. For instance, the Iran-Contra policy was vastly different from Operation Staunch against Iran, which came just one year later; constructive engagement toward Iraq was dramatically different from subsequent policies toward Iraq; and the twin pillar policy was radically different from invading Iraq to produce regime change and democratization. As one twenty-five-year veteran of policy making for the Persian Gulf described it, "most new initiatives or policy pronouncements were driven principally by events in the region that required a new U.S. response, often because the region lacked its own security mechanisms or institutions. What can be seen as a US hegemonic agenda is therefore more hegemony by default than by design."[5]

Sixth, insofar as it involves any approach, reactive engagement presumes that one major approach will be much more likely than the others: balance-of-threat policy. Like Edwardian Britain and imperial Spain, the United States faced rising threats.[6] Washington was much more likely to respond to prevailing threats, as they arose, than it was, for instance, to respond to prevailing power, to seek hegemony, or to pursue collective security. But it is fair to stress that balance-of-threat policy sometimes was at play and sometimes was not.

Seventh, the belief that states create and pursue grand strategies is based partly on an implicit faith in rationalism, on the notion that actors are purposeful, that they identify options, weigh their costs and benefits, and choose or try to choose the best option. Reactive engagement suggests that we should be careful about easily ascribing grand designs to U.S. foreign policy which assume careful, deliberate, and long-range planning. In an earlier book, *Explaining Foreign Policy*, I argued that we should not be quick to assume that states act in line with the assumptions of the rational actor model. I tried to show, drawing on a host of primary documents and on interviews with the key high-level decision makers, that we would be misled if we assumed that the United States did so in its decisions during the 1990–91 Persian Gulf crisis. The book showed how and explained why it was important to draw upon and apply multiple models, including the rational actor model, for understanding how states make decisions, and it developed an integrated theoretical approach for doing so.[7]

This book has a similar metatheoretical theme, though an entirely different goal. It is not about decision making that produces foreign policy actions but rather about how we conceptualize the actual foreign policies of states. The evidence from this book and the concept of reactive engagement caution against assuming that states use single, grand strategies.

However, to be clear, all this discussion is not to impugn the study of grand strategy. This book, first off, has focused on the American experience in the Persian Gulf. Its conclusions about grand strategy apply chiefly in that context. Certainly, there are cases in world politics in which grand strategy has been significantly at play. American containment strategy during the Cold War appears to be a case in point,[8] and this may be the case in various regions of the world at certain periods of history as well.

Moreover, the study of grand strategy is very valuable, irrespective of whether states often pursue such strategies. It is an important enterprise, a critical process of thought. It frames the big questions; it forces us to assess and examine the larger picture; it sketches possible cause and effect; it may help us see things that we otherwise would have overlooked; and it serves as a foil for weighing how states do behave. In addition, understanding different grand strategies is like having multiple tools in one's intellectual tool kit. These tools can then be used as perspectives on reality, as perspectives for analysis, as a way to inform us about how states might behave in theory.

That said, we need to do much more to test our interesting theories, concepts, and grand strategies against reality. We need to weigh them against the historical and contemporary record of actual state behavior. Doing so may yield a richer view of how states actually behave, a view that draws upon and reflects aspects of multiple grand strategies.

Ultimately, however, I would suggest that randomness all too often parades as design. The behavior of states, even great powers, seems to be a messy affair, shaped not only by the mix of complex factors related to the "black box" of decision making but also by a combination of external realities to which states must react. In this perspective, decision makers may want to react within an ordered architecture of thought, but that becomes a challenge. Instead, they may be forced to react without much preparation and with an admixture of behaviors that at best reflect aspects of multiple grand strategies and which may not last long in the overall evolution of foreign policy.

It may become a historical truism that great powers start with grand ideas but end up with a high dose of reality. Alas, they may strike up notions of grand strategy and get struck down by the caprice endemic in the human condition.

Appendix: Core Interviews

Scott Armstrong, phone interview, August 23, 1997.

James Baker, secretary of state, Washington, D.C., July 26, 1996.

Guy Caruso, Energy Information Administration director, Washington, D.C., August 8, 2003.

Sandra Charles, National Security Council analyst, Washington, D.C., June 5, 1997.

Lawrence Eagleburger, secretary of state, phone interview, July 10, 2001.

Chas W. Freeman Jr., U.S. ambassador to Saudi Arabia, Washington, D.C., February 19, 1999.

Richard Haass, special assistant to the president for Near East and South Asian Affairs, Washington, D.C., February 19, 1999.

Kenneth Juster, undersecretary of commerce, phone interview, July 29, 1999.

Ellen Laipson, National Security Council analyst, Washington, D.C., August 8, 2006.

Richard Murphy, assistant secretary of state, phone interview, August 24, 1998.

Thomas Pickering, U.S. ambassador to the United Nations, Washington: D.C., March 2, 2001.

Kenneth Pollack, CIA analyst, Washington, D.C., June 30, 2005.

Brent Scowcroft, national security adviser, Washington, D.C., February 19, 1999.

Bandar bin Sultan, Saudi ambassador to the United States, Washington, D.C., October 28, 1997.

William Webster, CIA director, Washington, D.C., October 1, 1999.

Notes

Abbreviations Used in the Notes and Bibliography

CDSP	*Current Digest of the Soviet Press*
CIA	U.S. Central Intelligence Agency
CRS	Congressional Research Service
DSR	Declassified, U.S. Department of State EO Systematic Review (June 30, 2005), National Archives
FBIS	Foreign Broadcast Information Service
GBPL	George Bush Presidential Library, Texas A&M University, College Station, Texas
GPO	Government Publishing Office
JPRS	Joint Publications Research Service
MEA	Middle East and Africa
MECS	*Middle East Contemporary Survey*
MEED	*Middle East Economic Digest*
MEES	*Middle East Economic Survey*
NA	National Archives
NENA	Near East and North Africa
NESA	Near East and South Asia
NIC	National Intelligence Council
NIE	National Intelligence Estimate
NSA	National Security Archive, Washington, D.C.
NSC	National Security Council
NSDD	National Security Decision Directive

INTRODUCTION: No Grand Strategy

1. For a brief discussion of the literature on bandwagoning, see Schweller, "Bandwagoning for Profit," 72–74.

2. Because the weaker side has more need for assistance, new members can increase their influence much more by joining it instead of the stronger side and can reap more gains because the weaker side will value their support more. Walt, *Origins of Alliances*, 18–19.

3. Taliaferro, *Balancing Risks*, 228. For an overview of the variants of realism, see Taliaferro, "Security Seeking under Anarchy," 132–35.

4. See Layne, *Peace of Illusions*, esp. 19. Indeed, this claim is sometimes made even

regarding structural realism. See Elman, "Horses for Courses," 10–11. See also Layne, *Peace of Illusions*, esp. 19.

5. Dueck, *Reluctant Crusaders*, 11.

6. Robert Art identifies eight strategies: dominion aims, to rule the world; global collective security, to keep peace everywhere; regional collective security, to keep the peace in some places; cooperative security, to reduce the occurrence of war by limiting the offensive military capabilities of states; containment, to hold the line against a specific aggressor state; offshore balancing, to do that and, in addition, to cut down any emerging Eurasian hegemon; and selective engagement, to do a selected number of critical tasks. Art, *Grand Strategy for America*, chap. 3. See Layne, *Peace of Illusions*, chap. 8, on the differences between hegemony, offshore balancing, and selective engagement.

On various grand strategies, see Kupchan, *Vulnerability of Empire*. For a good discussion of how to define grand strategy and for an analysis of what the author considers to be the four main grand strategies — strategic disengagement, balance of power, primacy, and liberal internationalism — see Dueck, *Reluctant Crusaders*, chaps. 1 and 5. On definitions, see Kennedy, *Grand Strategies in War and Peace*, 2–4. In addition, see Lieber, *Eagle without a Cause*. For an analysis of various grand strategies, see Posen and Ross, "Competing U.S. Grand Strategies."

7. Dueck, *Reluctant Crusaders*, 11. On the need for American grand strategy in the post–9/11 world, see Lieber, *American Era*.

8. See Barylski, "Collapse of the Soviet Union," 98; on Central America, Walt, *Origins of Alliances*, 23; on Europe, Khalilzad, "Losing the Moment"; and on Asia broadly, Ott, "Dragon's Reach," 118–26.

9. Betts, "Wealth, Power, and Instability," 34–77. See also Perlez, "U.S. Competes with China."

10. Thomas, "South Asian Security Balance," 305.

11. See, for instance, Indyk et al., "Symposium on Dual Containment," 2, and Lake, "Confronting Backlash States," esp. 48–50.

12. Telhami, "Are We Stuck in Iraq?"

13. For instance, Said, "Potential Egyptian Contribution." On the Bush Doctrine, see Monten, "Roots of the Bush Doctrine."

14. Russell, "Persian Gulf's Collective Security Mirage," 77.

15. Ibid., 82.

16. These actions capture roughly what this book means by balance-of-power behavior for an external actor. However, many different definitions of balance of power exist. Ernst Haas discovered eight different meanings of this concept; Martin Wight found nine. Haas, "Balance of Power," 442–77; Wight, "Balance of Power."

17. See Halper and Clarke, *America Alone*, 76–77.

18. See n. 6 above.

19. Layne, *Peace of Illusions*, 5.

20. Ibid., 178–79.

21. For Mearsheimer, the offshore balancer tends to focus more on how great powers will try to prevent other great powers from becoming hegemons in distant regions and less so on how great powers will prevent rising states within distant regions from gaining power. Mearsheimer, *Tragedy of Great Power Politics*.

22. On the differences between these schools of realism, see Mearsheimer, *Tragedy of Great Power Politics*. Wohlforth, *Elusive Balance*. On the United States as an offshore bal-

ancer, Layne, *Peace of Illusions*, 193, 23–28. John Mearsheimer's variant of offensive realism may appear to predict a hegemonic strategy. However, Mearsheimer asserts that great powers may want to be global hegemons but that hegemony faces limits, that "the best outcome a great power can hope for is to be a regional hegemon and possibly control another region that is nearby and accessible over land," but, in essence, "if a potential hegemon emerges . . . the distant hegemon would take the appropriate measures to deal with the threatening state" as an offshore balancer, provided that local great powers could not "do the job." See Mearsheimer, *Tragedy of Great Power Politics*, 41–42, 236–37.

23. Art, *Grand Strategy for America*, 176.

24. Mearsheimer, *Tragedy of Great Power Politics*, 237, 252, 139.

25. Joffe, *Überpower.* For a brief description of this policy, see 132–41.

26. On the characteristics of a credible balancer, see Sheehan, "Place of the Balancer," 128–29.

27. See Knock, *To End All Wars.*

28. Art, *Grand Strategy for America*, 206.

29. On the offshore balancer and preventing hegemony, Layne, *Peace of Illusions*, 160.

30. Kissinger, *Diplomacy*, 70.

31. On Roosevelt's views, see Kissinger, *Does America Need a Foreign Policy?*

32. Ikenberry and his colleagues explain why other states are not balancing much against the power of United States at the global level. See Ikenberry, *America Unrivaled.* For an argument that states in fact are balancing against the United States but in ways that are not militarily based, see Pape, "Soft Balancing against the United States," and Paul, "Soft Balancing in the Age of U.S. Primacy," esp. 58–59.

33. For a brief elaboration, see Layne, *Peace of Illusions*, 19–22.

34. Ibid., 3.

35. Ibid., 11. For a brief argument on how the United States pursued a hegemonic strategy in Asia after the Cold War, see Mastanduno, "Incomplete Hegemony and Security Order," esp. 193–96.

36. Many, of course, would agree that the United States became a hegemon in this sense after the fall of the Soviet Union. See, for instance, Posen, "Command of the Commons," 5–46. See the varied contributions in Lieber, *Eagle Rules*, xii. Ikenberry, *America Unrivaled.*

37. It is a neoclassical realist theory that incorporates systemic and domestic-level variables and assumes that the balance of power at the systemic level, as well as domestic factors such as ideology and perception, explains outcomes. See Layne, *Peace of Illusions*, 28–36.

38. Ranke (on European history) cited in Ferguson, *Colossus*, 296.

39. Robert Art identifies a grand strategy that he refers to as "dominion" and which he cautions Washington not to pursue. The strategy reflects the use of "American military power in an imperial fashion to effect the transformation." Art, *Grand Strategy for America*, 83. Stephen Walt and others refer to primacy, which Art does not consider a grand strategy but which shares the characteristics of hegemony as discussed by Layne. See Walt, *Taming American Power*, 40–60.

A voluminous literature exists on hegemony, empire, and imperialism, and many different definitions and terms are used. Some of the works refer directly to the Persian Gulf, and others are cast more generally but include the Gulf region. It is important not to conflate hegemony, empire, imperialism, and primacy, although they certainly do share some characteristics. On this literature, see, for instance, Craig, "American Realism versus American Imperialism," 143–71. Maier, *Among Empires*. See also Ferguson (*Colossus*, esp. 286–88), who believes that the United States has sought empire but has not been very good at doing so, being too constrained in its efforts. As he puts it, in "many respects, the American empire shares the same aspirations and ambitions as the last great Anglophone hegemon"—but there were "clear limits to American stamina" (288).

40. For polling information on this image, see Kohut and Stokes, *America against the World*.

41. For instance, Layne, *Peace of Illusions*, 3, 25.

42. Of all the existing grand strategies that scholars have identified, this would be closest to Robert Art's notion of selective engagement, although still quite different from it. Art, *Grand Strategy for America*.

43. For instance, Art does not include it in his sweeping typology. Ibid.

44. For those interested in theory, reactive engagement does share with defensive realism the notion that states are far more likely to react to threat than to be hegemonic. However, they differ markedly in that reactive engagement is not a theory, much less an international relations theory. Nor does reactive engagement share the assumptions that states are necessarily rational and driven by security concerns. It portrays states as driven by multiple motivations that are highly variable.

45. As regularly forecast by the U.S. Department of Energy. See its *International Energy Outlook*.

46. Merry, *Sands of Empire*.

47. *Cato Handbook for Congress, 105th Congress*, Persian Gulf Policy.

48. Walt, *Taming American Power*. Layne, *Peace of Illusions*.

49. For a good discussion of different grand strategies, see Art, *Grand Strategy for America*, chap. 3.

50. Kissinger, *Diplomacy*, 24.

51. The neoclassical literature challenges or revises balance-of-power theory; an example is Schweller, *Deadly Imbalances*. On the development of balance-of-risk theory, see Taliaferro, *Balancing Risks*. See also David, "Explaining Third World Alignment," 233–56. For a broader discussion of the central works through 1993, see Schweller, "Bandwagoning for Profit," esp. 249–56. Papayoanou, *Power Ties*. Niou and Ordeshook, "Theory of the Balance of Power in International Systems," 685–715.

On empirical challenges, for instance, see Miller, "Bringing the Leader Back In." See also Kaufman, "To Balance or to Bandwagon," 417–47. For a scholarly challenge to neorealist theory and an argument that states usually bandwagon, see Schroeder, "Historical Reality," 108–48. Walt addresses the empirical and theoretical challenges prior to 1987 in *Origins of Alliances*, 6–11.

52. For a brief discussion, see Schweller, "Bandwagoning for Profit," esp. 72–74. See also Schroeder, "Historical Reality," 108–48.

53. Walt, *Origins of Alliances*, 5. For a critical analysis of Walt's work, see Keohane, "Alliances, Threats, and the Uses of Neorealism," 169–76.

54. Namely, Walt, *Origins of Alliances*. David, "Explaining Third World Alignment."

55. Walt, *Origins of Alliances*, 149.

56. For full or partial exceptions, see Layne, *Peace of Illusions*. See Elman, "Extending Offensive Realism," 575. Walt, *Origins of Alliances*. Schroeder, "Historical Reality." Posen, *Sources of Military Doctrine*. To some extent, see Mastanduno, "Preserving the Unipolar

Moment," 49–88. For an exception that draws on mathematics rather than empirics, see Simowitz, *Logical Consistency and Soundness of Balance of Power Theory*.

57. Layne, *Peace of Illusions*.

58. David, "Explaining Third World Alignment," 252.

59. Indeed, in a lengthy annotated bibliography on Gulf security, no work identified deals seriously with it. Cordesman, *After the Storm*, 757–71. Although he excellently explores the distribution of capabilities, none of his work examines balancing in practice or theory. For an exception on the period of 1955–79, see Walt, *Origins of Alliances*.

60. On this endeavor, see Paul, Wirtz, and Fortmann, *Balance of Power*.

CHAPTER ONE: Exploring Great Powers in Regions

1. On the assertion, see Yetiv, *Crude Awakenings*, chaps. 6 and 7.

2. For interesting works on regionalism, regional subsystems, and/or regional security complexes which include excellent bibliographical references, see Gamble and Payne, *Regionalism and World Order*. Lake and Morgan, *Regional Orders*, esp. 46–52. Buzan, "Regional Security." Mansfield and Milner, "New Wave of Regionalism," 589–627. Wriggins et al., *Dynamics of Regional Politics*. Others have advanced the notion of security communities for subregional and broader analyses. See Adler and Barnett, *Security Communities*.

3. See Thompson, "Regional Subsystem."

4. Ibid.

5. Buzan, "Regional Security."

6. Lake and Morgan, "Regional Security Complexes," 48–50.

7. For instance, see Gamble and Payne, *Regionalism and World Order*.

8. Mansfield and Milner, "New Wave," 591. See also Lake and Morgan, *Regional Orders*, chaps. 8 and 12.

9. For a concise description of the various schools within the constructivist paradigm which includes an excellent bibliography, see Schwandt, "Constructivist, Interpretivist Approaches to Human Inquiry," esp. 128–29. See also Wendt, *Social Theory of International Politics*.

10. Lake and Morgan, *Regional Orders*.

11. Buzan, "Regional Security."

12. See Jackson, *Quasi-States*, and Philpott, *Revolutions in Sovereignty*.

13. For a good discussion, see Sheehan, *Balance of Power*, 91–93.

14. Game theory might treat this as a nested game in future work.

15. Churchill, *Gathering Storm*, 207–8. The active balancer is expected to balance chiefly against power but also against threat. Kissinger, *Diplomacy*, 72–73. Sheehan, *Balance of Power*, 138.

16. Walt, *Origins of Alliances*, 157–58.

17. See Yetiv, *Crude Awakenings*, chap. 6.

18. On the refinements of other scholars, see Schweller, "Bandwagoning for Profit."

19. Walt, *Origins of Alliances*. Schroeder, "Historical Reality."

20. As opposed to "soft balancing," which is primarily not militarily based. See Pape, "Soft Balancing against the United States," and Paul, "Soft Balancing in the Age of U.S. Primacy," esp. 58–59.

21. See Sheehan, "Place of the Balancer," esp. 124.

22. Ibid. See also Gulick, *Europe's Classical Balance of Power*, 67–70.

23. Sheehan, *Balance of Power*, 2–4, 11–15, and chap. 2.

24. Kissinger, *Diplomacy*, 72.

25. On how the administration of George W. Bush deviated from this approach, see Layne, *Peace of Illusions*, 120–24.

26. On balancing motivations in traditional balance-of-power theory, see Gulick, *Europe's Classical Balance of Power*; Claude, *Power and International Relations*, chaps. 2 and 3; and Waltz, *Theory of International Politics*, esp. chap. 6. Morgenthau and Thompson, *Politics Among Nations*, 6th ed., esp. chp. 11. Liska, *Nations in Alliance*, 13.

27. Walt, *Origins of Alliances*, 21–26.

28. For insights into the importance of the perception of the balance of power, see Christensen, "Perceptions and Alliances in Europe," 65–97.

29. Walt, *Origins of Alliances*, 22.

30. Schweller, *Deadly Imbalances*, 26–31.

31. That is what measures of power, such as COW, seek to capture. On COW, see Schweller, *Deadly Imbalances*, esp. 26–27.

32. I have argued that Saudi Arabia became a weaker third pole, but this occurred only in the 1990s. Yetiv, *Crude Awakenings*, chap. 4.

33. See Moore, "Assessment of the Iranian Military Rearmament Program," 377, fig. 1.

34. See ibid., 381, fig. 4.

35. See King, Keohane, and Verba, *Designing Social Inquiry*, chap. 6.

36. Lijphart, "Comparative Politics and the Comparative Method," 689.

37. Levy, "What Do Great Powers Balance against and When," 46.

CHAPTER TWO: The Nixon Administration's Twin Pillars

1. This paragraph is based partly on Palmer, *Guardians of the Gulf*, 27–29, 46–47. Yergin, *The Prize*, 391–400.

2. See Darby, *British Defense Policy East of Suez*. Bartlett, *Long Retreat*.

3. On the nature of the agreement, see CIA, "Moscow and the Persian Gulf," memo, May 12, 1972, IR00766. This document, as well as others cited in this book, is drawn from NSA and Chadwyck-Healey (publisher).

4. U.S. Department of State, "South and Southwest Asia: New Policy Perspectives," report, December 31, 1976, IR01136, NSA, 20.

5. Bill, *Eagle and the Lion*, esp. 200–204.

6. U.S. Department of State, "The Evolution of the U.S.-Iranian Relationship," report, January 29, 1980, IR03555, NSA.

7. See Cordesman, *Gulf and the Search for Strategic Stability*, 160.

8. See Nixon, *U.S. Foreign Policy for the 1970's*, 55–56.

9. For a good discussion of the twin pillars, see Haass, "Saudi Arabia and Iran," chap. 8. See also Bill, *Eagle and the Lion*, esp. 200–204. On protecting the status quo, Kissinger, *White House Years*, 1263–64. For official statements on the Nixon Doctrine, see U.S. Congress, House, Committee on Foreign Affairs, Subcommittee on the Near East and South Asia, *New Perspectives on the Persian Gulf*, 1973.

10. Palmer, *Guardians of the Gulf*, 85.

11. On these sales, see Bill, *Eagle and the Lion*, 200–201. Sick, *All Fall Down*, 13–15. Vance, *Hard Choices*, 315.

12. Kissinger to Ford, memo, "Strategy for Your Discussion with the Shah of Iran," May 13, 1975, IR00955, NSA, 3.

13. American Embassy in Tehran to Secretary of State, memo, "Iranian Involvement in World Affairs Deepens," August 22, 1974 (1974TEHRAN07081), DSR.

14. Bill, *Eagle and the Lion*, 202–3. Ramazani, *United States and Iran*, 47–48.

15. See U.S. Department of State, "Evolution of the U.S.-Iranian Relationship," 20. This document provides a list of major weapons systems delivered to Iran between 1972 and 1978.

16. Palmer, *Guardians of the Gulf*, 88.

17. Kissinger to Ford memo, "Strategy for Your Discussion with the Shah of Iran."

18. Kissinger, *White House Years*, 1263–64.

19. Ibid., 1263.

20. See Litwak, *Détente and the Nixon Doctrine*.

21. See Nelson, *Making of Détente*.

22. Kissinger, *White House Years*, 1263–64.

23. On Soviet objectives and efforts, see, for instance, CIA, "The Soviets in the Persian Gulf/Arabian Peninsula," IR01127, Secret Report, December 1976, NSA.

24. Omani officials in particular took this Soviet threat seriously. See Salalah Domestic Service, August 27, 1981, in FBIS: MEA, August 27, 1981, C1.

25. Middleton, "Arabian Anxieties."

26. For the views of key American officials on the role of Iran in American security, see Vance, *Hard Choices*, chaps. 14, 15.

27. American Embassy in Tehran to Secretary of State, memo, "Successor to Canada on ICCS," July 14, 1973 (1973TEHRAN04915), DSR.

28. American Embassy in Tehran to Secretary of State, memo, "Iran's Foreign Ministry Publishes Annual Report on GOI Foreign Relations," June 28, 1973 (1973TEHRAN04574), DSR.

29. U.S. Department of State, "Evolution of the U.S.-Iranian Relationship," 20–21; on the shah's open call, see American Embassy in Tehran to Secretary of State, memo, "Shah's Press Interview," November 26, 1973 (1973TEHRAN08305), DSR.

30. CIA, "Moscow and the Persian Gulf."

31. Kissinger to Ford memo, "Strategy for Your Discussion with the Shah of Iran," 4.

32. American Embassy in Tehran to Secretary of State, memo, "Soviet Ambassador's Audience with Shah," July 18, 1973 (1973TEHRAN05011), DSR.

33. American Embassy in Tehran to Secretary of State, memo, "Iranian Involvement in World Affairs Deepens."

34. See Rosati, *Carter Administration's Quest for Global Community*.

35. See Skidmore, *Reversing Course*, 29–30.

36. Vance, *Hard Choices*, 319–21; Sick, *All Fall Down*, 26–27.

37. See Secretary of State to USINT Cairo, memo, "Possibility of Decrease in Oil Prices," December 27, 1973 (1973TEHRAN250751), DSR.

38. U.S. Department of State, "Iran's Role in Oil Price Increases and U.S. Actions," report, January 29, 1980, IR03567, NSA.

39. American Embassy in Tehran to Secretary of State memo, "Iranian Involvement in World Affairs Deepens."

40. American Embassy in Tehran to Secretary of State, memo, "Iranian Shah's Views on Oil Prices, Other Matters," July 24, 1974 (1974TEHRAN06142), DSR.

41. See Yergin, *The Prize*, 645–46. Vance, *Hard Choices*, 22.

42. U.S. Department of State, "Evolution of the U.S.-Iranian Relationship," 23.

43. See Palmer, *Guardians of the Gulf*, 90.

44. American Embassy in Jidda to Secretary of State, memo, "Prince Sultan Presents Views on SAG Role in Gulf," July 17, 1973 (1973TEHRAN02981), DSR. See also memo, "Prince Sultan Speaks Further on Sag Role in Gulf," July 24, 1973 (1973Jidda03105).

45. See Ramazani, *Persian Gulf*, 143–48, for transcript of the January 29, 1972, press conference held by the shah of Iran. On Washington's understanding of the point, American Embassy in Tehran to Secretary of State memo, "Iranian Involvement in World Affairs Deepens."

46. On Khomeini's views, see Blumberg, *Reinventing Khomeini*.

47. Aden Domestic Service, in FBIS: MEA, January 4, 1979, C1–C2.

48. See "Comments by Sultan Qabus of Oman," *Oslo Arbeiderbladet*, in FBIS: MEA, February 16, 1979, C2. See *MEED*, March 9, 1979, 14.

49. For his speeches in 1979 and 1980s, see Rajaee, *Islamic Values and World View*, 48, 82–33.

50. For a concise description of Khomeini's worldview, see Ramazani, *Revolutionary Iran*, 19–31.

51. See ibid.

52. On the Saudi view, see *London Al-Hawadith*, in JPRS: NENA (73101), 107.

53. See *MEES*, August 6, 1979, 3. Iran praised the Gulf states for rejecting the Omani plan, which called for increased cooperation with Washington. See *Al-Ray'y Al-'Amm*, in JPRS: NENA (74695), September 23, 1979, 23.

54. Skoçpol, *States and Social Revolutions*.

55. For a good discussion of the twin pillars, see Haass, "Saudi Arabia and Iran," chap. 8.

56. See Safran, *Saudi Arabia*.

57. See comments by Oman's Qabus, *Oslo Arbeiderbladet*, in FBIS: MEA, February 16, 1979, C2, and Middleton, "Arabian Anxieties," A2; "Saudi Arabia and the United States," CRS Report, 8, prepared for the Subcommittee on Europe and the Middle East of the Committee on Foreign Affairs, August 1981.

58. Quandt, *Saudi Arabia in the 1980s*, 40.

59. On Saudi security perceptions, see Safran, *Saudi Arabia*.

60. On the Egyptian response to attempts to isolate it, see *MEES*, April 16, 1979, 3.

61. Lesch, *1979*, 82–94.

62. For a factual record of the Mecca crisis, see *MECS* 4 (1979–80): 682–88.

63. See U.S. Congress, Senate, Committee on Foreign Relations, *Security Interests and Policy in Southwest Asia*, February 6, 1980, 275–76.

64. For details, see *MEED*, December 7, 1979, 24.

65. A small rally supported Khomeini. See Manama Gulf News Agency, in FBIS: MENA, February 23, 1979, C1.

66. Prince Bandar bin Sultan, Saudi ambassador to the United States, interview with author, Washington, D.C., October 28, 1997.

67. See Goldberg, "Saudi Arabia," 130–31.

68. Ibid. See also Eilts, "Security Considerations in the Persian Gulf," 102.

69. See Kissinger, *Diplomacy*, 713.

CHAPTER THREE: The Reagan Administration and the Iran-Iraq War

1. See Lesch, *1979*.

2. Gwertzman, "U.S. Officials React Warily."

3. Vance, *Hard Choices*, 343.

4. On these American efforts, see Rubin, *Paved with Good Intentions*, 295–96, 253, 260.

5. Chronology in ibid., 370.

6. See Sick, *All Fall Down*, 188, 215–16, 241. Also, for a discussion of the impact of the embassy seizure, see Chubin, *Security in the Gulf*, 16–21.

7. On his view in October, U.S. Congress, House, *Chronologies*, 1979, 198.

8. Johnson, *Military as an Instrument of U.S. Policy*, 9 (citing interview with Komer).

9. On this episode, see Sick, *All Fall Down*, chap. 13.

10. Regarding the hostage crisis, a Defense Department team was sent to the Gulf in December, prior to the Soviet invasion, for exploratory talks on access to facilities in the Middle East. U.S. Congress, House, *Chronologies*, 1979, 208.

11. See U.S. Congress, House, *Chronologies*, 1979, 170.

12. Wilson, "Carter Budget Envisions a Force for Quick, Long-Distance Reaction."

13. Burt, "U.S. Studying Ways to Bolster Strength in Mideast."

14. Newsome, "America Engulfed," 27.

15. On this effort, see testimony by Harold Saunders in U.S. Congress, House, Subcommittee on Europe and the Middle East of the Committee on Foreign Affairs, *U.S. Policy toward Iran*, January 17, 1979, 43.

16. For details, see Chubin, "Soviet Policy toward Iran and the Gulf," 11.

17. Sick, *All Fall Down*, 95–97. See also CIA, "Soviet Efforts to Benefit from the U.S.-Iran Crisis," report, December 15, 1979, IR03508, NSA.

18. See U.S. Congress, House, Subcommittee on Europe and the Middle East of the Committee on Foreign Affairs, *U.S. Policy toward Iran*, January 17, 1979, 34.

19. See "Saudi Arabia and the United States," CRS Report, 8, prepared for the Subcommittee on Europe and the Middle East of the Committee on Foreign Affairs, August 1981, 12.

20. Iran's ambassador cited in *Pravda*, November 27, 1979, in *CDSP*, December 26, 1979, 21.

21. Gromyko cited in Anderson, "Double-Dealing on Iran Laid to Soviets."

22. See Keddie and Gasiorowski, *Neither East nor West*.

23. For a good discussion of the "Great Game," see Curzon, *Russia in Central Asia in 1889*. Hauner, "Last Great Game."

24. Prince Bandar bin Sultan, Saudi ambassador to the United States, interview with author, Washington, D.C., October 28, 1997. See *Kuwait Ar-Ra'y Al-Amm*, January 9, 1979, in FBIS: MEA, January 12, 1979, C1. See also *MECS* 3 (1978–79), 22. Even the shah blamed Washington for his demise. Sick, *All Fall Down*, 179. Also, on America's loss of credibility, see *MECS* 3 (1978–79), 751. See also *MEED*, March 9, 1979, 13.

25. Ibid.

26. On the Nixon and Carter doctrines, see Palmer, *Guardians of the Gulf*, 85–111.

27. On deterring "outside" pressure, see the statement by Nicholas Veliotes, assistant secretary for Near Eastern and South Asian Affairs, in U.S. Congress, House, Subcommittee on Foreign Affairs and the Joint Economic Committee, *U.S. Policy toward the Persian Gulf*, May 10, 1982, 9.

28. In Reagan, *Public Papers of the Presidents, 1982*, 873, 952.

29. For extensive details and tables on logistical support, see Yetiv, *America and the Persian Gulf*.

30. See statement by Harold Brown, secretary of defense, and by General Jones, former chairman of the Joint Chiefs of Staff, in U.S. Congress, House, *Foreign Assistance Legisla-*

tion for Fiscal Year 1981, pt. I (Washington, DC: GPO, 1980), 202–3, 221. See also U.S. Congress, House, *US Congress, Rapid Deployment Forces: Policy and Budgetary Implications* (Washington, DC: Congressional Budget Office, 1983), XIV, 4, 8, 11. See also interview with Secretary Brown, *Wall Street Journal*, July 1, 1980, 22.

31. On naval force deployment, address by Secretary of Defense Brown, in *Department of State Bulletin* 80 (May 1980): 66.

32. Scott Armstrong, phone interview with author, August 23, 1997; Armstrong originally broke this story for the *Washington Post* and then revisited it for *Mother Jones*.

33. See Yetiv, "How the Soviet Military Intervention in Afghanistan Improved the U.S. Strategic Position in the Persian Gulf," 62–81.

34. Ultimately, Iraq's new Shiite-led government publicly acknowledged in May 2005 for the first time that Iraq was to blame for the war, inflaming the sentiments of Iraq's Sunnis, who supported Saddam Hussein.

35. On the origins of the war, see Chubin and Tripp, *Iran And Iraq at War*, chap. 2.

36. See Cottam, "Revolutionary Iran and the War with Iraq," esp. 5–9.

37. On the differences between Iraq's and Iran's Shiites, see Nakash, *Shi'is of Iraq*.

38. See Lebow, *Between Peace and War*, 254–57; see also Niou and Ordeshook, "Preventive War and the Balance of Power," 327–419.

39. See "Interview with King Fahd," *London Al-Hawadith*, in FBIS: NESA, February 14, 1992, 21.

40. Lavy, "Economic Embargo of Egypt," 421.

41. On its increased influence over Saudi Arabia, see *MECS* 3 (1978–79): 236.

42. "Aziz Interview," *London Al-Tadamun*, in FBIS: NESA, September 26, 1990, 31.

43. For a more lengthy discussion of the origins of war, see MECS 14 (1990): 73–82.

44. See Freedman and Karsh, *Gulf Conflict*, 21.

45. On these relations, see Sick, *All Fall Down*. Bill, *Eagle and the Lion*, esp. 313–14.

46. See Chubin and Tripp, *Iran And Iraq at War*, 206–8.

47. For more details, see Shultz, *Turmoil and Triumph*. See also Karsh, *Iran-Iraq War*.

48. Freedman and Karsh, *Gulf Conflict*, 25.

49. On the benefits of the intelligence, Pollack, *Persian Puzzle*, 206–8.

50. Shultz, *Turmoil and Triumph*, 235–37.

51. See, for instance, Veliotes to Eagleburger, memo, U.S. Department of State, October 7, 1983, NSA.

52. On perceptions of the Iranian threat, see U.S. Congress, House, *Report of the Congressional Committees Investigating the Iran-Contra Affair*, 159 (hereafter the *Iran-Contra Affair* report).

53. On the consideration of options, see Veliotes to Eagelburger memo.

54. See Waas, "What Washington Gave Saddam for Christmas," 85–90. See also Phythian, *Arming Iraq*, 35.

55. Rumsfeld Mission, London 27572: U.S. Department of State, January 13, 1994, release.

56. Ibid.

57. See Cooley, *Alliance against Babylon*, 165.

58. Secretary of State to American Embassy in Baghdad, memo, "Secretary's Meeting with Iraqi Deputy Prime Minister Tariq Aziz," November 26, 1984, Department of State, NSA.

59. On the difference between the hawks and doves, see Yetiv, *Crude Awakenings*.

60. On Iran's moderation of its foreign policy, see Sick, "Iran's Quest for Superpower Status," 697–715. See also *London Al-Awsat* in FBIS: NESA, March 6, 1995, 13.

61. The U.S. effort to cultivate moderates in Iran is clear in various declassified memos. See Graham E. Fuller to Director of Central Intelligence, memo, "Toward a Policy on Iran," NIC 02545-85, May 17, 1985.

62. Washington also requested that Iran quit its support of terrorism. U.S. National Security Council, Oliver North Notebook Entries for November 27, 1985, IC-01922, NSA.

63. Poindexter to Reagan, memo, "Covert Action Finding Regarding Iran," January 6, 1983, IC-0201, NSA. On the Iranian side of the affair, see Ramazani, *Revolutionary Iran*, epilogue.

64. See Tower, *Tower Commission Report*, chap. 4.

65. Rumsfeld Mission, London 27572.

66. Tower, *Tower Commission Report*, xv.

67. "U.S. Policy toward Iran," NSDD, NSC/ICS 402010, June 11, 1985, declassified memo to Robert McFarlane.

68. Tower, *Tower Commission Report*, 20.

69. Powell, *My American Journey*, 294.

70. Ibid.

71. Weinberger to McFarlane, "U.S. Policy toward Iran," July 16, 1985, IG-00266, NSA.

72. Ibid.

73. Shultz to McFarlane, "U.S. Policy toward Iran: Comment on Draft NSDD," June 29, 1985, IG-00261, NSA.

74. Powell, *My American Journey*, 300.

75. U.S. Department of State, Bureau of Near Eastern and South Asian Affairs, "The Gulf War, Secret, Briefing Paper," February 27, 1986, IG-00311, NSA.

76. Michael H. Armacost to Office of the Secretary of State, "Arms Sales to Iran," May 3, 1986, IC-02759, NSA.

77. See Cordesman, *The Iran-Iraq War and Western Security*, 93–102.

78. U.S. Department of State, Bureau of Near Eastern and South Asian Affairs, "The Gulf War, Secret, Briefing Paper."

79. Armacost to Office of the Secretary of State, "Arms Sales to Iran."

80. See Walsh, *Iran-Contra: The Final Report*, 16–24. He was the independent council on Iran-Contra.

81. Pollack, *Persian Puzzle*, 219.

82. See "U.S. Policy Toward Iran," NSDD, NSC/ICS 402010, June 11, 1985.

83. Ibid.

84. Fuller memo, "Toward a Policy on Iran."

85. Ibid., 928.

86. On U.S. motivations for cultivating moderates, see Bill, "U.S. Overture to Iran."

87. See Walsh, *Iran-Contra: The Final Report*, 1–24.

88. Tower, *Tower Commission Report*, 36. See also Strober and Strober, *Reagan Presidency*, esp. 390.

89. See *Iran-Contra Affair* report, 277–78.

90. Strober and Strober, *Reagan Presidency*, 403.

91. Quoted in Pollack, *Persian Puzzle*, 212.

92. Ibid., 212–13.

93. Rothkopf, *Running the World*, 244.

94. Strober and Strober, *Reagan Presidency*, 449.

95. Tower, *Tower Commission Report*, 225. See also *Iran-Contra Affair* report, chaps. 9, 10. In addition, on the vice president's role, see *Iran-Contra Affair* report, 247–48.

96. For instance, "U.S. Policy toward Iran," NSDD, NSC/ICS 402010, June 11, 1985. Fuller memo, "Toward a Policy on Iran." See also Walsh, *Iran-Contra: The Final Report*, 1–24, and *Iran-Contra Affair* report, chap. 9.

97. Top-secret memo from Robert McFarlane, The White House, June 17, 1985.

98. Strober and Strober, *Reagan Presidency*, 439–40.

99. *Iran-Contra Affair* report, 193. Also, on the role of high-level administration officials, see Walsh, *Firewall*.

100. Tower, *Tower Commission Report*, 225.

101. On Reagan's involvement, ibid., esp. 28, 36–39, 220–225. See also *Iran-Contra Affair* report, 277–78. On the 1985 authorization, U.S. National Security Council, Oliver North Notebook Entries for November 26, 1985, IC-01909, NSA. On the 1986 authorization, Reagan to Casey, "Top Secret Presidential Finding," January 17, 1986, IC-02182, NSA. On the August 1985 decision, see *Iran-Contra Affair* report, 163, 167.

102. Rothkopf, *Running the World*, 246 (Shultz), 250 (Poindexter).

103. See *New York Times*, February 11, 1987, A-8.

104. Chubin and Tripp, *Iran and Iraq at War*, 196–97.

105. For quotation, see *Department of State Bulletin* 87 (October 1987), 38. See also text of interview with Assistant Secretary Murphy in ibid. In addition, see U.S. Department of State, statement by Armacost before the Senate Foreign Relations Committee on June 16, 1987, in *Department of State Bulletin* 87 (August 1987), and "US Navy: Iran Triples Gulf Deployed Missiles," Reuters, July 20, 1996.

106. On GCC assistance, see witness statement by Crist in U.S. Congress, Senate, Subcommittee of the Committee on Appropriations, *Department of Defense Appropriations for Fiscal Year 1989*, 1988, table 2, 178.

107. For example, see "U.S. Intelligence for Iraq," memo, December 15, 1986, IG-00383, NSA.

108. Ibid.

109. See *MECS* 11 (1987): 29–35, for a good summary of the reflagging mission. On the U.S. team, Sandra Charles, National Security Council analyst, interview with author, Washington, D.C., June 5, 1997. Charles was part of that team.

110. Quotation from Richard Murphy, assistant secretary of state, phone interview with author, August 24, 1998.

111. Former high-level National Security Council official, interview with author.

112. Quoted in the *New York Times*, August 5, 1987, A1, A12.

113. For more on how the United States altered its rules of engagement, see *New York Times*, December 22, 1987, A7, and April 23, 1988, A1.

114. Blumberg, *Reinventing Khomeini*, 142.

115. On the visits, *New York Times*, September 23, 1987, A15. On Iran's reaction to the U.S. reflagging mission, see Ramazani, "The Iran-Iraq War and the Persian Gulf Crisis," 63–64.

116. U.S. Congress, House, Committee on Foreign Affairs, House Joint Resolution 216, *Overview of the Situation in the Persian Gulf*, 1987, 302. See also U.S. Congress, Senate,

"War in the Persian Gulf: The U.S. Takes Sides," staff report to the Committee on Foreign Relations, November 1987.

117. See Jentleson, *With Friends Like These*, 46.

118. On conflicting evidence, Cordesman, *Gulf and the West*, 370–71.

119. Quoted in Kifner, "Iranian Officials Urge 'Uprooting' of Saudi Royalty."

120. On the link between the Hajj and U.S. reflagging, see Chubin and Tripp, *Iran and Iraq at War*, 175–76.

121. Ibid., 1.

122. Presidential Determination no. 87–20, September 23, 1987, 52 Fed. Reg. 36749 (1987).

CHAPTER FOUR: The Bush Administration and Constructive Engagement

1. Richard Haass, *Frontline* interview, broadcast January 9 and 10, 1996. For more extensive analysis on this period, see Karabell, "Backfire," esp. 32–38.

2. Bush and Scowcroft, *World Transformed*, 305–6. See also Wilson, *Politics of Truth*, 81–82.

3. Baker, *Politics of Diplomacy*, 263.

4. Pollack, *Threatening Storm*, 29.

5. See "Saddam Hussein's Speech to the Arab Cooperation Council," *Baghdad Al-Thawrah*, in FBIS: NESA, February 27, 1990, in FBIS: NESA, September 12, 1990. See also "Aziz Recounting Saddam's July 16, 1990 Speech," *Baghdad INA*, in FBIS: NESA, September 12, 1990, 30. See also Telhami, "Middle East Politics in the Post Cold War Era," and "Iraqi Transcript of the Meeting between President Saddam Hussein and U.S. Ambassador April Glaspie," *New York Times*, September 23, 1990. On how Saddam was concerned about U.S. hegemony, see Saddam Hussein, interview, Mexico City XEW Television Network, in FBIS: NESA, December 26, 1990, 20.

6. See Spector, *Nuclear Ambitions*, 191.

7. On the United States' earlier estimation, see Albright and Hibbs, "Iraq's Bomb," 30–40.

8. This is made clear in critical staff reports to the Senate Committee on Foreign Relations. See U.S. Congress, Senate, staff reports to the Committee on Foreign Relations, "Chemical Weapons," and ibid., "Kurdistan."

9. Cited in Sifry and Serf, *Gulf War Reader*, 102.

10. Quotation from ibid.

11. Speech by Saddam Hussein to the Arab Summit Conference in Baghdad, in FBIS: NESA, May 29, 1990, 5.

12. "Aziz Recounting Saddam's July 16, 1990 Speech," 30.

13. General Colin Powell, *Frontline* interview, broadcast January 9 and 10, 1996.

14. Hare to the Secretary, March 23, 1989, fiche 123, Iraqgate Collection, NSA.

15. Robert Gates, *Frontline* interview, broadcast January 9 and 10, 1996.

16. James Baker, *Frontline* interview, broadcast January 9 and 10, 1996.

17. Baker to Glaspie, April 12, 1990, fiche 198, Iraqgate Collection, NSA.

18. See Gordon and Trainor, *General's War*, 11–13.

19. Brent Scowcroft, national security adviser, interview with author, Washington, D.C., February 19, 1999.

20. Baker, *Politics of Diplomacy*, 267.

21. For instance, Washington had solid intelligence that the Saudis were considering pocketbook diplomacy to appease Iraq after it invaded Kuwait. William Webster, CIA director, interview with author, Washington, D.C., October 1, 1999.

22. Kenneth Pollack, CIA analyst, interview with author, Washington, D.C., June 30, 2005.

23. This motivation is clear in U.S. Department of State, "CCC Credits for Iraq," memorandum to the secretary of state, October 11, 1989, in *Congressional Record*, March 2, 1992.

24. Scowcroft interview with author.

25. For a brief recapitulation of this approach, see Karabell, "Backfire," esp. 31–33.

26. Baker, *Politics of Diplomacy*, 266–67.

27. Sandra Charles, National Security Council analyst, interview with author, Washington, D.C., June 5, 1997.

28. Kenneth Juster, undersecretary of commerce, phone interview with author, July 29, 1999.

29. See Freedman and Karsh, *Gulf Conflict*, 27.

30. See Salinger, *Secret Dossier*, 4.

31. Pollack interview.

32. See statement by John H. Kelly, assistant secretary of state for Near East and South Asian affairs, in U.S. Congress, Senate, Foreign Relations Committee, *U.S. Relations with Iraq*, May 23, 1990.

33. U.S. Department of State, "Memorandum for Brent Scowcroft," May 16, 1990, IG-01379, NSA.

34. Freedman and Karsh, *Gulf Conflict*, 37.

35. For a diplomat's account, see Wilson, *Politics of Truth*, 86–106.

36. FBIS: NESA-88-140, July 21, 1988.

37. On Iranian economic problems, see Karshenas and Pesaran, "Economic Reform and the Reconstruction of the Iranian Economy," 89–111.

38. For extensive data on war damage, see Amirahmadi, "Economic Destruction and Imbalances in Post-revolutionary Iran."

39. Pollack interview.

40. See Ibrahim, "Rebounding Iranians Are Striving for Regional Leadership in Gulf," 6. Iranian moderates did well in elections for Iran's Fourth Islamic Majlis in April and May 1992. The elections were a resounding victory for Rafsanjani, whose supporters won an absolute majority in the Majlis. Sarabi, "Post-Khomeini Era in Iran," 104.

41. Hunter, "Iran from the August 1988 Cease-Fire to the April 1992 Majlis Election," 200.

42. On its interest in joining, *OPEC Bulletin* (June 2000): 7.

43. Television interview with Professor Shaul Bakhash, *Near East Report*, March 6, 2000.

44. See Sick, "Iran's Quest for Superpower Status," 697–715. In response to Iran's foreign policy shift, Riyadh sent Saudi foreign minister Saud al-Faisal on a formal visit to Iran, which marked the beginning of improvement in relations. *London Al-Awsat*, in FBIS: NESA, March 6, 1995, 13.

45. "Thinking about a Policy for Iraq," January 12, 1990, fiche 179, Iraqgate Collection, NSA.

CHAPTER FIVE: The Iraq War of 1991

1. On Iraq's view, see "Aziz Recounting Saddam's July 16, 1990 Speech," *Baghdad INA*, in FBIS: NESA, September 12, 1990, 26–32.

2. Quoted in Bengio, *Saddam's Word*, 37.

3. Quoted in ibid., 155.

4. *Cairo MENA*, in FBIS: NESA, August 13, 1990, 5.

5. In a letter to Iran's President Rafsanjani on August 15, Saddam even called on Iran to help Iraq confront the "evil doers who seek to inflict evil on Muslims and the Arab nation." Baghdad, Republic of Iraq Radio, August 15, 1990, in BBC Summary of World Broadcasts, August 16, 1990.

6. Speech by Saddam Hussein to the Arab Summit Conference in Baghdad, in FBIS: NESA, May 29, 1990, 5. Iraq recognized that Kuwait did change its position on oil production quotas but said that Kuwait's behavior suggested that the change was a ploy. See "Interview with Iraqi First Deputy Prime Minister Taha Yasin Ramadan," in *London Al-Tadamun*, in FBIS: NESA, October 30, 1990, 24.

7. Wilson, *Politics of Truth*, 84.

8. On Iraq's view, see "Aziz Recounting Saddam's July 16, 1990 Speech," 30–31.

9. Quoted in "Saddam Says He Won the War," *APS Diplomat Recorder*, January 20, 2001.

10. Saddam Hussein, interview, *Wall Street Journal*, June 16, 1990.

11. BBC Special Report, "The Gulf War," January 16, 1991.

12. For the text of the transcript of the Glaspie meeting, see "Excerpts from Iraqi Document on Meeting with U.S. Envoy," *New York Times*, September 23, 1990, A19.

13. On this interview, see Baram, "Iraqi Invasion of Kuwait," 21–25.

14. For an in-depth analysis, see ibid.

15. The agreement on the waterway, however, was ambiguous in terms of how concessionary Iraq intended to be. See *London Keyhan*, in FBIS: NESA, September 19, 1990, 67. On resumption of diplomatic relations, see *Tehran IRNA*, in FBIS: NESA, September 19, 1990, 25.

16. Sultan, *Desert Warrior*, esp. 19.

17. Fahd speech on the Gulf Crisis, broadcast on August 9, 1990, *Middle East*, 371–72. See also General Norman Schwarzkopf, interview with Brian Lamb, C-SPAN-2, Book TV, October 1, 1990. Schwarzkopf interacted closely with the Saudis in the region.

18. See Hiro, *Desert Shield to Desert Storm*, 114–15. See *Baghdad INA*, in FBIS: NESA, September 12, 1990, 32.

19. Sultan, *Desert Warrior*, esp. 19, 189.

20. Chas W. Freeman Jr., U.S. ambassador to Saudi Arabia, interview with author, Washington, D.C., February 19, 1999. Freeman worked with General Schwarzkopf in the region.

21. Fahd was also aware of Saddam's Machiavellian nature. After all, he suggested to Fahd twice in the 1980s that they divide the small Arab Gulf states between them. Baram and Rubin, *Iraq's Road to War*.

22. Freeman interview.

23. George H. W. Bush, interview with Sir David Frost, PBS, January 16, 1996.

24. "Press Conference by the President," August 8, 1990, OA/ID, CF 0703, Roman Popadiuk Files, Office of the Press Secretary, GBPL.

25. See Yetiv, *Explaining Foreign Policy*. Colin Powell, "Our Troops Are Giving Bush All His Options," interview with *USA Today*, December 18, 1990. James Baker, interview, ABC News, *This Week with David Brinkley*, August 12, 1990.

26. Brent Scowcroft, national security adviser, interview with author, Washington, D.C., February 19, 1999. Scowcroft, *Frontline* interview, broadcast January 9 and 10, 1996. Statement by the Honorable Richard Cheney, GBPL.

27. James Baker, *Frontline* interview, broadcast January 9 and 10, 1996.

28. Statement by Secretary of State James A. Baker III, GBPL.

29. Bush and Scowcroft, *World Transformed*, 491. See also Bush to Marlin Fitzwater, memo, September 25, 1991, OA/ID PR010 202278, Philip Brady Files, GBPL; includes attachment of Bush's proposed answers to an interview by Kenneth Walsh.

30. See Miller and Yetiv, "New World Order."

31. Collective security also differs from collective defense. See Wolfers, *Discord and Collaboration*, 182–84.

32. For a transcript of this speech, http://net.lib.byu.edu/rdh7/wwi/1918/14points .html.

33. Buehrig, *Woodrow Wilson and the Balance of Power*, 260.

34. On his assertion, see MacMillan, *Paris 1919*, 12–14.

35. Link, *Woodrow Wilson and a Revolutionary World*.

36. See Kissinger, *World Restored*.

37. See Kissinger, *Does America Need a Foreign Policy?*

38. Link, *Public Papers of Woodrow Wilson*, 41:356–57; 43:360; 47:105.

39. George Washington, Farewell Address, September 17, 1796, reprinted as Senate Document 3, 1991.

40. Quoted in MacMillan, *Paris 1919*, 33.

41. See Claude, *Swords into Plowshares*. Bull, *Anarchical Society*, 239. Mearsheimer, "False Promise of International Institutions," esp. 26–34. See Doyle, "Balancing Power Classically."

42. On the nature of collective security, see Wolfers, *Discord and Collaboration*. Claude, *Swords into Plowshares*. Downs, *Collective Security beyond the Cold War*.

43. For a good discussion, see Art, *Grand Strategy for America*, 92–99.

44. See Kupchan and Kupchan, "Concerts, Collective Security, and the Future of Europe," esp. 119.

45. For UN Security Council Resolutions in 1990, see www.un.org/Docs/scres/1990/ scres90.htm.

46. Bush, *Public Papers of the Presidents: 1991*, 60.

47. Ibid., 221.

48. Bush and Scowcroft, *World Transformed*, 400.

49. Ibid., 491.

50. Quoted in Freedman and Karsh, *Gulf Conflict*, 404.

51. For interviews with the key actors, see Yetiv, *Explaining Foreign Policy*, 219–21.

52. Quoted in Powell, *My American Journey*, 512.

53. See Yetiv, *Explaining Foreign Policy*.

54. In dozens of hours of *Frontline* interviews with decision makers, the word "balance" was used only twice; the words "balance of power" were used only once.

55. James Baker, secretary of state, interview with author, Washington, D.C., July 26,

1996. There is no apparent reason for him to say this, other than that it was a factor. It would have been better for the record to suggest that the administration was concerned about the balance of power issue.

56. Interview with author (off the record).

57. Powell, *My American Journey*, 508.

58. Robert Gates, *Frontline* interview, broadcast January 9 and 10, 1996.

59. Powell, *My American Journey*, 521.

60. This paragraph is based on Freeman interview.

61. Bush and Scowcroft, *World Transformed*, 370.

62. Transcript of President Bush's address "Kuwait Is Liberated," February 27, 1991, in Bush, *Public Papers of the Presidents: 1991*, 187–88.

CHAPTER SIX: The Clinton Administration and Saddam Hussein

1. Art, *Grand Strategy for America*, 83.

2. See Kenneth Katzman, "Iran: U.S. Policy and Options." CRS Report for Congress, January 14, 2000.

3. For the texts of major UN resolutions adopted in 1991, see *U.N. Security Resolutions on Iraq: Compliance and Implementation. Report to the Committee on Foreign Affairs by the CRS* (Washington, DC: GPO, March 1992).

4. Ibid.

5. The UN Security Council allowed Iraq to sell Jordan seventy thousand barrels of oil per day. In addition, small amounts of oil were sold illegally across the Turkish and Iranian borders and on oil-smuggling barges that proceeded undetected along the Gulf coastline.

6. U.S. Congress, House, Subcommittee on Europe and the Middle East, Committee on Foreign Affairs, *Developments in the Middle East, July 1993*, July 27, 1993, 26.

7. See U.S. Congress, House, Subcommittee on Europe and the Middle East, Committee on Foreign Affairs, *U.S. Policy toward Iraq Three Years after the Gulf War*, February 23, 1994, 15. For a detailed record of Saddam's government purges between November 1990 and early 1994, see Cordesman, *Iran and Iraq*, 120–27.

8. For details on the coup, see Sciolino, "Failed Plot to Overthrow Hussein," *New York Times*.

9. This discussion is based on a personal correspondence with Dr. Amatzia Baram, August 14, 2000.

10. On Iraq's conventional capability, see U.S. Department of Defense, *Conduct of the Persian Gulf War: Final Report to Congress* (April 1992), 148–59; Eisenstadt, *Like a Phoenix*, chap. 3.

11. See Albright and Hibbs, "Iraq's Bomb," 30–40.

12. See statement by Robert L. Galluci, assistant secretary for politico-military affairs, Department of State, in U.S. Congress, House, Subcommittee on Europe and the Middle East, Committee on Foreign Affairs, *Iraq's Nuclear Weapons Capability and IAEA Inspections in Iraq*, June 29, 1993.

13. See Eisenstadt, *Like a Phoenix*, 24.

14. Woolsey, cited in ibid., 33; this paragraph is based on ibid., 30–34.

15. For the text of such an argument, see "Iraq Calls for Lifting of UN Embargo," *MEES*, July 20, 1992, D1.

16. Address by Ronald Neumann, director, Office of Northern Gulf Affairs, Department of State, "United States Policy toward Iraq," Meridian International Center, Washington, D.C., January 27, 1994, 1.

17. On Kuwait's position, see *Cairo MENA*, in FBIS: NESA, April 24, 1992, 13. See also *Cairo MENA*, in FBIS: NESA, May 7, 1992, 15–16.

18. *Riyadh SPA*, in FBIS: NESA, July 12, 1993, 16.

19. An Iranian official asserted in 1995 that the three islands will remain Iran's forever. *Baghdad Al-'Iraq*, in FBIS: NESA, April 3, 1995, 32.

20. *Paris AFP*, in FBIS: NESA, March 2, 1995, 64.

21. Ibid.

22. U.S. Department of Defense, "Remarks by Secretary of Defense William H. Perry to the Washington State China Relations Council," *Defense Issues* 10 (1995). "US Navy: Iran Triples Gulf Deployed Missiles," Reuters, July 20, 1996.

23. Cited in *World Oil Market and Oil Price Chronologies: 1970–2000* (www.eia.doe.gov/emeu/cabs/chron.html), 19.

24. For a readable work on Iran's history, see Mackey, *The Iranians*.

25. Ibrahim, "To Counter Iran, Saudis Seek Ties with Ex-Soviet Islamic Republics."

26. Quoted in Isenberg, "Desert Storm Redux," 430.

27. See Gerges, *America and Political Islam*, chap. 6, esp. 116–17.

28. Freedman and Karsh, *Gulf Conflict*.

29. On the factors driving the rapprochement, see Ramazani, "Emerging Arab-Iranian Rapprochement."

30. See Litwak, "Iraq and Iran," 176.

31. See Ansari, *Confronting Iran*, chap. 5.

32. For a good brief overview of this period, see Amuzegar, "Iran's Crumbling Revolution."

33. Albright, *Madam Secretary*, 408.

34. On the administration's description, see Alikhani, *Sanctioning Iran*, esp. 166–70.

35. Pollack, *Threatening Storm*, 66.

36. See Clinton's foreword in Soderberg, *Superpower Myth*.

37. Kenneth Pollack, CIA analyst, interview with author, Washington, D.C., June 30, 2005.

38. Statement by Edward Djerejian, assistant secretary for Near Eastern and South Asian Affairs, in U.S. Congress, House, Subcommittee on Europe and the Middle East, Committee on Foreign Affairs, *Developments in the Middle East*, March 9, 1993, 4. On GCC states and European Union, *Kuwait KUNA*, in FBIS: NESA, May 9, 1994, 2–3.

39. On the range of U.S. sanctions against Iran from 1995 and 1996, see Alikhani, *Sanctioning Iran*, chaps. 7–8.

40. On Iran rebuffing Iraq, *London Al-Awsat*, in FBIS: NESA, March 3, 1994, 38.

41. *Paris AFP*, in FBIS: NESA, April 4, 1994, 26.

42. Quoted in *MEED*, November 6, 1998, 21.

43. See Pollack, *Threatening Storm*, 63.

44. For a good brief on regime change policy and Iraqi opposition groups, see U.S. Congress, House, CRS Report for Congress, *Iraq: U.S. Regime Change Efforts and Post-Saddam Governance* (Washington, DC: GPO, March 7, 2006).

45. See Gerges, *America and Political Islam*, 122–23, 132.

46. Indeed, Robert Art distinguishes containment from balancing, and dual contain-

ment is even further intellectually from containment. See Art, *Grand Strategy for America*, esp. 82–83.

47. Lake, "Confronting Backlash States," 48.

48. Indyk et al., "Symposium on Dual Containment," 2, 15.

49. Quoted in Pollack, *Persian Puzzle*, 216.

50. Lake, "Confronting Backlash States," 46.

51. Ellen Laipson, National Security Council analyst, interview with author, Washington, D.C., August 8, 2006.

52. Indyk, speech to the Washington Institute for Near East Policy, May 18, 1993. For the most recent critique of dual containment, see Brzezinski, Scowcroft, and Murphy, "Differentiated Containment," 20–30.

53. Lake, "Confronting Backlash States," 52.

54. Gause, "Illogic of Dual Containment," 60.

55. Brent Scowcroft, national security adviser, interview with author, Washington, D.C., February 19, 1999.

56. Laipson interview.

57. See Pollack, *Persian Puzzle*, 269–70.

58. Ibid., 260–61.

59. U.S. Department of State, "Peter Tarnoff, Under Secretary of Political Affairs," in *US Department of State Dispatch*, November 13, 1994, 832. See also Lake, "Confronting Backlash States," and, for a more recent statement, Pelletreau, "American Objectives in the Middle East," 286.

CHAPTER SEVEN: Containment-Plus and Regime Change in Iraq

1. For a detailed account, see Pollack, *Threatening Storm*, 77–108.

2. On Iran, see Alikhani, *Sanctioning Iran*, esp. chap. 10.

3. Richard Murphy, assistant secretary of state, phone interview with author, August 24, 1998.

4. Butler, *Greatest Threat*, 201, 202.

5. Tripp, *History of Iraq*, 259–64, 278–84.

6. On Russia's loss, "Iraq, Russia Discuss Ways to Enhance Oil Sector Cooperation," Xinhua News Agency, January 31, 2001.

7. Quoted in Shanker, "Rumsfeld Warns That Iraq Ties Will Hurt Russian Pocketbooks."

8. See Albright, *Madam Secretary*, 357–62.

9. Ibid., 349.

10. Ibid., 365.

11. Pollack, *Threatening Storm*, 94.

12. Quoted in Albright, *Madam Secretary*, 365.

13. Ibid.

14. Pollack, *Threatening Storm*, 95.

15. Kenneth Pollack, CIA analyst, interview with author, Washington, D.C., June 30, 2005.

16. See United States Information Agency transcript, President Clinton and British prime minister Blair, The White House, February 5, 1998.

17. Testimony of Secretary of State Colin L. Powell, in U.S. Congress, Senate, Budget

Hearing before the Senate Budget Committee, February 12, 2002.

18. Thomas Pickering, U.S. ambassador to the United Nations, interview with author, Washington, D.C., March 2, 2001.

19. Vassiliev, "Russia and Iraq," 127–28.

20. U.S. Department of State, press briefing by Secretary of State Colin Powell, February 23, 2001.

21. For a good treatment of the notion of regime change after 9/11, see Litwak, *Regime Change.*

22. Testimony of Secretary Powell at Budget Hearing before the Senate Budget Committee, February 12, 2002.

23. Kissinger, *World Restored,* esp. 139. See also Gulick, *Europe's Classical Balance of Power,* esp. chap. 3. Walt, *Origins of Alliances,* 18. Doyle, "Balancing Power Classically," 135, 145. Sheehan, *Balance of Power,* 126–27. Bull, *Anarchical Society,* 101–6.

24. Quoted in Layne, *Peace of Illusions,* 124.

25. To be sure, Walt considers ideology in his formulation. However, he does so in attempting to understand why states align with one another, rather than why they balance against others. This is a fundamental difference. On balancing motivations, see Gulick, *Europe's Classical Balance of Power.* Claude, *Power and International Relations,* chaps. 2 and 3; Waltz, *Theory of International Politics,* esp. chap. 6. Morgenthau and Thompson, *Politics among Nations,* esp. chap. 11. Liska, *Nations in Alliance,* 13.

26. Woodward, *Plan of Attack,* 13.

CHAPTER EIGHT: The Iraq War of 2003

1. See Gordon and Trainor, *Cobra II,* 64–65, 121.

2. On UN politics and the Iraq crisis, see Malone, *International Struggle over Iraq.*

3. The transcript appears at www.whitehouse.gov/news/releases/2002/09/20020912-1.html.

4. For the text of the resolution, see http://ods-dds-ny.un.org/doc/UNDOC/GEN/N02/682/26/PDF/N0268226.pdf?OpenElement.

5. On this jockeying and for the draft of the resolution at this time, see *New York Times,* October 23, 2002.

6. Hans Blix, "An Update on Inspection," Report of the Executive Chairman of UNMOVIC to the United Nations Security Council, New York, January 27, 2003, at www.un.org/Depts/unmovic/Bx27.htm.

7. See www.state.gov/r/pa/prs/ps/2002/16118pf.htm.

8. Powell's statement in front of the United Nations, excerpted in the *New York Times,* February 23, 2003.

9. Linzer, "Iraq Approves Inspectors' Use of U-2 Surveillance Planes, Iraqi Ambassador Says," Associated Press February 6, 2003.

10. Gustafson, *Changing Course,* 2–3.

11. On the legality of the war, see Thornberry, "On the Legal Case for Invading Iraq."

12. See Gordon and Trainor, *Cobra II,* 64–65, 121.

13. See Bodansky, *Secret History of the Iraq War,* 5.

14. On the war's motivations, see Freedman, "War in Iraq."

15. Woodward, *Plan of Attack,* 155.

16. Cited in Freedman, "War in Iraq," 24.

17. CIA, "National Intelligence Estimate: Iraq's Continuing Programs for Weapons of Mass Destruction," October 2002, NIE 2002–16HC. Redacted, declassified version released under Freedom of Information Act to George Washington University's National Security Archive, posted July 9, 2004.

18. The White House, "President Bush Outlines Iraqi Threat," October 7, 2002, http://www.whitehouse.gov/news/releases/2002/10/20021007-8.html.

19. Remarks by President Bush on Iraq in the Rose Garden, September 26, 2002, http://www.whitehouse.gov/news/releases/2002/09/20020926-7.html.

20. See CIA, "National Intelligence Estimate: Iraq's Continuing Programs for Weapons of Mass Destruction."

21. Kenneth Katzman, "Iraq: U.S. Efforts to Change the Regime," CRS Report for Congress, October 3, 2002, 10–11.

22. On how the war was sold, see Kaufmann, "Threat Inflation and the Failure of the Marketplace of Ideas."

23. On how 9/11 changed the U.S. approach toward Iraq, see Ross, *Statecraft*, esp. 104–10. See Tenet, *At the Center*, esp. 305–9.

24. Dick Cheney, "The Risks of Inaction Are Far Greater Than the Risk of Action," address to the 103rd National Convention of the Veterans of Foreign Wars, August 26, 2002.

25. The full text of the State of the Union address appears at www.whitehouse.gov/news/releases/2003/01/20030128-19.html.

26. Radio Address by the President to the Nation, Office of the Press Secretary, September 28, 2002.

27. Tenet, *At the Center*, 305.

28. See Gordon, "Iraq," 15. For an argument that this connection did exist, see Mylroie, *Bush vs. the Beltway*.

29. On suggestions to take action, Richard A. Clarke to Condoleezza Rice, National Security Council, memo, Washington, D.C., January 25, 2001.

30. Woodward, *Bush at War*, 34–35.

31. Clarke, *Against All Enemies*, 26, 237–38.

32. Ibid.

33. Dick Cheney, "Speech to the Council on Foreign Relations," Washington, D.C., February 15, 2002, www.whitehouse.gov/vicepresident/news-speeches/speeches/vp200 20215.html.

34. This paragraph is based on Gordon and Trainor, *Cobra II*.

35. Downing Street Memo text, www.downingstreetmemo.com/memos.html.

36. See Kaufmann, "Threat Inflation and the Failure of the Marketplace of Ideas." For a view that the Al Qaeda connection to Iraq was real, see Bodansky, *Secret History of the Iraq War*, chap. 3.

37. Quoted in Woodward, *Plan of Attack*, 27.

38. Testimony by Secretary of Defense Donald H. Rumsfeld, Senate Armed Services Committee, Washington, D.C., July 9, 2003, www.defenselink.mil/speeches/2003/sp20 030709-secdef0364.html.

39. U.S. Department of State, Secretary Colin L. Powell, "Remarks to the United Nations Security Council," February 5, 2003, 19.

40. For some inside information on this point, see Suskind, *One Percent Doctrine*.

41. See Tenet, *At the Center*, esp. 305–9. Certainly, Colin Powell appeared reluctant about invading Iraq, although he eventually argued for it in front of the United Nations.

42. See the account by former counterterrorism chief Richard Clarke in Clarke, *Against All Enemies*, 30.

43. Testimony by national security adviser Condoleezza Rice to the 9/11 Commission, April 8, 2004, transcript available at www.cnn.com/2004/ALLPOLITICS/04/08/rice .transcript/. See also Freedman, "War in Iraq," 18–19. On the impact of 9/11, see Woodward, *Bush at War*, 34–35, and "U.S. Decision on Iraq Has Puzzling Past: Opponents of War Wonder When, How Policy Was Set," *Washington Post*, January 12, 2003.

44. On Bush and Iraq's involvement, Woodward, *Bush at War*, 99. On the ties to terrorist groups, Radio Address by the President to the Nation, Office of the Press Secretary, December 7, 2002.

45. On this debate, see Merry, *Sands of Empire*.

46. "Statement by the President in His Address to the Nation," September 11, 2001.

47. Albright, *Madam Secretary*, 416.

48. Weisman, "Rice Urges Egyptians and Saudis to Democratize."

49. See "Excerpts from President Bush's Remarks at the Air Force Academy Graduation Ceremony," *New York Post*, June 3, 2004, 33.

50. *New York Times*, February 3, 2005, A1.

51. Tenet, *At the Center*, 321–22.

52. See Gurtov, *Superpower on Crusade*, 40–41. Also, see Litwak, *Regime Change*, esp. 325–26.

53. Quoted in Woodward, *Plan of Attack*, 12.

54. See Freedman, "War in Iraq," 15–16.

55. Presidential debate between Al Gore and George W. Bush, University of Massachusetts, Boston, October 3, 2000.

56. See Katzman, "Iraq" (CRS Report), esp. 7–12.

57. On this doctrine, see Freedman, *Deterrence*. The full text of the State of the Union address appears at www.whitehouse.gov/news/releases/2002/01/20020129–11.html.

58. See George W. Bush, "National Strategy to Combat Weapons of Mass Destruction," The White House, 2002.

59. See www.defenselink.mil/transcripts/2003/tr20030509-depsecdef0223.html.

60. Remarks by the President and British Prime Minister Tony Blair, White House, January 31, 2003 www.whitehouse.gov/news/releases/2003/01/20030131–23.html.

61. The White House, "President Bush Outlines Iraqi Threat."

62. Haass, *The Opportunity*.

63. As CIA director George Tenet notes, the U.S. intelligence community partly "paved" the "road to war" with "flawed performance"; Tenet, *At the Center*, 493. See Jehl, "Report Says White House Ignored C.I.A. On Iraq Chaos."

64. Colin Powell on C-SPAN, December 8, 2004.

65. A number of thinkers make the case for manipulation. For instance, see Suskind, *One Percent Doctrine*. For a sober assessment, see Pfiffner, "Did President Bush Mislead the Country in His Arguments for War With Iraq?"

66. U.S. Congress, Senate, Select Committee on Intelligence, "Report on the U.S. Intelligence Community's Prewar Intelligence Assessments on Iraq," July 7, 2004, at www .gpoaccess.gov/serialset/creports/iraq.html. The Commission on the Intelligence Ca-

pabilities of the United States Regarding Weapons of Mass Destruction, "Report to the President of the United States," March 31, 2005, at www.wmd.gov/report/index.html.

67. For instance, regarding Iraq's obtainment of nuclear materials from Niger. See Wilson, Politics of Truth, chap. 15.

68. CIA, "National Intelligence Estimate: Iraq's Continuing Programs for Weapons of Mass Destruction," October 2002, NIE 2002–16HC.

69. See Jehl, "Report Warned Bush Team about Intelligence Doubts."

70. Tenet, *At the Center*, 341–49.

71. See, for instance, Dunn, "Myths, Motivations and 'Misunderestimations.'"

72. Cited in ibid., 280.

73. Telhami, "Return of the State," 112.

74. Osama bin Laden, *Frontline* interview, "Hunting the Enemy," at http://userhome .brooklyn.cuny.edu/sschaar/Hunting.htm.

75. See, for instance, Whitlock, "Commandos Free Hostages Being Held in Saudi Arabia."

76. U.S. Office of the President, National Security Directive 54, The White House, January 15, 1991. Yetiv, *Explaining Foreign Policy*.

77. On Iraq's potential, see Lauerman, "Gulf War II."

78. "Oil Prices-Short-Term Strength Masking Longer-Term Weakness," *World Oil Report — 2002*, no. 2 (Dresdner, Kleinwort, Wasserstein research: July 24, 2002).

79. See Chalabi, "Iraq and the Future of World Oil."

80. Chalabi, *Iraqi Oil Policy*.

81. Lauerman, "Gulf War II."

82. See Duffield, "Oil and the Iraq War."

83. On how most of the remaining oil is in the Gulf, see Duncan, "Three World Oil Forecasts Predict Peak Oil Production."

84. On how the administration tended to ignore their views, see Desch, "Bush and the Generals."

85. For a polemical argument that the Pentagon shaped American foreign policy to its own interests, see Carroll, *House of War*, esp. 434–38 on the 2003 Iraq invasion.

86. For an argument along the same vein, see Philips, *American Theocracy*.

87. On this cynical view, see, for instance, Ratner, Green, and Olshansky, *Against War in Iraq*. On the war's motivations, see Freedman, "War in Iraq," esp. 9.

88. Quoted in Unger, *House of Bush, House of Saud*, 225.

89. See Eckholm, "Now You See It."

90. Glanz, "Army Plans to End Contentious Halliburton Logistics Pact."

91. See Driody, *The Halliburton Agenda*.

92. For instance, George W. Bush and First Lady Laura Bush, interview on *Larry King Live*, CNN, July 7, 2006.

93. Remarks by President Bush on Iraq in the Rose Garden, September 26, 2002.

94. Scowcroft, "Don't Attack Saddam."

95. On the "Lord's Hands," Bacevich and Prodromou, "God Is Not Neutral," 49. On Bush's rhetoric, *New York Times*, February 15, 2003. On his religious interpretation in general, Juergensmeyer, "Religious Terror and Global War."

96. See Peters, "The Firanj Are Coming — Again," 3–19.

97. See Karam, *Transnational Political Islam*.

98. See www.bsos.umd.edu/sadat.

99. Gerges, *America and Political Islam*, esp. chap. 3.

100. See Pagden, "Imperialism, Liberalism and the Quest for Perpetual Peace." On exceptionalism, see McDougall, *Promised Land, Crusader State*. Mead, *Special Providence*.

101. On the first hundred years of exceptionalism, see Brands, *What America Owes the World*, chap. 1.

102. On the sources of exceptionalism, see Monten, "Roots of the Bush Doctrine."

103. Quoted in MacMillan, *Paris 1919*, 14.

104. See Monten, "Roots of the Bush Doctrine."

105. The White House, "President Bush Outlines Iraqi Threat." A version of this quotation was first used by Condoleezza Rice.

106. On containment as problematic, see Woodward, *Plan of Attack*, 12. On Iraq as not an urgent threat, see Freedman, "War in Iraq," 15–16.

107. See Katzman, "Iraq" (CRS Report), esp. 7–12.

108. Woodward, *Plan of Attack*, 146–48, 154–55.

109. See ibid., 206.

110. Woodward, *Plan of Attack*, 150–51; see also Daalder and Lindsay, *America Unbound*, 132–42.

111. For a succinct view, see Nakash, "The Shiites and the Future of Iraq."

112. For a concise description of these developments, see Wong, "Iraq Dances with Iran, While America Seethes."

113. Woodward, *Plan of Attack*, 228–31.

114. Fukuyama, *America at the Crossroads*, 37.

115. The Pew Global Attitudes Project, at www.pewtrusts.com/pdf/vf_pew_research_global_attitudes_0603.pdf. Also, on these polls, see Munson, "Lifting the Veil."

116. Baer, *Sleeping with the Devil*, xxvii.

117. See www.usatoday.com/news/attack/2002/02/27/usat-pollside.htm. Also, for opinion polls of the Arab world in 2002–3, see Abdallah, "Causes of Anti-Americanism in the Arab World," 70–71.

118. See www.bsos.umd.edu/sadat.

119. On this clash, see Layne, *Peace of Illusions*, 120–24.

120. Remarks by the president at the 2002 graduation exercise of the U.S. Military Academy, West Point, N.Y. The full text can be found at www.whitehouse.gov/news/releases/2002/06/20020601-3.html.

121. See Woodward, *Plan of Attack*, 87–88.

122. Downing Street Memo text.

123. See, for instance, the analysis of neoconservatives in Halper and Clarke, *America Alone*.

124. See Timmerman, *Countdown to Crisis*.

125. See Sanger, "Bush's Shift."

CHAPTER NINE: The Decline of Balance-of-Power Policy

1. On the arguments for continuing containment, see Mearsheimer and Walt, "Can Saddam Be Contained?"

2. Palazchenko, *My Years with Gorbachev*, esp. 215. Bush, *Public Papers of the President, 1990*, 1206.

3. See Medvedev, *Post-Soviet Russia*.

4. James Baker, *Frontline* interview, broadcast January 9 and 10, 1996.

5. Palazchenko, *My Years with Gorbachev*, 215. Freedman, "Moscow and the Iraqi Invasion Of Kuwait," 81–82.

6. See Freedman, "Moscow and the Iraqi Invasion Of Kuwait," 88–89, 95. See also Baker, *Politics of Diplomacy*, 294. For another participant's analysis, see Palazchenko, *My Years with Gorbachev*, esp. 214–15.

7. On this period, see Freedman, "Soviet Union, the Gulf War, and Its Aftermath," 374–76.

8. *Pravda*, in *CDSP*, May 18, 1988, 14. *Tass* statement in *CDSP*, August 3, 1988, 18.

9. *Pravda*, in *CDSP*, August 17, 1988, 23.

10. Vorontsov, quoted in *Pravda*, in *CDSP*, August 17, 1988, 23.

11. Reported in *Pravda*, in *CDSP*, February 22, 1989, 19.

12. *Tass* political observer in FBIS: USSR, March 2, 1989, 27. His view coincides with the official view.

13. Excerpt of the agreements, cited in Moscow International Service, in FBIS: USSR, August 3, 1989, 11. For Moscow's justification to Arab states of this sale, see *Kuwait Al-Qabas*, in FBIS: NESA, July 28, 1989, 18.

14. For example, see *Pravda*, in FBIS: USSR, July 20, 1989, 30, and *Tass*, August 20, 1989, in FBIS: USSR, August 21, 1989, 25.

15. Yetiv, "Persian Gulf."

16. U.S. Office of the President, The National Security Strategy of the United States, September 2002.

17. Remarks by National Security Adviser Condoleezza Rice on Terrorism and Foreign Policy, Office of the Press Secretary, April 29, 2002.

18. Iran is a case in point. See Bill, *Eagle and the Lion*. See also Sullivan, *American Adventurism Abroad*.

19. Brands, *What America Owes the World*, 315.

20. On how the United States compared with other great powers in history, see Ferguson, *Colossus*, 14–19.

21. Ikenberry, *America Unrivaled*, 1.

22. For a good discussion of the debate at the time, over the U.S. decline, see Nye, *Bound to Lead*.

23. For details on Saddam's foreign policy actions prior to his invasion of Kuwait, see Freedman and Karsh, *Gulf Conflict*, 45–50. Iran, and Iranian commentators, also often refer to the United States as a hegemon. For example, see *Tehran Salam* in FBIS: NESA, April 25, 1995, 50.

24. See Yetiv, *America and the Persian Gulf*.

25. Kennedy, *Rise and Fall of the Great Powers*, 15. In addition, Zakaria, *From Wealth to Power*.

26. See U.S. Office of the President, The National Security Strategy of the United States, September 2002.

27. This argument is developed in Monten, "Roots of the Bush Doctrine." Some classical realists assume this view as well, but they would not necessarily see the promotion of democracy as a likely strategy.

28. See Hardt and Negri, *Empire*. Gurtov, *Superpower on Crusade*, 33–39. Boot, *Savage Wars of Peace*.

29. Krasner and Pascual, "Addressing States Failure," 153.

30. Ajami, "Iraq and the Arabs' Future."

31. On how jihad became transnational, see Gerges, *Far Enemy*.

32. See Fuller, *Future of Political Islam*, chap. 8. For bin Laden, jihad is a holy war against the infidels; in mainstream Islam, jihad means a struggle against oneself for self-improvement. Radicalism is built on the writings of Sayyid Qutb, who was imprisoned by President Nasser and executed in 1966 and wrote many volumes while in prison, and Hassam al-Banna, who founded the Muslim Brotherhood in 1928. For an English translation of Qutb's famous book, *Milestones*, see the 1990 publication by American Trust. On the writings of extremists, see Schweitzer and Shay, *Globalization of Terror*, chap. 1. For a brief argument that Qutb has been misunderstood, see Khan, "Radical Islam, Liberal Islam."

33. Thomas, "South Asian Security Balance," 326.

34. Barnett, *Pentagon's New Map*, 92.

35. Miller and Yetiv, "New World Order."

36. See Nye, *Soft Power*.

37. Ibid.

38. "Anonymous" [Michael Scheuer], *Imperial Hubris*.

39. Ibid., chap. 4.

40. See Schweitzer and Shay, *Globalization of Terror*, 3–7.

41. A complete transcript is online at www.nytimes.com/international.

42. Testimony of Secretary Powell at Budget Hearing before the Senate Budget Committee, February 12, 2002.

43. *Baghdad INA*, in FBIS: October 10, 1990, 27.

44. Quoted in *New York Times*, December 27, 2001, B4. See also Coll, *Ghost Wars*, 222–23.

45. The transcript also appears in Rubin and Rubin, *Anti-American Terrorism and the Middle East*, 137–42.

46. Ibid.

47. On foreign occupation as the primary cause of terrorism, see Pape, *Dying to Win*.

48. See Gause, "Saudi Arabia Challenged."

49. Department of the Treasury official, phone interview with author, July 16, 2004 (off the record).

50. On the crackdown on militants, Guy Caruso, Energy Information Administration director, interview with author, Washington, D.C., August 8, 2003.

51. Ambah, "Saudi Raids Uncover Network of Extremists' Sleeper Cells."

52. See Ambah, "Saudis Hint al-Qaida Presence," and "Bush Denies Saudi Request to Release 9/11 Information."

53. On how big changes in the way states view the world are generated by domestic struggles to redefine the national interest, see Legro, *Rethinking the World*.

54. On the clash with balance of power, see Layne, *Peace of Illusions*, 120–24. On the rise of neoconservatives, see Mann, *Rise of the Vulcans*. Fukuyama, *America at the Crossroads*. Ehrman, *Rise Of Neoconservatism*.

55. Sheehan, *Balance of Power*, 104.

56. See Kissinger, *White House Years*, 58.

57. See Friedman, *Neoconservative Revolution*, chap. 8.

58. See Monten, "Roots of the Bush Doctrine."

59. On the impact of neoconservative views on foreign policy, see Ehrman, *Rise Of Neoconservatism*.

60. See Halper and Clarke, *America Alone*, 326.

61. Ibid., 92.

62. Ibid., 326.

63. See Monten, "Roots of the Bush Doctrine," esp. 149.

64. See Bacevich, *American Empire*, 7–8, 122.

65. Haass, *Reluctant Sheriff.*

66. Kristol and Kagan, "National Interest and Global Responsibility."

67. This could be the basis for a neoclassical realist theory for explaining the U.S. invasion of Iraq, although it was far more complex than that.

68. Quoted in Halper and Clarke, *America Alone*, 81.

69. See the letter to the president, January 26, 1998, at www.newamericancentury.org/iraqclintonletter.htm.

70. Contrary to popular view, they were not part of this original movement; nor did they, with the possible exception of Cheney, identify themselves as neoconservatives.

71. Fukuyama, *America at the Crossroads*, 37.

72. Although the president was not a neoconservative per se, some evidence suggests he was not cognitively flexible. See Renshon, *Why Some Leaders Choose War*, esp. 115–17.

73. Halper and Clarke, *America Alone.*

74. See the analysis of a former Clinton NSC official in Soderberg, *Superpower Myth.*

75. Halper and Clarke, *America Alone*, 146.

CHAPTER TEN: The Balance Sheet, So to Speak

1. Richard Haass, special assistant to the president for Near East and South Asian Affairs, interview with author, Washington, D.C., February 19, 1999.

2. Walt, *Origins of Alliances*, 153.

3. Ellen Laipson, National Security Council analyst, interview with author, Washington, D.C., August 8, 2006. See also Ansari, *Confronting Iran*, 136–37.

4. See Halper and Clarke, *America Alone*, esp. 92. Ehrman, *Rise Of Neoconservatism.*

5. See Hoogland, "Policy of the Reagan Administration toward Iran," esp. 190–92.

6. For instance, see Graham E. Fuller to Director of Central Intelligence, memo, "Toward a Policy on Iran," NIC 02545-85, May 17, 1985.

7. See Yetiv, *Explaining Foreign Policy.*

8. On Bush's critical role in the 1990–91 Gulf crisis, see ibid.

9. Layne, *Peace of Illusions.*

10. Posen, "Command of the Commons," 6.

11. On hegemony, see, for instance, Ferguson, *Colossus*, and Wohlforth, "Stability of a Unipolar World." On nonhegemonic strategies, see Layne, *Peace of Illusions*, and Huntington, "Lonely Superpower." For a good application of selective engagement strategy, see Posen, "Command of the Commons."

12. Art, *Grand Strategy for America*, 82 and, for an explanation of these strategies, chap. 3; Layne, *Peace of Illusions*, 5 and chap. 8. See also Layne's chapter 8 for the differences between hegemony, offshore balancing, and selective engagement.

13. Layne, *Peace of Illusions*, 116, 170.

14. Ibid., *Peace of Illusions*, 160.

15. Joffe, *Uberpower*, 144.

16. On temptations to conquer and annex, see Kennedy, *Rise and Fall of the Great Powers*. Gilpin, *War and Change in World Politics.* Doyle, *Empires.*

17. See Krasner, *International Regimes*. See also Gulick, *Europe's Classical Balance of Power*. Albrecht-Carrie, *Diplomatic History of Europe*.

18. On earlier in the twentieth century Palmer, *Guardians of the Gulf*, 27–29, 46–47, and Yergin, *The Prize*, 391–400; on expansion of its interests, see Palmer, *Guardians of the Gulf*. Yergin, *The Prize*. Stoff, *Oil, War, and American Security*. Lesch, *Middle East and the United States*.

19. Armstrong, "Saudis' AWACs Just a Beginning of a New Strategy."

20. For details on this infrastructure, see U.S. Department of Defense, *Conduct of the Persian Gulf War: Final Report to Congress* (April 1992), app. F.

21. Ibid., 116, 170.

22. See U.S. Office of the President, *National Security Strategy of Engagement and Enlargement* (Washington, DC: The White House, 1995).

23. U.S. Department of Defense, *Report of the Quadrennial Defense Review* (May 1997).

24. Books that illuminate this point include Halper and Clarke, *America Alone*; Daalder and Lindsay, *America Unbound*; and Mann, *Rise of the Vulcans*.

25. For instance, see the analysis in Dueck, *Reluctant Crusaders*, 152–62.

26. On this doctrine, see Freedman, *Deterrence*.

27. Robert Art identifies four periods when the United States pursued "semblances" of what he refers to as a "full-fledged policy of dominion," one of which was under Bush. Art, *Grand Strategy for America*, 87–90.

28. Laipson interview.

29. On such an interpretation, see Craig, "American Realism versus American Imperialism," 143–71.

30. Cover letter to the National Security Strategy.

31. On this motivation in foreign policy and on prospect theory, see Welch, *Painful Choices*.

32. Freedman and Karsh, *Gulf Conflict*, chap. 29.

33. U.S. Office of the President, National Security Directive 54, The White House, January 15, 1991. Yetiv, *Explaining Foreign Policy*.

34. Barnett, *Pentagon's New Map*, 359.

35. On how true empires do exceed these requirements, see Craig, "American Realism versus American Imperialism," esp. 165.

36. Layne, *Peace of Illusions*, 3.

37. Dueck, *Reluctant Crusaders*, 1–5.

38. See Gordon, "The End of the Bush Revolution."

39. See Fukuyama, *America at the Crossroads*, 182.

40. Sanger, "Bush's Shift."

41. Stephen Toulmin refers to postdiction as retrodiction in that it aims to "predict the nature of things yet to be discovered about the past." Toulmin, *Foresight and Understanding*, 26.

CHAPTER ELEVEN: Theory, Strategy, and Realism

1. See Yetiv, *Crude Awakenings*, chap. 6.

2. Ikenberry, *America Unrivaled*, 284–310.

3. On the rising importance of civil wars and the challenges of addressing them, see David, *Civil Nightmares*.

4. See, for instance, Kissinger, *Diplomacy*, 70–72.

5. On the strategic model, see Doyle, "Balancing," 144–46. On semiautomatic conceptions, see Claude, *Power and International Relations*, esp. 47–49.

6. In Keohane, *Neorealism and Its Critics*, 123.

7. Waltz, *Theory of International Politics*, 68, 71, 121–23.

8. Keohane, *Neorealism and Its Critics*, 172–73.

9. Author's correspondence with Lake, September 2, 2000.

10. Mastanduno, "Preserving the Unipolar Moment," 52–53.

11. See ibid. and also Layne, *Peace of Illusions*, 193. He notes, for instance, that since "the early 1940s, the United States has pursued a grand strategy of extraregional hegemony. From the standpoint of neorealist theory, this is puzzling." Walt, *Origins of Alliances*. Thus, using neorealism, one scholar predicts that China will balance the United States after the Cold War. See Johnston, "International Structures and Chinese Foreign Policy," esp. 60.

12. See Elman, "Horses For Courses," 10–11. For Waltz's rebuttal, see Waltz, "International Politics Is Not Foreign Policy," 54–57.

13. See Layne, *Peace of Illusions*, esp. 19.

14. See Ikenberry, *America Unrivaled*. On how states may be balancing against the United States nonmilitarily, see Pape, "Soft Balancing against the United States." Paul, "Soft Balancing in the Age of U.S. Primacy," esp. 58–59.

15. On conditions under which states balance, see Walt, *Origins of Alliances*, 28–30. On domestic variables, see Schweller, "Bandwagoning for Profit."

16. See Ramazani, "Iran's Foreign Policy," 204–8, and Sick, *All Fall Down*.

17. Few, if any, theories exist to help answer this question, a shortcoming recognized by some who helped fashion the U.S. approach toward Iraq after the Iran-Iraq War. Author's discussion with Richard Haass, New York, April 17, 1997.

18. See Cottam, "Revolutionary Iran and War with Iraq," esp. 5–9.

19. For works that see realism as obsolete, see Kapstein, "Is Realism Dead?" and Legro and Moravcsik, "Is Anybody Still a Realist." On how balancing is exaggerated, to the neglect of bandwagoning, see Schweller, "Bandwaging for Profit."

20. See Miller and Yetiv, "New World Order."

CONCLUSION: Reactive Engagement

1. For instance, for recent work, see Legro, *Rethinking the World*, and Welch, *Painful Choices*. For a neoclassical view of how international pressures and American strategic culture have acted together to shape U.S. grand strategy, see Dueck, *Reluctant Crusaders*.

2. For instance, see Art, *Grand Strategy for America*, and Dueck, *Reluctant Crusaders*. See Mastanduno, "Preserving the Unipolar Moment." He believes that the United States pursued a realist grand strategy after the end of the Cold War.

3. Layne, *Peace of Illusions*, 193, 25.

4. Dueck, *Reluctant Crusaders*.

5. Ellen Laipson, National Security Council analyst, interview with author, Washington, D.C., August 8, 2006.

6. Kennedy, *Rise and Fall of the Great Powers*, esp. 515.

7. Yetiv, *Explaining Foreign Policy*.

8. See Kupchan, *Vulnerability of Empire*. Gaddis, *Strategies of Containment*.

Bibliography

Abdallah, Abdel Mahdi. "Causes of Anti-Americanism in the Arab World: A Socio-Political Perspective." *Middle East Review of International Affairs* 7 (December 2003).

Adler, Emanuel, and Michael Barnett, eds. *Security Communities*. Cambridge: Cambridge University Press, 1998.

Ajami, Fouad. "Iraq and the Arabs' Future." *Foreign Affairs* (January/February 2003).

Albrecht-Carrie, Rene. *A Diplomatic History of Europe since the Congress of Vienna*. New York: Harper and Row, 1958.

Albright, David, and Mark Hibbs. "Iraq's Bomb: Blueprints and Artifacts." *Bulletin of the Atomic Scientists* (January/February 1992).

Albright, Madeleine. *Madam Secretary: A Memoir*. New York: Hyperion, 2003.

Alikhani, Hossein. *Sanctioning Iran: Anatomy of a Failed Policy*. London: I. B. Tauris, 2000.

Ambah, Faiza Saleh. "Bush Denies Saudi Request to Release 9/11 Information." Knight Ridder News Service, July 30, 2003.

———. "Saudi Raids Uncover Network of Extremists' Sleeper Cells." Associated Press, August 14, 2003.

———. "Saudis Hint al-Qaida Presence." Associated Press, July 30, 2003.

Amirahmadi, Hooshang. "Economic Destruction and Imbalances in Post-revolutionary Iran." In Hooshang Amirahmadi and Nader Entessar, eds., *Reconstruction and Regional Diplomacy in the Persian Gulf*. London: Routledge, 1992.

Amirahmadi, Hooshang, and Nader Entessar, eds. *Reconstruction and Regional Diplomacy in the Persian Gulf*. London: Routledge, 1992.

Amirsadeghi, Hossein, ed. *The Security of the Persian Gulf*. New York: St. Martin's Press, 1981.

Amuzegar, Jahangir. "Iran's Crumbling Revolution." *Foreign Affairs* 82 (January/February 2003).

Anderson, Jack. "Double-Dealing on Iran Laid to Soviets." *Washington Post*, December 31, 1979.

"Anonymous" [Michael Scheuer]. *Imperial Hubris: Why the West Is Losing the War on Terror*. London: Brassey's, 2004.

Ansari, Ali M. *Confronting Iran: The Failure of American Foreign Policy and the Next Great Crisis in the Middle East*. New York: Basic Books, 2006.

Armstrong, Scott. "Saudis' AWACs Just a Beginning of a New Strategy." *Washington Post*, November 1, 1981.

Art, Robert J. *A Grand Strategy for America*. Ithaca, NY: Cornell University Press, 2003.

Bacevich, Andrew J. *American Empire: The Realities and Consequences of U.S. Diplomacy*. Cambridge, MA: Harvard University Press, 2002.

Bacevich, Andrew J., and Elizabeth H. Prodromou. "God Is Not Neutral: Religion and U.S. Foreign Policy after 9/11." *Orbis* 48 (Winter 2004).

Baer, Robert. *Sleeping with the Devil.* New York: Crown Publishers, 2003.

Baker, James A. *The Politics of Diplomacy: Revolution, War, and Peace, 1989–1992.* New York: G. P. Putnam's Sons, 1995.

Baram, Amatzia. "The Iraqi Invasion of Kuwait: Decision-making in Baghdad." In Amatzia Baram and Barry Rubin, eds., *Iraq's Road to War.* New York: St. Martin's Press, 1993.

Baram, Amatzia, and Barry Rubin, eds. *Iraq's Road to War.* New York: St. Martin's Press, 1993.

Barnett, Thomas P. M. *The Pentagon's New Map: War and Peace in the Twenty-first Century.* New York: G. P. Putnam's Sons, 2004.

Bartlett, C. J. *The Long Retreat: A Short History of British Defense Policy, 1945–1970.* London: Macmillan, 1972.

Barylski, Robert V. "The Collapse of the Soviet Union and Gulf Security." In David E. Long and Christian Koch, eds., *Gulf Security in the Twenty-first Century,* London: I. B. Tauris, 1997.

Bengio, Ofra. *Saddam's Word: Political Discourse in Iraq.* New York: Oxford University Press, 1998.

Betts, Richard K. "Wealth, Power, and Instability: East Asia and the United States after the Cold War." *International Security* 18 (Winter 1993/94).

Bill, James A. *The Eagle and the Lion: The Tragedy of American-Iranian Relations.* New Haven, CT: Yale University Press, 1988.

——. "The U.S. Overture to Iran, 1985–1986: An Analysis." In Nikki R. Keddie and Mark J. Gasiorowski, eds., *Neither East nor West: Iran, the Soviet Union, and the United States.* New Haven, CT: Yale University Press, 1990.

Blumberg, Daniel. *Reinventing Khomeini: The Struggle for Reform in Iran.* Chicago: University of Chicago Press, 2001.

Bodansky, Yossef. *The Secret History of the Iraq War.* New York: HarperCollins, 2004.

Boot, Max. *The Savage Wars of Peace: Small Wars and the Rise of American Power.* New York: Basic Books, 2003.

Brands, H. W. *What America Owes the World: The Struggle for the Soul of Foreign Policy.* Cambridge: Cambridge University Press, 1998.

Breslauer, George, Harry Kreisler, and Ben Ward, eds. *Beyond the Cold War: Conflict and Cooperation in the Third World.* Berkeley: Institute of International Studies, University of California, 1992.

Brzezinski, Zbigniew, Brent Scowcroft, and Richard Murphy. "Differentiated Containment." *Foreign Affairs* (May/June 1997).

Buehrig, Edward H. *Woodrow Wilson and the Balance of Power.* Bloomington: Indiana University Press, 1955.

Bull, Hedley. *The Anarchical Society: A Study of Order in World Politics.* New York: Columbia University Press, 1977.

Burt, Richard. "U.S. Studying Ways to Bolster Strength in Mideast." *New York Times,* December 10, 1979.

Bush, George. *Public Papers of the Presidents of the United States: George Bush, 1990.* Vol. 2. Washington, DC: GPO, 1991.

——. *Public Papers of the Presidents of the United States: George Bush, 1991.* Vol. 1. Washington, DC: GPO, 1992.

Bush, George, and Brent Scowcroft. *A World Transformed.* New York: Knopf, 1998.

Butler, Richard. *The Greatest Threat: Iraq, Weapons of Mass Destruction, and the Growing Crisis Of Global Security.* New York: Public Affairs, 2001.

Buzan, Barry. "Regional Security as a Policy Objective: The Case of South and Southwest Asia." In Alvin Z. Rubinstein, ed., *The Great Game: Rivalry in the Persian Gulf and South Asia.* New York: Praeger, 1983.

Carpenter, Ted Galen, and James A. Dorn, eds. *China's Future: Constructive Partner or Emerging Threat?* Washington, DC: Cato Institute, 2000.

Carroll, James. *House of War: The Pentagon and the Disastrous Rise of American Power.* New York: Houghton Mifflin, 2006.

Cato Handbook for Congress, 105th Congress. Washington, DC: Cato Institute, 1997.

Chalabi, Fadhil J. "Iraq and the Future of World Oil." *Middle East Policy* 7 (October 2000).

Chalabi, Issam al-. *Iraqi Oil Policy: Present and Future Perspectives.* Cambridge, MA: Cambridge Energy Research Associates, 2003.

Christensen, Thomas J. "Perceptions and Alliances in Europe, 1865–1940." *International Organization* 51 (Winter 1997).

Chubin, Shahram. *Security in the Gulf: The Role of Outside Powers.* Aldershot, England: Gower Publishing Co., 1982.

——. "Soviet Policy toward Iran and the Gulf." *Adelphi Papers* 157 (Spring 1980).

Chubin, Shahram, and Charles Tripp. *Iran and Iraq at War.* Boulder, CO: Westview Press, 1988.

Churchill, Winston S. *The Gathering Storm.* Vol. I of *The Second World War.* Boston: Houghton Mifflin, 1948.

Clarke, Richard A. *Against All Enemies: Inside America's War on Terror.* New York: Free Press, 2004.

Claude, Inis L. *Power and International Relations.* New York: Random House, 1962.

——. *Swords into Plowshares: The Problems and Progress of International Organization.* 4th ed. New York: Random House, 1971.

Coll, Steve. *Ghost Wars: The Secret History of the CIA, Afghanistan, and bin Laden from the Soviet Invasion of Afghanistan to September 10, 2001.* New York: Penguin, 2004.

Cooley, John K. *An Alliance against Babylon: The U.S., Israel, and Iraq.* London: Pluto Press, 2005.

Cordesman, Anthony H. *After the Storm: The Changing Military Balance in the Middle East.* Boulder, CO: Westview Press, 1993.

——. *The Gulf and the Search for Strategic Stability: Saudi Arabia, the Military Balance in the Gulf, and Trends in the Arab-Israeli Military Balance.* Boulder, CO: Westview Press, 1984.

——. *The Gulf and the West: Strategic Relations and Military Realities.* Boulder, CO: Westview Press, 1988.

——. *Iran and Iraq: The Threats from the Northern Gulf.* Boulder, CO: Westview Press, 1994.

——. *The Iran-Iraq War and Western Security, 1984–87: Strategic Implications and Policy Options.* London: Jane's Publishing Co., 1987.

Cottam, Richard W. "Revolutionary Iran and the War with Iraq." *Current History* 80 (January 1981).

Craig, Campbell. "American Realism versus American Imperialism." *World Politics* 57 (October 2004).

Curzon, George N. *Russia in Central Asia in 1889 and the Anglo-Russian Question*. London: Frank Cass and Co., 1967.

Daalder, Ivo H., and James M. Lindsay. *America Unbound: The Bush Revolution in Foreign Policy*. Washington, DC: Brookings Institution Press, 2003.

Darby, Phillip. *British Defense Policy East of Suez, 1947–1968*. London: Oxford University Press, 1973.

David, Steven R. *Civil Nightmares*. Forthcoming.

——. "Explaining Third World Alignment." *World Politics* 43 (January 1991).

Denizen, Norman K., and Yvonna S. Lincoln, eds. *Handbook of Qualitative Research*. London: Sage, 1994.

Desch, Michael C. "Bush and the Generals." *Foreign Affairs* 86 (May/June 2007).

Downs, George W., ed. *Collective Security beyond the Cold War*. Ann Arbor: University of Michigan Press, 1994.

Doyle, Michael W. "Balancing Power Classically: An Alternative to Collective Security." In George W. Downs, ed., *Collective Security beyond the Cold War*. Ann Arbor: University of Michigan Press, 1994.

——. *Empires*. Ithaca, NY: Cornell University Press, 1986.

Driody, Dan. *The Halliburton Agenda: The Politics of Oil and Money*. New York: John Wiley and Sons, 2004.

Dueck, Colin. *Reluctant Crusaders: Power, Culture, and Change in American Grand Strategy*. Princeton, NJ: Princeton University Press, 2006.

Duffield, John S. "Oil and the Iraq War: How the United States Could Have Expected to Benefit, and Might Still." *Middle East Review of International Affairs* 9 (June 2005).

Duncan, Richard. "Three World Oil Forecasts Predict Peak Oil Production." *Oil & Gas Journal*, May 26, 2003.

Dunn, David Hastings. "Myths, Motivations and 'Misunderestimations': The Bush Administration and Iraq." *International Affairs* 79 (March 2003).

Eckholm, Erik. "Now You See It: An Audit Of KBR." *New York Times*, March 20, 2005.

Ehrman, John. *The Rise of Neoconservatism*. New Haven, CT: Yale University Press, 1995.

Eilts, Hermann. "Security Considerations in the Persian Gulf." *International Security* 5 (Fall 1980).

Eisenstadt, Michael. *Like a Phoenix from the Ashes? The Future of Iraqi Military Power*. Policy Paper No. 36. Washington, DC: Washington Institute for Near East Policy, 1993.

Elman, Colin. "Extending Offensive Realism: The Louisiana Purchase and America's Rise to Regional Hegemony." *American Political Science Review* 98 (November 2004).

——. "Horses for Courses: Why Not Neorealist Theories of Foreign Policy?" *Security Studies* 6 (Autumn 1996).

Ferguson, Niall. *Colossus: The Rise and Fall of the American Empire*. New York: Penguin, 2005.

Freedman, Lawrence. *Deterrence*. London: Polity, 2004.

——. "War in Iraq: Selling the Threat." *Survival* 46 (Summer 2004).

Freedman, Lawrence, and Efraim Karsh. *The Gulf Conflict, 1990–1991: Diplomacy and War in the New World Order*. Princeton, NJ: Princeton University Press, 1993.

Freedman, Robert O., ed. *The Middle East after Iraq's Invasion of Kuwait*. Gainesville: University Press of Florida, 1993.

——. "Moscow and the Iraqi Invasion of Kuwait." In Robert O. Freedman, ed., *The Middle East after Iraq's Invasion of Kuwait*. Gainesville: University Press of Florida, 1993.

———. "The Soviet Union, the Gulf War, and Its Aftermath: A Case Study in Limited Superpower Cooperation." In David W. Lesch, ed., *The Middle East and the United States: A Historical and Political Reassessment.* Boulder, CO: Westview Press, 1996.

Friedman, Murray. *The Neoconservative Revolution: Jewish Intellectuals and the Shaping of Public Policy.* Cambridge: Cambridge University Press, 2005.

Fukuyama, Francis. *America at the Crossroads: Democracy, Power, and the Neoconservative Legacy.* New Haven, CT: Yale University Press, 2006.

Fuller, Graham E. *The Future of Political Islam.* New York: Palgrave, 2003.

Gaddis, John. *Strategies of Containment.* New York: Oxford University Press, 1982.

Gamble, Andrew, and Anthony Payne, eds. *Regionalism and World Order.* New York: St. Martin's Press, 1996.

Gause, F. Gregory, III. "The Illogic of Dual Containment." *Foreign Affairs* 73 (March/April 1994).

———. "Saudi Arabia Challenged." *Current History* 103 (January 2004).

Gerges, Fawaz A. *America and Political Islam: Clash of Cultures or Clash of Interests?* Cambridge: Cambridge University Press, 1999.

———. *The Far Enemy: Why Jihad Went Global.* New York: Cambridge University Press, 2005.

Gilpin, Robert. *War and Change in World Politics.* Cambridge: Cambridge University Press, 1981.

Glanz, James. "Army Plans to End Contentious Halliburton Logistics Pact and Split Work among Companies." *New York Times,* July 13, 2006.

Goldberg, Jacob. "Saudi Arabia: The Bank Vault Next Door." In Amatzia Baram and Barry Rubin, eds., *Iraq's Road to War.* New York: St. Martin's Press, 1993.

Gordon, Michael R., and Bernard E. Trainor. *Cobra II: The Inside Story of the Invasion and Occupation Of Iraq.* New York: Pantheon Books, 2006.

———. *The General's War: The Inside Story of the Conflict in the Gulf.* Boston: Little, Brown and Co., 1995.

Gordon, Philip H. "The End of the Bush Revolution." *Foreign Affairs* 85 (July/August 2006).

———. "Iraq: The Transatlantic Debate." Institute for Security Studies Occasional Papers, No. 39 (November 2002).

Gulick, Edward Vose. *Europe's Classical Balance of Power.* New York: W. W. Norton, 1955.

Gurtov, Mel. *Superpower on Crusade: The Bush Doctrine in US Foreign Policy.* Boulder, CO: Lynne Rienner, 2006.

Gustafson, Thane. *Changing Course? Iraq and The "New" US-Russian Relationship.* Cambridge, MA: Cambridge Energy Research Associates, 2003.

Gwertzman, Bernard. "U.S. Officials React Warily; Put Bakhtiar Odds at 50–50." *New York Times,* January 17, 1979.

Haas, Ernst B. "The Balance of Power: Prescription, Concept, or Propaganda?" *World Politics* 5 (July 1953).

Haass, Richard N. *The Opportunity: America's Moment to Alter History's Course.* New York: PublicAffairs, 2005.

———. *The Reluctant Sheriff: The United States after the Cold War.* New York: Council on Foreign Relations Press, 1997.

———. "Saudi Arabia and Iran: The Twin Pillars in Revolutionary Times." In Hossein Amirsadeghi, ed., *The Security of the Persian Gulf.* New York: St. Martin's Press, 1981.

Halper, Stefan, and Jonathan Clarke. *America Alone: Neo-conservatives and the Global Order*. Cambridge: Cambridge University Press, 2004.

Hardt, Michael, and Antonio Negri. *Empire*. Cambridge, MA: Harvard University Press, 2003.

Hauner, Milan. "The Last Great Game." *Middle East Journal* 38 (Winter 1984).

Hiro, Dilip. *Desert Shield to Desert Storm: The Second Gulf War*. New York: Routledge, 1992.

Hoogland, Eric. "The Policy of the Reagan Administration toward Iran." In Nikki R. Keddie and Mark J. Gasiorowski, eds., *Neither East nor West: Iran, the Soviet Union, and the United States*. New Haven, CT: Yale University Press, 1990.

Hunter, Shireen T. "Iran from the August 1988 Cease-Fire to the April 1992 Majlis Election." In Robert O. Freedman, ed., *The Middle East after Iraq's Invasion of Kuwait*. Gainesville: University Press of Florida, 1993.

Huntington, Samuel P. "The Lonely Superpower." *Foreign Affairs* 78 (March–April 1999).

Ibrahim, Youssef M. "Rebounding Iranians Are Striving for Regional Leadership in Gulf." *New York Times*, November 7, 1992.

———. "To Counter Iran, Saudis Seek Ties with Ex-Soviet Islamic Republics." *New York Times*, February 22, 1992.

Ikenberry, G. John, ed. *America Unrivaled: The Future of the Balance of Power*. Ithaca, NY: Cornell University Press, 2002.

Indyk, Martin, Graham Fuller, Anthony Cordesman, and Phebe Marr. "Symposium on Dual Containment: U.S. Policy toward Iran and Iraq." *Middle East Policy* 3 (1994).

Isenberg, David. "Desert Storm Redux." *Middle East Journal* 47 (Summer 1993).

Jackson, Robert H. *Quasi-States: Sovereignty, International Relations, and the Third World*. Cambridge: Cambridge University Press, 1990.

Jehl, Douglas. "Report Says White House Ignored C.I.A. On Iraq Chaos," *New York Times*, October 13, 2005.

———. "Report Warned Bush Team about Intelligence Doubts." *New York Times*, November 6, 2005.

Jentleson, Bruce W. *With Friends Like These: Reagan, Bush, and Saddam, 1982–1990*. New York: W. W. Norton, 1994.

Joffe, Josef. *Überpower: The Imperial Temptation of America*. New York: W. W. Norton, 2006.

Johnson, Maxwell Orme. *The Military as an Instrument of U.S. Policy in Southwest Asia*. Boulder, CO: Westview Press, 1983.

Johnston, Alastair Ian. "International Structures and Chinese Foreign Policy." In Samuel S. Kim, ed., *China and the World: Chinese Foreign Policy Faces the New Millennium*. Boulder, CO: Westview Press, 1998.

Juergensmeyer, Mark. "Religious Terror and Global War." In Craig Calhoun, Paul Price, and Ashley Timmer, eds., *Understanding September 11*. New York: New Press, 2002.

Kapstein, Ethan B. "Is Realism Dead? The Domestic Sources of International Politics." *International Organization* 99 (Autumn 1995).

Karabell, Zachary. "Backfire: US Policy toward Iraq, 1988–2 August 1990." *Middle East Journal* 49 (Winter 1995).

Karam, Azza, ed. *Transnational Political Islam*. London: Pluto Press, 2004.

Karsh, Efraim, ed. *The Iran-Iraq War: Impact and Implications*. New York: St. Martin's Press, 1989.

Karshenas, Massoud, and M. Hashem Pesaran. "Economic Reform and the Reconstruction of the Iranian Economy." *Middle East Journal* 49 (Winter 1995).

Kaufman, Robert G. "To Balance or to Bandwagon? Alignment Decisions in 1930s Europe." *Security Studies* 1 (Spring 1992).

Kaufmann, Chaim. "Threat Inflation and the Failure of the Marketplace of Ideas: The Selling of the Iraq War." *International Security* 29 (2004).

Keddie, Nikki R., and Mark J. Gasiorowski, eds. *Neither East nor West: Iran, the Soviet Union, and the United States.* New Haven, CT: Yale University Press, 1990.

Kennedy, Paul, ed. *Grand Strategies in War and Peace.* New Haven, CT: Yale University Press, 1991.

———. *The Rise and Fall of the Great Powers.* New York: Random House, 1989.

Keohane, Robert O. "Alliances, Threats, and the Uses of Neorealism." *International Security* 13 (Summer 1988).

———, ed. *Neorealism and Its Critics.* New York: Columbia University Press, 1986.

Khalilzad, Zalmay. "Losing the Moment? The United States and the World after the Cold War." *Washington Quarterly* 18 (Spring 1995).

Khan, M. A. Muqtedar. "Radical Islam, Liberal Islam." *Current History* 102 (December 2003).

Kifner, John. "Iranian Officials Urge 'Uprooting' of Saudi Royalty." *New York Times,* August 3, 1987.

King, Gary, Robert O. Keohane, and Sidney Verba. *Designing Social Inquiry: Scientific Inference in Qualitative Research.* Princeton, NJ: Princeton University Press, 1994.

Kissinger, Henry. *Diplomacy.* New York: Simon and Schuster, 1994.

———. *Does America Need a Foreign Policy? Toward a Diplomacy for the Twenty-first Century.* New York: Simon and Schuster, 2001.

———. *White House Years.* Boston: Little, Brown and Co., 1979.

———. *A World Restored: Metternich, Castlereagh and the Problems of Peace, 1812–1822.* Boston: Houghton Mifflin, 1973.

Knock, Thomas. *To End All Wars: Woodrow Wilson and the Quest for a New World Order.* New York: Oxford University Press, 1992.

Kohut, Andrew, and Bruce Stokes. *America against the World: How We Are Different and Why We Are Disliked.* New York: Times Books, 2006.

Krasner, Stephen, ed. *International Regimes.* Ithaca, NY: Cornell University Press, 1983.

Krasner, Stephen D., and Carlos Pascual. "Addressing State Failure." *Foreign Affairs* 84 (July/August 2005).

Kristol, William, and Robert Kagan. "National Interest and Global Responsibility." In Irwin Stelser, ed., *The Neo-con Reader.* New York: Atlantic Books, 2004.

Kupchan, Charles. *Vulnerability of Empire.* Ithaca, NY: Cornell University Press, 1994.

Kupchan, Charles A., and Clifford A. Kupchan. "Concerts, Collective Security, and the Future of Europe." *International Security* 16 (Summer 1991).

Lake, Anthony. "Confronting Backlash States." *Foreign Affairs* 73 (March–April 1994).

Lake, David A., and Patrick M. Morgan, eds. *Regional Orders: Building Security in a New World.* University Park: Pennsylvania State University Press, 1997.

———. "Regional Security Complexes: A Systems Approach." In Lake and Morgan, eds., *Regional Orders: Building Security in a New World.* University Park: Pennsylvania State University Press, 1997.

Lauerman, Vincent. "Gulf War II: Longer Term Implications for the World Oil Market." *Geopolitics of Energy* (April 2003).

Lavy, Victor. "The Economic Embargo of Egypt by Arab States: Myth and Reality." *Middle East Journal* 38 (Summer 1984).

Layne, Christopher. *The Peace of Illusions: American Grand Strategy from 1940 to the Present.* Ithaca, NY: Cornell University Press, 2006.

Lebow, Richard Ned. *Between Peace and War: The Nature of International Crisis.* Baltimore: Johns Hopkins University Press, 1981.

Legro, Jeffrey W. *Rethinking the World: Great Power Strategies and International Order.* Ithaca, NY: Cornell University Press, 2005.

Legro, Jeffrey W., and Andrew Moravcsik. "Is Anybody Still a Realist?" *International Security* 24 (Fall 1999).

Lesch, David W., ed. *The Middle East and the United States: A Historical and Political Reassessment.* Boulder, CO: Westview Press, 1996.

———. *1979: The Year That Shaped the Modern Middle East.* Boulder, CO: Westview Press, 2001.

Levy, Jack S. "What Do Great Powers Balance against and When?" In T. V. Paul, James J. Wirtz, and Michel Fortmann, eds., *Balance of Power: Theory and Practice in the Twenty-first Century.* Stanford, CA: Stanford University Press, 2004.

Lieber, Robert J. *The American Era: Power and Strategy for the Twenty-first Century.* Cambridge: Cambridge University Press, 2005.

———, ed. *Eagle Adrift: American Foreign Policy at the End of the Century.* New York: Longman, 1997.

———, ed. *Eagle Rules? Foreign Policy and American Primacy in the Twenty-first Century.* Upper Saddle River, NJ: Prentice Hall, 2002.

———. "Eagle without a Cause: Making Foreign Policy without the Soviet Threat." In Lieber, ed., *Eagle Adrift: American Foreign Policy at the End of the Century.* New York: Longman, 1997.

Lijphart, Arend. "Comparative Politics and the Comparative Method." *American Political Science Review* 65 (September 1971).

Link, Arthur, ed. *The Public Papers of Woodrow Wilson.* Princeton, NJ: Princeton University Press, 1983–84.

———, ed. *Woodrow Wilson and a Revolutionary World, 1913–1921.* Chapel Hill: University of North Carolina Press, 1982.

Linzer, Dafna. "Iraq Approves Inspectors' Use of U-2 Surveillance Planes, Iraqi Ambassador Says." Associated Press, February 6, 2003.

Liska, George. *Nations in Alliance: The Limits of Interdependence.* Baltimore: Johns Hopkins University Press, 1962.

Litwak, Robert S. *Détente and the Nixon Doctrine: American Foreign Policy and the Pursuit of Stability, 1969–76.* Cambridge: Cambridge University Press, 1984.

———. "Iraq and Iran: From Dual to Differentiated Containment." In Robert J. Lieber, ed., *Eagle Rules? Foreign Policy and American Primacy in the Twenty-first Century.* Upper Saddle River, NJ: Prentice Hall 2002.

———. *Regime Change: U.S. Strategy through the Prism of 9/11.* Baltimore: Johns Hopkins University Press, 2007.

Mackey, Sandra. *The Iranians: Persia, Islam, and the Soul of a Nation.* New York: Plume, 1996.

MacMillan, Margaret. *Paris 1919: Six Months That Changed the World*. New York: Random House, 2002.

Maier, Charles S. *Among Empires: American Ascendancy and Its Predecessors*. Cambridge, MA: Harvard University Press, 2006.

Malone, David M. *The International Struggle over Iraq: Politics in the UN Security Council, 1980–2005*. New York: Oxford University Press, 2006.

Mann, Jim. *Rise of the Vulcans: The History of Bush's War Cabinet*. New York: Viking, 2004.

Mansfield, Edward D., and Helen V. Milner. "The New Wave of Regionalism." *International Organization* 53 (Summer 1999).

Mastanduno, Michael. "Incomplete Hegemony and Security Order in the Asia-Pacific." In G. John Ikenberry, ed., *America Unrivaled: The Future of the Balance of Power*. Ithaca, NY: Cornell University Press, 2002.

——. "Preserving the Unipolar Moment: Realist Theories and U.S. Grand Strategy after the Cold War." *International Security* 21 (Spring 1997).

McDougall, Walter A. *Promised Land, Crusader State: The American Encounter with the World since 1776*. New York: Houghton Mifflin, 1997.

Mead, Walter Russell. *Special Providence: American Foreign Policy and How It Changed the World*. New York: Knopf, 2002.

Mearsheimer, John J. "The False Promise of International Institutions." *International Security* 19 (Winter 1994–95).

——. *The Tragedy of Great Power Politics*. New York: W. W. Norton, 2001.

Mearsheimer, John J., and Stephen M. Walt. "Can Saddam Be Contained? History Says Yes." Belfer Center for Science and International Affairs, John F. Kennedy School of Government, Harvard University, November 12, 2002, posted on the Belfer Center's Web site (http://bcsia.ksg.harvard.edu/).

Medvedev, Roy. *Post-Soviet Russia: A Journey through the Yeltsin Era*. New York: Columbia University Press, 2000.

Merry, Robert W. *Sands of Empire: Missionary Zeal, American Foreign Policy, and the Hazards of Global Ambition*. New York: Simon and Schuster, 2005.

The Middle East. 7th ed. Washington, DC: Congressional Quarterly Press, 1991.

Middleton, Drew. "Arabian Anxieties: What Soviets Might Do and What U.S. Might Not." *New York Times*, June 16, 1979.

Miller, Eric A. "Bringing the Leader Back In: Internal Threats and Alignment Theory in the Commonwealth of Independent States." *Security Studies* 14 (Winter 2005).

Miller, Eric A., and Steve Yetiv. "The New World Order in Theory and Practice: The Bush Administration's World View." *Presidential Studies Quarterly* 31 (March 2001).

Monten, Jonathan. "The Roots of the Bush Doctrine: Power, Nationalism, and Democracy Promotion in U.S. Strategy." *International Security* 29 (Spring 2005).

Moore, James W. "An Assessment of the Iranian Military Rearmament Program." *Comparative Strategy* 13 (1994).

Morgenthau, Hans, and Kenneth Thompson. *Politics among Nations*. 6th ed. New York: Knopf, 1985.

Munson, Henry. "Lifting the Veil: Understanding the Roots of Islamic Militancy." *Harvard International Review* 25 (Winter 2004).

Mylroie, Laurie. *Bush vs. the Beltway: How the CIA and the State Department Tried to Stop the War on Terror*. New York: ReganBooks, 2003.

Nakash, Yitzhak. *The Shi'is of Iraq*. Princeton, NJ: Princeton University Press, 1994.

——. "The Shiites and the Future of Iraq." *Foreign Affairs* 82 (July/August 2003).

Nelson, Keith L. *The Making of Détente: Soviet-American Relations in the Shadow of Vietnam.* Baltimore: Johns Hopkins University Press, 1995.

Newsome, David. "America Engulfed." *Foreign Policy* 43 (Summer 1981).

Niou Emerson, M. S., and Peter C. Ordeshook. "Preventive War and the Balance of Power: A Game-Theoretic Approach." *Journal of Conflict Resolution* 31 (September 1987).

——. "A Theory of the Balance of Power in International Systems." *Journal of Conflict Resolution* 30 (December 1996).

Nixon, Richard. *U.S. Foreign Policy for the 1970's: A New Strategy for Peace.* Report to the Congress, February 18, 1970. Washington, DC: GPO, 1970.

Nye, Joseph S., Jr. *Bound to Lead: The Changing Nature of Power.* New York: Basic Books, 1990.

——. *Soft Power: The Means to Success in World Politics.* New York: PublicAffairs, 2004.

Ott, Marvin C. "The Dragon's Reach: China and Southeast Asia." In Ted Galen Carpenter and James A. Dorn, eds., *China's Future: Constructive Partner or Emerging Threat?* Washington, DC: Cato Institute, 2000.

Pagden, Anthony. "Imperialism, Liberalism and the Quest for Perpetual Peace." *Daedalus* 134 (Spring 2005).

Palazchenko, Pavel. *My Years with Gorbachev and Shevardnadze: The Memoir of a Soviet Interpreter.* University Park: Pennsylvania State University Press, 1997.

Palmer, Michael A. *Guardians of the Gulf: A History of America's Expanding Role in the Persian Gulf, 1833–1992.* New York: Free Press, 1992.

Papayoanou, Paul A. *Power Ties: Interdependence, Balancing, and War.* Ann Arbor: University of Michigan Press, 1999.

Pape, Robert A. *Dying to Win: The Strategic Logic of Suicide Terrorism.* New York: Random House, 2005.

——. "Soft Balancing against the United States." *International Security* 30 (Summer 2005).

Paul, T. V. "Soft Balancing in the Age of U.S. Primacy." *International Security* 30 (Summer 2005).

Paul, T. V., James J. Wirtz, and Michel Fortmann, eds. *Balance of Power: Theory and Practice in the Twenty-first Century.* Stanford, CA: Stanford University Press, 2004.

Pelletreau, Robert H. "American Objectives in the Middle East." *US Department of State Dispatch* 7 (June 3, 1996).

Perlez, Jane. "U.S. Competes with China for Vietnam's Allegiance." *New York Times*, June 19, 2006.

Peters, Edward. "The Firanj Are Coming—Again." *Orbis* 48 (Winter 2004).

Pfiffner, James P. "Did President Bush Mislead the Country in His Arguments for War with Iraq?" *Presidential Studies Quarterly* 34 (March 2004).

Philips, Kevin. *American Theocracy: The Peril and Politics of Radical Religion, Oil, and Borrowed Money in the Twenty-first Century.* New York: Viking, 2006.

Philpott, Daniel. *Revolutions in Sovereignty: How Ideas Shaped Modern International Relations.* Princeton, NJ: Princeton University Press, 2001.

Phythian, M. *Arming Iraq: How the U.S. and Britain Secretly Built Saddam's War Machine.* Boston: Northeastern University Press, 1997.

Pollack, Kenneth M. *The Persian Puzzle: The Conflict between Iran and America.* New York: Random House, 2004.

——. *The Threatening Storm: The Case for Invading Iraq.* New York: Random House, 2002.

Posen, Barry R. "Command of the Commons: The Military Foundation of U.S. Hegemony." *International Security* 28 (Summer 2003).

——. *The Sources of Military Doctrine: Britain, France, and Germany between the World Wars.* Ithaca, NY: Cornell University Press, 1984.

Posen, Barry R., and Andrew L. Ross. "Competing U.S. Grand Strategies." In Robert J. Lieber, ed., *Eagle Adrift: American Foreign Policy at the End of the Century.* New York: Longman, 1997.

Powell, Colin. *My American Journey.* New York: Random House, 1995.

Quandt, William B. *Saudi Arabia in the 1980s: Foreign Policy, Security, and Oil.* Washington, DC: Brookings Institution, 1981.

Qutb, Sayyid. *Milestones.* Indianapolis: American Trust, 1990.

Rajaee, F. *Islamic Values and World View: Khomeini on Man, the State, and International Politics.* Lanham, MD: University Press of America, 1983.

Ramazani, Rouhoullah K. "The Emerging Arab-Iranian Rapprochement: Towards an Integrated U.S. Policy in the Middle East." *Middle East Policy* 4 (June 1998).

——. "The Iran-Iraq War and the Persian Gulf Crisis." *Current History* 87 (February 1988).

——. "Iran's Foreign Policy: Contending Orientations." *Middle East Journal* 43 (Spring 1989).

——. *The Persian Gulf: Iran's Role.* Charlottesville: University Press of Virginia, 1972.

——. *Revolutionary Iran: Challenge and Response in the Middle East.* Baltimore: Johns Hopkins University Press, 1986.

——. *The United States and Iran: The Patterns of Influence.* New York: Praeger, 1982.

Ratner, Michael, Jennie Green, and Barbara Olshansky. *Against War in Iraq: An Anti-War Primer.* New York: Seven Stories Press, 2003.

Reagan, Ronald. *Public Papers of the Presidents of the United States: Ronald Reagan.* Washington, DC: GPO, 1981.

Renshon, Jonathan. *Why Some Leaders Choose War: The Psychology of Prevention.* Westport, CT: Praeger, 2006.

Rosati, Jerel. *The Carter Administration's Quest for Global Community: Beliefs and Their Impact on Behavior.* Columbus: University of South Carolina Press, 1991.

Ross, Dennis. *Statecraft: And How to Restore America's Standing in the World.* New York: Farrar, Straus, and Giroux, 2007.

Rothkopf, David J. *Running the World: The Inside Story of the National Security Council and the Architects of American Power.* New York: PublicAffairs, 2004.

Rubin, Barry. *Paved with Good Intentions: The American Experience and Iran.* New York: Oxford University Press, 1980.

Rubin, Barry, and Judith Colp Rubin, eds. *Anti-American Terrorism and the Middle East.* New York: Oxford University Press, 2002.

Russell, Richard L. "The Persian Gulf's Collective Security Mirage." *Middle East Policy* 12 (Winter 2005).

Safran, Nadav. *Saudi Arabia: The Ceaseless Quest for Security.* Cambridge, MA: Harvard University Press, 1985.

Said, Mohamed Kadry. "Potential Egyptian Contribution to a Security Framework in the Persian Gulf." *Middle East Policy* 11 (Fall 2004).

Salinger, Pierre (with Eric Laurent). *Secret Dossier: The Hidden Agenda behind the Gulf War*. London: Penguin, 1991.

Sanger, David E. "Bush's Shift: Being Patient with Foes." *New York Times*, July 10, 2006.

Sarabi, Farzin. "The Post-Khomeini Era in Iran: The Election of the Fourth Islamic Majlis." *Middle East Journal* 48 (Winter 1994).

Schroeder, Paul. "Historical Reality vs. Neo-Realist Theory." *International Security* 19 (Summer 1994).

Schwandt, Thomas A. "Constructivist, Interpretivist Approaches to Human Inquiry." In Norman K. Denizen and Yvonna S. Lincoln, eds., *Handbook of Qualitative Research*. London: Sage, 1994.

Schweitzer, Yoram, and Shaul Shay. *The Globalization of Terror: The Challenge of Al-Qaida and the Response of the International Community*. New Brunswick, NJ: Transaction Publishers, 2003.

Schweller, Randall L. "Bandwagoning for Profit: Bringing the Revisionist State Back In." *International Security* 19 (Summer 1994).

———. *Deadly Imbalances: Tripolarity and Hitler's Strategy of World Conquest*. New York: Columbia University Press, 1998.

Sciolino, Elaine. "A Failed Plot to Overthrow Hussein Is Reported in Iraq." *New York Times*, March 14, 1995.

Scowcroft, Brent. "Don't Attack Saddam." *Wall Street Journal*, August 15, 2002.

Shanker, Thom. "Rumsfeld Warns That Iraq Ties Will Hurt Russian Pocketbooks." *New York Times*, August 22, 2002.

Sheehan, Michael. *The Balance of Power: History and Theory*. London: Routledge, 1996.

———. "The Place of the Balancer in Balance of Power Theory." *Review of International Studies* 15 (1989).

Shultz, George P. *Turmoil and Triumph: My Years as Secretary of State*. New York: Charles Scribner's Sons, 1993.

Sick, Gary. *All Fall Down: America's Tragic Encounter with Iran*. New York: Random House, 1985.

———. "Iran's Quest for Superpower Status." *Foreign Affairs* 65 (Spring 1997).

Sifry, M. L., and C. Cerf, eds. *The Gulf War Reader: History, Documents, Opinions*. New York: Random House, 1991.

Simowitz, Roslyn. *The Logical Consistency and Soundness of Balance of Power Theory*. Monograph Series in World Affairs. Denver, CO: University of Denver, 1982.

Skidmore, David. *Reversing Course: Carter's Foreign Policy, Domestic Politics, and the Failure of Reform*. Nashville, TN: Vanderbilt University Press, 1996.

Skoçpol, Theda. *States and Social Revolutions: A Comparative Analysis of France, Russia, and China*. New York: Cambridge University Press, 1979.

Soderberg, Nancy. *The Superpower Myth: The Use and Misuse of American Might*. New York: John Wiley and Sons, 2005.

Spector, Leonard (with Jaqueline Smith). *Nuclear Ambitions: The Spread of Nuclear Weapons, 1989–1990*. Boulder, CO: Westview Press, 1999.

Stelser, Irwin, ed. *The Neo-con Reader*. New York: Atlantic Books, 2004.

Stoff, Michael B. *Oil, War, and American Security: The Search for a National Policy on Foreign Oil, 1941–47*. New Haven, CT: Yale University Press, 1980.

Strober, Deborah Hart, and Gerald S. Strober. *The Reagan Presidency: An Oral History of the Era*. Washington, D.C.: Brassey's, 2003.

Sullivan, Michael J., III. *American Adventurism Abroad: Thirty Invasions, Interventions, and Regime Changes since World War II.* Westport, CT: Greenwood, 2004.

Sultan, HRH General Khaled Bin (with Patrick Seale). *Desert Warrior: A Personal View of the Gulf War by the Joint Forces Commander.* New York: HarperCollins, 1995.

Suskind, Ron. *The One Percent Doctrine: Deep inside America's Pursuit of Its Enemies since 9/11.* New York: Simon and Schuster, 2006.

Taliaferro, Jeffrey W. *Balancing Risks: Great Power Intervention in the Periphery.* Ithaca, NY: Cornell University Press, 2004.

———. "Security Seeking under Anarchy: Defensive Realism Reconsidered." *International Security* 25 (Winter 2000).

Telhami, Shibley. "Are We Stuck in Iraq?" *Thawra Net-Watch*, March 21, 2005.

———. "Middle East Politics in the Post Cold War Era." In George Breslauer, Harry Kreisler, and Ben Ward, eds., *Beyond the Cold War: Conflict and Cooperation in the Third World.* Berkeley: Institute of International Studies, University of California, 1992.

———. "The Return of the State." *National Interest* (Summer 2006).

Tenet, George. *At the Center of the Storm: My Years at the CIA.* New York: HarperCollins, 2007.

Thomas, Raju G. C. "The South Asian Security Balance in a Western Dominant World." In T. V. Paul, James J. Wirtz, and Michel Fortmann, eds., *Balance of Power: Theory and Practice in the Twenty-first Century.* Stanford, CA: Stanford University Press, 2004.

Thompson, William R. "The Regional Subsystem: A Conceptual Explication and a Propositional Inventory." *International Studies Quarterly* 17 (March 1973).

Thornberry, Patrick. "On the Legal Case for Invading Iraq." In Alex Danchev and John MacMillan, eds., *The Iraq War and Democratic Politics.* New York: Routledge, 2005.

Timmerman, Kenneth R. *Countdown to Crisis: The Coming Nuclear Showdown with Iran.* New York: Crown Forum, 2005.

Toulmin, Stephen. *Foresight and Understanding: An Enquiry into the Aims of Science.* New York: Harper and Row, 1961.

Tower, John. *The Tower Commission Report.* New York: Bantam Books, 1987.

Tripp, Charles. *A History of Iraq.* 2nd ed. Cambridge: Cambridge University Press, 2002.

Unger, Craig. *House of Bush, House of Saud: The Secret Relationship between the World's Two Most Powerful Dynasties.* New York: Scribner, 2004.

Vance, Cyrus. *Hard Choices: Critical Years in America's Foreign Policy.* New York: Simon and Schuster, 1983.

Vassiliev, Alexei. "Russia and Iraq." *Middle East Policy* 7 (October 2000).

Waas, M. "What Washington Gave Saddam for Christmas." In M. L. Sifry and C. Cerf, eds., *The Gulf War Reader: History, Documents, Opinions.* New York: Random House, 1991.

Walsh, Lawrence E. *Firewall: The Iran-Contra Conspiracy and Cover-Up.* New York: W. W. Norton, 1997.

———. *Iran-Contra: The Final Report.* New York: Random House, 1994.

Walt, Stephen M. *The Origins of Alliances.* Ithaca, NY: Cornell University Press, 1987.

———. *Taming American Power: The Global Response to U.S. Power.* New York: W. W. Norton, 2005.

Waltz, Kenneth N. "International Politics Is Not Foreign Policy." *Security Studies* 6 (Autumn 1996).

———. *Theory of International Politics.* Reading, MA: Addison-Wesley, 1979.

Weisman, Steven R. "Rice Urges Egyptians and Saudis to Democratize." *New York Times*, June 21, 2005.

Welch, David A. *Painful Choices: A Theory of Foreign Policy Change.* Princeton, NJ: Princeton University Press, 2006.

Wendt, Alexander. *Social Theory of International Politics.* New York: Cambridge University Press, 1999.

Whitlock, Craig. "Commandos Free Hostages Being Held in Saudi Arabia." *Washington Post*, May 30, 2004.

Wight, Martin. "The Balance of Power." In H. Butterfield and Martin Wight, eds., *Diplomatic Investigations: Essays in the Theory of International Politics.* London: Allen and Unwin, 1966.

Wilson, George C. "Carter Budget Envisions a Force for Quick, Long-Distance Reaction." *Washington Post*, November 27, 1979.

Wilson, Joseph. *The Politics of Truth: Inside the Lies That Put the White House on Trial and Betrayed My Wife's CIA Identity.* New York: Carroll and Graf, 2005.

Wohlforth, William. *The Elusive Balance: Power and Perceptions during the Cold War.* Ithaca, NY: Cornell University Press, 1993.

——. "The Stability of a Unipolar World." *International Security* 24 (Summer 1999).

Wolfers, Arnold. *Discord and Collaboration: Essays on International Politics.* Baltimore: Johns Hopkins University Press, 1962.

Wong, Edward. "Iraq Dances with Iran, While America Seethes." *New York Times*, July 31, 2005.

Woodward, Bob. *Bush at War.* New York: Simon and Schuster, 2002.

——. *Plan of Attack.* New York: Simon and Schuster, 2004.

Wriggins, W. Howard, F. Gregory Gause, III, Terrence P. Lyons, and Evelyn Colbert. *Dynamics of Regional Politics: Four Systems on the Indian Ocean Rim.* New York: Columbia University Press, 1992.

Yergin, Daniel. *The Prize: The Epic Quest for Oil, Money, and Power.* New York: Simon and Schuster, 1992.

Yetiv, Steve A. *America and the Persian Gulf: The Third Party Dimension in World Politics.* New York: Praeger, 1995.

——. *Crude Awakenings: Global Oil Security and American Foreign Policy.* Ithaca, NY: Cornell University Press, 2004.

——. *Explaining Foreign Policy: U.S. Decision-Making and the Persian Gulf War.* Baltimore: Johns Hopkins University Press, 2004.

——. "How the Soviet Military Intervention in Afghanistan Improved the U.S. Strategic Position in the Persian Gulf." *Asian Affairs: An American Review* 18 (Summer 1990).

——. "The Persian Gulf: A Bivariable Analysis." *Defense Analysis* 6 (September 1990).

Zakaria, Fareed. *From Wealth to Power: The Unusual Origins of America's World Role.* Princeton, NJ: Princeton University Press, 1998.

Index